Kanya •

Pietersbu

EAST

AFRICA

• Derdeport

Pitsani

T R A N S V A A L

Limpopo River

Oliphants R

Mauchberg

Lydenburg

• Zeerust

Magaliesberg Rustenburg

PRETORIA

Balmoral Middelburg

Belfast

Machadodorp *Waterval Onder*

Komati Poort

Mafeking
aaipan Cypherfontein

Nooitgedacht

Lichtenburg *Witwatersrand*
Doornkop

Ventersdorp

Diamond Hill

JOHANNESBURG

• Carolina

Barberton

Lourenço Marques
Delagoa Bay

Mari's R

Potchefstroom *Gatsrand*

Modderfontein

Bakenlaagte
Ermelo •

S W A Z I -
L A N D

Klerksdorp

Vereeniging

eebosch

Rhenoster R • Wolvehoek

Standerton

Bothaville •
Roodewal

Heilbron

Frankfort

Piet Retief

Vaal R

O R A N G E

Kroonstad

Valsch R

Reitz

• Vrede

Volksrust

Utrecht

Vet R

Senekal

Lindley

Brandwater

Botha's Pass *Laing's Nek*

Newcastle

• Vryheid

F R E E

Bethlehem

Harrismith

Blood R

brove *Abraham's Kraal*

Winburg

Tweefontein *Roodebergen*
Wittebergen

Glencoe
• Dundee

Fort Itala

Fourlesburg

Ladysmith

Elandslaagte

Brandfort
Karee Siding

Zand R D

Fort Prospect

MFONTEIN

Colenso
Chieveley

Buffalo R

Sannah's Post

Thabanchu • Ladybrand

Frere

Z U L U L A N D

Tugela R

T A T E

Estcourt

N A T A L

nie

• De Wetsdorp

Wepener •

B A S U T O L A N D

Pietermaritzburg

Bethulie

• DURBAN

Caledon R *Kiba Drift*

Herschel

Aliwal
North

Mordenaars Poort

Stormbergen

P O N D O -
L A N D

I N D I A N

O C E A N

berg
nction
land's R-
Poort

Dordrecht

• Queenstown

Tarkastad

T R A N S K E I

Kei R

ter's Nek

Great Fish R

• East London

• Port Alfred

Elizabeth

0   100   200
                              miles

FROM WAR
TO
WILDERNESS

Cyril Shelford

SHELFORD PUBLISHING

Canadian Cataloguing in Publication Data

Shelford, Cyril, 1921-
  From war to wilderness

  ISBN 1-55056-533-8

  1. Shelford, Jack. 2. Pioneers--British Columbia--Ootsa Lake Region--Biography. 3. Trappers--Alaska--Biography. 4. Frontier and pioneer life--British Columbia. 5. Frontier and pioneer life--Alaska. 6. Ootsa Lake Region (B.C.)--Biography. 7. Alaska--Biography. I. Title.
  FC3845.O68Z49 1997   971.1'8203'092   C97-910712-1
  F1089.O68S54 1997

Photograph Credits:
   British Columbia Archives — pp.82,105
   Ann Chamberlain — pp.216,234
   Liz Hardey — p.vi
   Pakenham, Thomas. *The Boer War.* London: Weidenfeld and
      Nicolson, 1979. — front endsheet, pp.14,16,17,22,24,29
   Cyril Shelford — pp.134,186,233
   Telegraph Line Survey Reports — pp.206,235

Cover photograph by Tim Cushman
Typesetting and design by Jean Robinson
Printed and bound in Canada by Friesens

Shelford Publishing
4210 Kincaid Street
Victoria, B.C. V8X 4K6
(250) 479-6827 (phone)
(250) 479-4656 (fax)

DEDICATION

This book is dedicated to my grandchildren, and all young people coming out of schools, in order to show that there is a bright future for them—providing they develop clear goals and strive towards attaining them. Goals in life seldom come easily, which makes them all the more rewarding once achieved.

It is helpful to consider the difficult experiences faced by the thousands of settlers like my Dad and Mother. They endured unbelievable hardships in order to reach success in building their homestead into a productive farm.

Happy communities were developed without any help from government—who played no part in their lives—in the building of the original schools, hospitals, churches, wagon roads...

Cyril M. Shelford
August 1997

SPECIAL THANKS

to

Barbara, my wife, for the many hours spent reading and
for urging me to keep going when things were difficult
during the development of the book;

Catriona Kaufman of Top Kat Services in Victoria, B.C.
for the hours of typing and, even more, the editing of
the original draft;

Mel Smith for reading the first draft and making many
needed corrections;

Liz Hardy, who came from Evenley where the Shelford
family originated, for writing the Foreword and
supplying photographs of the village;

Ann Chamberlain, my daughter, for the photographs of
the Ootsa and Eutsuk mountains;

John Zacarias (from Victoria), **Mary Zacarias and Paul
Thompson** (from Anchorage, Alaska) for giving me
names of contacts which were very helpful.

CONTENTS

Left: *Evenley School* Right: *"Shelfords' House"*
Evenley, Bedfordshire, England

Red Lion Pub in Evenley

FOREWORD
by Liz Hardey

I first met Cyril Shelford in 1980 and mentioned that I had heard of a much-respected village schoolmaster with the same surname. Cyril smiled and said that if the village was called Evenley then the schoolmaster was his grandfather.

In 1959, my family moved into the small village of Evenley, about 20 miles north of Oxford. The house next to the school was still called "Shelfords' House," which confused me as the family who lived there was called Fox. When I finally asked about this, one of the village old-timers, Bill Buggins, told me about Mr. and Mrs. Shelford. Mr. Charles Shelford, Cyril's grandfather, was the schoolmaster, organist and church choirmaster for over 50 years and he and his wife educated, nurtured and cared for generations of Evenley's young people. Although Mrs. Shelford died in the terrible influenza epidemic of 1919 and Mr. Shelford in 1935, their influence was still felt strongly in the village and many of the older residents had favourite stories.

During the Boer and First World Wars, Mr. Shelford would read the daily newspaper to pensioners gathered on the village green, some of whom were illiterate. He also drew maps of South Africa and Europe, marking in the battlefields where so many of England's young men, including some from the village, were fighting and dying. Now, as I read the schoolmaster's sons's letters, I can understand his personal interest and concern.

Other villagers told me that they had discussed world events, such as Bleriot's flight across the English Channel, the sinking of the *Titanic* and how wireless led to the arrest of the murderer Dr. Crippen, who had fled the country but was arrested when his ship arrived in New York. Cricket was then—and remains today—a passion in Evenley and Mr. Shelford would read out the exploits of legendary cricketers such as W.G. Grace, as great a hero in England in his time as Wayne Gretzky is in Canada today.

I sometimes think of how Mr. And Mrs. Shelford must have felt when they said their goodbyes to their two sons, Jack and Arthur. There were no telephones, no air mail and travel back and forth across Canada and by ship across the Atlantic took many weeks. The mail was the only way of keeping in touch and as the Shelford brothers moved around the country, even that must have been sporadic.

In the 60 years or so between Jack's departure for Canada and my own in 1966, travel and communications have changed the world beyond all recognition. When I left England, my parents knew they could pick up the phone and call me at any time. Or, if I wanted to return home, it was a short ride by taxi and a few hours by plane, to be met by my father in his car. On one epic journey in 1914, Jack travelled 120 miles by snowshoe from his homestead on Ootsa Lake to Fort Fraser, where he took the train to Montreal and a ship to England. As he was going home to propose to his sweetheart, Safie, this was truly an odyssey of love.

If Jack and his parents returned in spirit to Evenley today, they would still feel very much at home. The village pub still dispenses good locally-brewed beer and horse racing tips, cricket is still played on Evenley village green and the shop sells everything from nails to gourmet food. Unfortunately, the village school is closed and students now take a bus to Brackley and sit in large classes with much less discipline than Mr. Shelford imposed. The old school is now a busy village hall where arts, crafts, dances, concerts and plays flourish and contribute to the richness of village life.

History is often seen as a dry collection of dates of battles or kings and queens. Real history, I believe, is the story of people such as Jack and Arthur Shelford who left their homes to find a better and peaceful life far away from the clamour and ugliness of war. Their sense of adventure and refusal to let this vast and sometimes cruel land overwhelm them is a part of our own history that should be discussed in today's schoolrooms. We can imagine the schoolmaster Charles Shelford sharing his sons' letters and adventures with incredulous fellow villagers in England. That, too, has become part of our history.

PROLOGUE

The principal reason for writing this book is to record the life of my Dad for family, friends, and all those interested in a little history of early European settlement in North America. Most of the people who came left their home country with very little money—except their one-way fare. All they had was the driving hope of a better life for their family in a new land.

My task would have been impossible to complete without the many long letters Dad wrote home to England to his father and mother, two brothers (Percy and Arthur), a sister (Flora), and Cousin Herbert that survived the many years locked up in a trunk in England. Many of these letters had faded and many had pieces missing. However, after reading them many times, it renewed memories of Dad's stories when I was growing up and thus enabled me to put the story together.

The trail of letters started when Dad joined the Army Cavalry. He was quickly sent to South Africa, where the British were losing most of the battles against the Boers. The Boer War lasted from 1899 until 1902. There is no question that this war profoundly changed Dad's life. He became emotionally drained from hearing the cries of the wounded—some of whom lay in the scorching sun for hours until death or darkness came when rescue parties from both sides would creep to bring out their wounded.

Dad was also upset by the stupid leadership of many of the generals and senior officers who still wanted to fight a war and still use the outdated Aldershot Rules of Battle rather than adapt to new methods of a mobile war. These old rules meant sending men into battle where they advanced, shoulder to shoulder. Such tactics had been successful in Egypt and India against an enemy armed with spears and knives; however, they were a complete failure in the Boer War. As a result of using these tactics against the Boers, the British lost many early battles, with extremely heavy casualties. The Boers were armed with fast-firing magazine Mauser rifles which could shoot so quickly. The soldiers, bunched up in straight lines, did not stand a chance against a well dug-in and highly mobile enemy. The Boers also were all mounted on horses, while the British Army was mainly on foot. The Boers could move quickly before the British got their superior artillery into position and ride under cover of darkness to hit the slow moving oxen-drawn supply wagons. The Boers would take all they could carry away and then burn the rest. Later, they would stampede the oxen, which would take days to round up again.

Dad came out of the War with such a hatred for the stupidity of war and all its accompanying suffering that he resolved to get away from armies, wars and people. He wanted to get away into the wilderness, where he could get himself together—and where, for months on end, he wouldn't see anything, except wild animals and birds that he thought were more civilized than humans during wars.

After returning to England and family in 1902, Dad didn't stay there for long. He soon left for America, where he landed in April 1903. From New York, he made his way across the U.S., staying long enough in such places as Buffalo, Hayse City (Kansas) and San Francisco to buy a fare to another city.

In 1904, Dad moved from San Francisco to Vancouver (British Columbia) and worked for a short time. He lived at 109 Hastings Street (in what is now downtown Vancouver)—and in letters home, complained bitterly about the mud that hindered his walking to work down Hastings Street. The ruts in the mud, etc. were caused by oxen pulling big wagons loaded with logs that had been cut further up Hastings Street and were being hauled down to a sawmill in a bay close to where Stanley Park is today.

Dad left Vancouver in June of that year and went by coastal steamer to Nome (Alaska). He stayed in Nome for nearly two months before he caught a river steamer bound for Fairbanks for six years. (He travelled on one of the last boats before ice stopped them for the long winter.)

There are many interesting stories Dad related in his letters home about trapping up the Tanana, Kuskakwim, Salcha, Clear and

Kantishna and other Alaskan rivers. Often he would be several hundred miles away from supply centres for six or seven months of the year—and not even see another person until the ice went out of the river and he could float or raft back down to civilization. During the spring he would cut wood for the river steamers (a thriving business in those days).

Once the salmon came up the rivers, Dad fished and shot moose and caribou for the gold miners who were too busy searching for gold to hunt and fish. The salmon were mainly caught in fykes and fish wheels that Dad made himself. He also made many of his own nets during the long winter nights when he was not busy skinning and stretching his fur. He found the bought nets weren't as strong as the thread he bought by mail order from Chicago. (He would order in the spring to ensure delivery before fall when the rivers closed for travel.) The rivers were the highways for traffic—in the summer by river steamboats and in the winter by dog sleigh. A carpenter by trade, Dad made his own small riverboats, dog sleighs and snowshoes.

Dad had many good Indian friends and valued their advice—especially during the first year when, as a green Englishman, he knew nothing about trapping, hunting and, more importantly, survival in the long harsh winters. He spent the winters mainly in tents with only a tin folding woodstove, which was light and easy to carry on a dog sleigh. He used the dog sleigh to get supplies to a distant trap line, as well as to carry the traps while setting out the line. After that, Dad would cover the trap lines on snowshoes and left the dogs at base camp. From the base camp, Dad had four lines in different directions and would cover them once a week. If the going was tough on snowshoes, he would take enough food and stay overnight in a lean-to made of branches, then return the following day. That is, unless a bad storm had hit the area. In the event of that happening, Dad would stay put until the storm had blown over and then return to base camp.

In 1910, Dad reluctantly said goodbye to Alaska and joined up with his younger brother, Arthur, who had come over from England and was then working in a logging camp in Powell River. This was an excellent camp and Dad was served several lovely meals, which looked great to him after his "batching" in Alaska for six years!

Dad was anxious to find some land in an undeveloped area of British Columbia, where he could develop a farm, stop his wanderings, and raise a family in peace and quiet without too many people around. Dad and Uncle Arthur quickly decided to return to Vancouver and pick up much needed supplies (including Dad's carpentry tools that he had stored at 109 Hastings Street). The two brothers stays two days in Vancouver, then caught a steam ship going to Prince Rupert. From there, they boarded the *Port Simpson* to go up the Kitselas Canyon. Having negotiated the Canyon, the brothers travelled by riverboat to Hazelton (nearly 160 miles up the Skeena River).

On arrival at Hazelton, they bought one horse (by the name of Tom) from an Indian to help them carry supplies during their search for land. They then purchased only enough food that they could pack on the horse—as well as the 80 pounds each they carried on their backs! After leaving Hazelton, they followed the Bulkley River over 120 miles to the east—that is, as far as Houston. After this, they turned south, following the Buck River for over 20 miles, and then over to the Francois Lake watershed. They then crossed the Nadina River and travelled southeast over to the Ootsa Lake watershed.

Once on Ootsa Lake, they searched the north shore, which is 42 miles long, and managed to stake out several pieces of land that they thought might be suited to homesteading. The west end of Ootsa Lake, they felt, also looked good for trapping. Once satisfied with their claims, they returned to Hazelton to file their one-half section each. Both sections had beaver meadows and the rest was covered mainly with shrub poplars. (Most of the trees were 10"-12" tall.)

While in Hazelton, the two brothers bought enough food for the winter—not an easy task since they had to ensure that they remembered all the essentials like flour, rolled oats, dried beans, salt, pepper, baking powder, sugar and, most important of all, enough ammunition for Dad's .30-30 and .22 rifles. Dad reports that game was very scarce and that he only saw one deer in all their travels. He soon realized that their meat diet would come largely from ducks, grouse, beaver, muskrats and porcupines.

The first year they established themselves—bringing in most of their needed supplies and their first cattle from Bella Coola, nearly 180 miles away. They had to cross five rivers to get there. To cross two of the rivers, all the supplies had to be loaded onto rafts and then polled across. The horses and cattle had to swim! Bella Coola was the main supply base for most of the early settlers until the railway lines were linked up between Prince Rupert and Prince George—April 7th, 1914. The advent of the railway quickly changed the lives of the early pioneers because supplies could be obtained from either Houston (50 miles away) or Burns Lake (almost 60 miles away). The railway line also nearly brought to an end the pack trains over the mountains. The pack trains were replaced by wagons and sleighs, where two horses could bring as much as six or eight pack horses with much less time spent loading and unloading.

In 1914, Dad went to England and arranged for his fiancée to come over to Canada the following spring. The next year proved to be a year of big decisions, as Arthur and Herbert Plumb (a cousin) decided to join the Army. In the spring of 1915, a German submarine sunk the passenger ship, *Lusitania*. This event brought about quite a series of telegraph messages back and forth between Dad and Mother as to whether it was safe for her to travel to Canada.

It was decided that she should. Dad met her in Montreal, where they were married. They then travelled by rail across Canada on their honeymoon and arrived in Burns Lake. The 15-mile trip to Francois Lake was made by wagon over a rough stump road. Dad and Mother then stayed in a deserted cabin on Francois Lake, where they had for company a pack of rats running around all night.

The little freight boat took nearly two days to get up to Nadina because of rough weather. My parents then sent young Sam, an Indian boy, over to get Arthur. They spent the night under a good tree that kept the rain off and they all arrived at the ranch the following day.

Soon after this, letters reached England to say that they had arrived safely and were enjoying a new life on the ranch. Hard work was the order of the day, including extra work necessitated by the departure of my uncles Arthur and Herbert to help the war effort. My parents cleared land to feed the expanding cattle herd. There was no time to write many letters.

Thus, the letter trail was brought to an end.

Cyril Shelford

CHAPTER 1

BOER WAR
(1899-1902)

The letters in Chapter 1 written by my father cover going to work in Bedford as a carpenter, then joining the Army, training, the trip to South Africa, as well as the heartbreaking struggle to stay alive and find enough to eat due to enemy action cutting supply lines and destroying what they could not carry away.

Bedford, England
September 1899

Dear Dad,
     I managed to get a job working on a major building project in
Bedford, which is a few miles from where I board—a nice place and
the people are very friendly (they treat me as if I was one of the
family). I worked for a few days to get a little money, which, together
with my savings, gave me enough to buy a bicycle—a mode of
transport that saved me a lot of time getting to and from work. I soon
found the bicycle is the real thing to attract the attention of the girls, as
we can travel so fast compared to the horse—which seems to greatly
impress them. When I drive by, some of them wave madly to try to get
me to stop and give them a ride. This they can do by hanging on, as
there isn't much room on the seat. I stand up and try to pedal. The first
time I tried it wasn't too successful when I got going too fast down a
hill. We ended up in a hedge half way down the hill. We ended up with
a few scratches and torn clothes—which she didn't seem to appreciate
for some strange reason—and she didn't talk to me for several days.
     Many of the girls think a bicycle is the real thing compared to
an old horse, but the boys on the horses don't like it at all and get
really upset, as they are rated low on the list of eligible young men.
Some of the them get real mad and try to ride over some of us on
bicycles.
     Before I left home to go to work Mother was upset when I sat
and read the newspaper about a possible war in South Africa. You can
tell her I still read all about it, but she can relax as I plan to stay here
for a few months and make a little money before I move on to
something else. It does seem the Peace Talks are breaking down at
Bloemfontein, as neither side seems willing to give way—some-thing
that could ensure peace in the years ahead.
     Hope all is well at home.

                                   Jack

Aldershot, England
October 30th, 1899

D ear Percy,
        Since writing last, the newspapers here are all full of War News
since the war started on October 11th. It appears from the news that
Kruger, the President of the Transvaal Republic, has built up over the
last few years the largest explosive factory in the world—which could
very well keep his army going for a long time. The British explosives,
on the other hand, have to be shipped all the way out from England
(and that one-way trip from England to South Africa takes over two
weeks to make). I see that 8,000 troops have already left for South
Africa, where things are not going well by all reports. It seems the
Boers are moving quickly to try and take the Port of Durban before re-
enforcements arrive. Many people here at work are already talking
about joining the Army, since Ladysmith is already surrounded and
under siege by the Boers. In one battle outside the town of Nicholson's
Nek, the British lost over 1,200 men with 950 who had to surrender.
Also, the British garrison at Kimberley to the west is also surrounded
and could fall to the Boers at any time.

        Today, the newspaper reports that General Buller, the British
Commander in South Africa, seems very concerned that his men are
mainly on foot, with very little cavalry. The Boers, however, are very
mobile, since most of them are mounted and can hit hard at the slow
supply lines. Then they ride away before the infantry and artillery can
get into action. I gather we are trying to buy horses, mules and oxen to
try and speed up the movement of troops into areas being attacked.

        It seems the British Generals are finding the war so different
from what they found when fighting in Egypt and India—where they
mainly faced opposing armies that were equipped with spears, rawhide
shields, and on foot. They seem to be having a lot of difficulty fighting
the Boers, who strike so quickly then disappear in to the vast veldt (or
prairie), which is totally different from the Aldershot rules practised by
our Generals on Salisbury Plains.

        Another change they have to cope with is the magazine Mauser
Rifle brought in from Europe. This type of rifle can fire so fast that the

days of the shoulder-to-shoulder attacks used in India don't work, as so many men can be shot down so quickly by the enemy. The enemy fires from trenches dug out on the top of the hills that can't be touched except by Artillery shrapnel shells. Once it's dark, they ride away and hit another area.

The only means of transportation is on the single-track railway line from Cape Town north, and from Durban northwest to Pretoria, the capital of the Transvaal. The railway lines are very vulnerable to sabotage. The only other way for supply is by the slow oxen pulling the supply wagons—the main targets of the Boer Cavalry, who move quickly to take all the supplies they need, including oxen, if they have the time. If not, they burn the remaining supplies and stampede the oxen that are left behind.

Jack

H. Block Barracks
Aldershot, England
March 1900

Dear Flora,
   I quit my job, even thought it was a nice place to work and hope you won't get too upset when you hear that I've joined the Army with the 7th Battalion, 27th Devon Squadron, a Cavalry Regiment that is being formed to match the Boer Army in speed and mobility (that is, a regiment that can move quickly from place to place). The regiment will form part of the Imperial Yeomanry that was formed by the Government and a committee of fox hunters, which will be outside the control of the regular Army—the latter is trying to use the same methods that succeeded in India and Egypt. I understand some people in the War Office are furious. The need for such a force seems apparent to fight the new war, which is now called "The Invisibility"—because the Boers ride in shooting smokeless Mauser magazine rifles and the puff of smoke can no longer be seen. As one officer described it to us while training, the Boers would not play the game fairly so we have to change. They even use the officers' shiny brass buttons and buckles as targets so far more officers are getting killed than private soldiers. The result is that the officers now have to use the same dull looking buttons as the private soldiers. At the moment, we are waiting for General Buller to inspect all his new recruits.
   Most of our training consists of getting up early so we can get breakfast and be mounted by daylight. Most of the day is spent learning how to ride and shoot from the saddle until you get close enough—then you jump off the horse and take cover as best you can. Our training is to keep space between horses, which is supposed to give you a better chance than being close together where one rifleman can shoot four or five real fast. We are still trained to use a lance—something I hope we will never use as the thought of using it makes me shudder. We are camped in tents out in a pasture, as there are far too many of us to stay in the Army buildings. There are many rumours around that we will soon be moving, so you may not hear from me for some time because I gather the war is not going well in Africa.

One of the greatest problems facing us is where the Army is going to find 8,000 horses for us to ride. We were told yesterday the Government is searching in countries all over the world—even in North and South America. Most of the Boers come from the farms and have a good supply of horses in both the Orange Free State and the Transvaal. It appears they are excellent riders and have very capable men leading them. As very few wear uniforms, it's difficult to know who is a soldier and who is just a farm hand. Many go out to battle when they get information of a supply train or some other valuable target (e.g., heavy guns, food and ammunition) being moved by train and guarded by a small number of men once the task is completed. These men go back to their farm until another target appears.

Once we get to South Africa we will have to learn quickly what it's all about. Try not to worry about me as I'm getting good on a horse. There are too few rifles, however, for many of us to get practice—that will come later. Riding is the most important, especially in the dark. We practise this whenever there is a little light from the moon.

I gather the War Office and the regular Army leaders are quite upset by the formation of the Imperial Yeomanry and, in the paper today, claim that it will be a disaster to send untrained men who are not familiar with Army discipline out to Africa. A reply came from Lord Lansdowne, who answered the criticism by saying that the Boers are not highly trained, according to the Aldershot Rules of Discipline—yet they seem to fight only too well according to the recent defeats we have suffered over the last few weeks. The Yeomanry idea caught the imagination of the press and those in sporting circles who are rushing to abandon the fox hunt and turn to the pursuit of the Boers.

The City of London offered and paid for 1,000 volunteers to go to Africa—even 34 Members of Parliament (MPs) joined up quickly to serve in Africa. They joined the ranks, along with stockbrokers, journalists who have brought a feeling of democracy to the barracks and camps around Aldershot and the camp fires on the veldt in Africa. Our camp area is expanding every day as more and more people are flocking in to join the Army. There are still lots of rumours about moving, so we will see what happens next week.

With Love to All,

Jack

John Leo Shelford

7th Battalion
27th Devon Squadron
April 1900

My address is:
No 26623
Imperial Yeomanry
Field Force
South Africa

Dear Flora,
    I hope Mother got the letter from Aldershot that I wrote two days before we left. It seemed like a rushed move as we were wakened early to pack our gear (which wasn't much) and then got on the train bound for Southampton. As soon as all of us got on board our ship, The Garson, it left port and headed out to sea for the long journey to Africa.

    You will note the number 26623 in my new address is my personal number throughout the war and can identify me, if necessary. I'm just about recovering my equilibrium after three days of being seasick. We are packed on board but very comfortable, and I like sleeping in hammocks. We only have one blanket, so sleep in our clothes. No doubt it will be warm when we get further south. Our hammocks overlap, with 200 of us in a place about as big as a big room at school in Evenley.

    We sighted the most westerly point of Portugal on Monday. I enjoy sight-seeing with my field glasses, given to me by Mr. Allen with my name engraved on them. There is no doubt I will use them a lot during the months ahead.

    The bread and coffee are good, but the tea is so awful—even I can't stomach it. It tastes like burnt soupy tea. We watched a shoal of porpoises (Monday) and they played for some time just outside the vessel.

    We touch Las Palmas in the Canary Islands at 6 p.m. tonight, so I will post this letter—although we cannot land as some of us might not come back.

We have nearly as many horses as we have men on board the ship. The horses are kept in pens holding 10 horses. The pens are crowded so that the horses wouldn't fall down when the ship is in rough water.

The first few days of the voyage were very rough, so some of us had to take 12-hour shifts to stay down with the horses—not only to feed and water them but also to make sure one didn't get down and get trampled by the others. Horses are very vulnerable when down and they don't last long. This happened several times and help had to be called in to rope the other horses to enable us to get in the pen and get the downed horse back on its feet. Several men were hurt during the storm with other horses falling on them. I was lucky. When I was in the pen, I got knocked down and a horse stepped on my jacket and tore a big hole while I was trying to get up. The Guard Sergeant wasn't very sympathetic and told me to sew up the uniform, as it would be good practice to patch the uniform before landing and going into battle against the Boers.

Will write more later.

Love,

Jack

The following letter Dad started aboard the ship and finished after landing in Cape Town. It is printed from the original handwritten copy.

1901.

On the Ship at Present
April 4th

Dear Mam,

We are nearing the end of the voyage & I am glad as it is getting monotonous. We have not had half the work I expected to do been left to lay lazily about most of the time & any work has been half hearted. We have learnt a little saddlery & vedette duty & a little bit of physical drill but not ... of anything to keep us employed. The voyage has been very smooth in fact all except about 5 days. I ... a lot ... had a touch more of seasickness on ... two April 3rd after a very rough day so I cannot claim to be a very good sailor. The grub as far as you can say is excellent especially for variety. The equator was not so hot as I expected but it was cloudy & ... tell ... the sun going wrong way round

... clouds of flying fish
as many as a hundred rise out of the
water together. Some of them fly
60 yds without a fresh spring but
most of them fly about 20 yds & then
have a fresh spring from their
tails on the water & go on again
Las Palmas where we stopped was
grand. We did not go off the
ship but scores of natives came
off in boats selling. lost my
field service cap there. The oranges
were delicious, you never get one
in England like them, but when
you have been at sea a few days
they get just like ours tough
We have not sighted land since
though we were near enough
but it was night & we were
not allowed on deck for fear
of malaria fever. We are just
having our valises & black kit
bags, which have been stored

~~in the field, ~~served out to us
so ~~after a while~~

We have arrived at Cape Town or rather
~~the bay~~ in land 4th Easter Day.
I have been wondering whether you
were all together & what you are
doing. We do not disembark till
Tuesday morning so are rather
short. We had General pulled barrow
on board this morning to give
orders. We go straight up to
Johannesburgh good Friday was
~~yes~~ a funny one, we were on guard
with a rough wind & a concert
at night. I happened to be sentry
on the platform so I had to
shift, so I got in a good position
& so my two hrs pleasant went
we had tin whistle solo & that a flute
duet, sounded a treat. singing
one could listen to, singing awful
& real good singing & clog dancing.
Cape town through the glasses is
not what I quite expected. It is
formed ½ round a circular bay

topped by Table Mt & the Peak, the Peak is a pure cone a bell of white sand, then green scrub, then a ridge of high rocky hills besides the M to, with the town & shipping form the best landscape I have yet seen. The writing accomodation is so awful I must really conclude we have a prize to get round, a tin of pears, not comandeered but well paid for in secret.

It is 4 days rail to Joh——h you I shall be sick of that. Give my love to everybody, this is the only letter I write a——. There is most likely a bank of England 5£ note in this & I will put yes on the bottom if I do. Hope you can read this & hope you are well

Jack.

Know not address yet so do not write ——

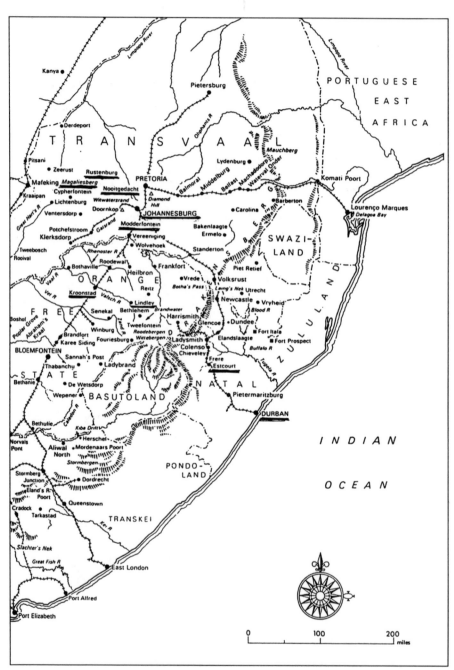

Transvaal and Orange Free State 1899

New Address:
Shelford 26623
27th Devon Squadron
Imperial Yeomanry
South Africa

Dear Arthur,
We just got settled at Gunniston Camp and, to our surprise, orders came down that we were being shipped by rail back to Cape Town. We would then proceed by ship up to Durban to reinforce mobile patrol troops protecting the railway line from Durban to Ladysmith from roving commando groups.

The trip by sea was very nice with smooth water all the way. Once we reached our destination, we stayed in camps for over three weeks waiting for enough horses to arrive on other ships before leaving for the front where no one seemed to know where it was.

Eventually, a ship came in with a limited number of horses. A small group of us rode out a few miles on patrol to see if there was any sign of Boers in the area north of here, as one of the Natives coming in told our officers that he had sighted dust trails between 8-10 miles out. We rode all day and saw nothing, so we came back to camp. The next morning a scout came in and reported a railway bridge across a small river had been blown up. The Boers must have sat quietly and watched us ride by. When darkness came they moved in and blew the bridge out, then rode away. There was soon a lot of activity going on around the Officers' tents during the morning and by 2 p.m. we were loading in railway box cars with all the available horses. We were taken out as far as the blown up bridge, where we unloaded and rode out to try and find the Boers on our way to Estcourt. That journey took several days, as the settlement is about 120 miles from where we started. We never did catch sight of the Boers' raiding party. We made camp in a small flat area that had low hills all around—an area that could be defended easily, with any luck.

Everything was going well in preparation for our main supplies which were due to arrive later in the day. By dark, we were wondering why they hadn't arrived. Then a scout rode in to tell us that a raiding

*South African Light Horse marching through Cape Town, early 1900
(inset: Lord Roberts)*

British reinforcements prepare for kit inspection at Cape Town.

Inspection before going into battle

party had come in behind and blown up a section of the railway line, including a bridge, with the result that further supplies would not get through for a day or so. Our food supply was only meant to last two days, so we had to go easy on our meals just in case the raiders returned and destroyed more railway line in order to try and starve us out of our position before the main force arrived to help us pursue the raiders and clear the area. The latter had been cleared twice before only to have the raiders return when they were least expected. All of this was a great surprise to us as, in Durban, we all thought the war was nearly over—Ladysmith had been relieved after a 118 day siege where they had to eat even their horses and oxen to stay alive. Naturally, the Cavalry men were reluctant to eat their horses, but they soon found they were tender compared to the oxen that pulled the heavy wagons and guns. Before the Boers retreated from the area, they crept in at night to the hill where the heavy guns were set up and soon cleared the guards from the hill. Later, they shot all the draft horses so the British when they were ready to move forward couldn't move the heavy guns. The British Army to the west had moved rapidly after capturing Bloemfontein and the wide areas to the north (mainly close the railway line). The railway had to be repaired before heavy supplies could be brought in. The Army mainly on foot could only advance as fast as the slow oxen could haul ammunition and food to the forward positions.

General French with his Cavalry had swept forward and relieved Kimberly after a long siege but had to come to a halt due to the heavy loss of horses. He lost 1,500 horses in less than one month and a further 200 trying to keep the Boers, under General De Wet and De la Rey, from taking much of the area captured back again. They have an army of over 6,000 tough men who knew every inch of the ground and could ride long distances to hit quickly in order to capture or destroy food and ammunition, which they couldn't pack away. They would be long gone before daylight. De Wet was both smart and tough. If any of his men fell asleep while on guard, they were quickly punished by making them sit on an ant hill for up to 20 minutes.

The British Generals still haven't grasped the mobile wars that started at the turn of the century. Many were still following the Aldershot Rules used for many years previous during Colonial Wars of the past. We soon found out that the war was only just starting. Since De Wet took command of the Mobile Army, he fully realized that the Boers could not win a fixed position war against our forces. The latter outnumbered the Boers five to one and we have more heavy artillery, which was nearly powerless against the quick raids that swept in then disappeared into the vast land with no roads. Many of the Boers were soldiers at night and worked their farms in the day time, if they were close enough to move back and forth. The raids in our area were carried out by small groups of less than 30 or 40 men. However, no matter how often we patrolled an area they seemed able to slip in under the cover of darkness and blow up bridges or sections of the railway line. We have been waiting over a month for sufficient horses to come in from as far away as Argentina and Burma. The horses coming from other countries are not as hardy as those raised on the veldt, where the grass is dry a good part of the year. The local horses can outwalk those brought in from overseas. The horses are more vulnerable than men during a battle, as the men can lay behind an ant hill, rock or a bank on the side of a river while the horse is out in the open nearby trying to get enough dead grass to eat. Much of the area is burned over by both sides in order to reduce the feed supply and the distance a horse can travel.

Once we were able to get a horse to ride and rid the area of roving commandoes so that the railway line could be used to carry the heavy supplies, we left the area and moved northwest over the Drakensberg Mountains to join forces with the British Army of 30,000 who had marched 260 miles from Bloemfontein to the Rand and Johannesburg. The Tigers (Cavalry) rode ahead until they met stiff resistance and waited for the main force to catch up. They reached their objective in only 26 days. The main objectives and concerns of the foot soldiers were not the great battles they won or the right or wrong side of the war. There were far more important things like survival, whether they could find wood for a fire during the cold nights, how to get a duck without getting caught, how to make biscuits last the long day, and above all, would they be able to find water to drink. Also, they thought about whether they could shoot a sparrow to make a cup of soup or whether the dead horse or oxen would still be good to eat.

One other concern that faced every foot soldier was will my shoes hold out till we reach Pretoria. There were five rivers to cross: the Vet, Zand, Valsch, Vaal and Rhenoster. The enemy was not the Boers—it was the veldt, the sun to fry you, and the frost to freeze you at night. Many days passed with too little trek ox to eat and too few biscuits when there were any rations at all. The main problem was always the supply trains crawling over the veldt, where De Wet had caught the British supply wagons at Waterval Drift and had captured or destroyed 180 wagons and turned the oxen, mules or hoses loose and chased away those they couldn't use. All five rivers had well dug trenches which had been abandoned and the Boers slipped into space, which left one British officer upset. He said, "Why don't they stay in the trenches they dug along the rivers and fight like gentlemen."

Hunger, typhoid and dysentery caused far more casualties than all the battles. Pretoria was captured by the British on June 5th before we got to the area. We were more than busy trying to keep the railway clear of Boer commando raiding parties. During some periods the repair of the railway line couldn't even keep up to the slow ox wagons. In several cases, the rail repairs were going well when a section of rail track 70 or 80 miles behind would be blown up. Our job was to ride between the many lookout positions to find out if anyone had seen a strange dust trail. If one was seen, we would get 20 or 30 men and ride fast to see who they were. It was a frustrating job, as three or four Boers would come in during the cover of darkness and look for a good area to blow up—preferably a bridge which would take longer to repair. Once they located the right place, they would send a rider back to get the explosives and lie low all day watching for patrols and how many there were. Once nightfall came, they could quickly put the explosives in place with a time fuse. They would then have time to get out of the area before the explosive went off. Sometimes they would leave two men to make sure they had done a good job. They seldom did the same thing twice, which made it far more difficult. If the British patrol got careless and sent only a small number of men, the Boers would get in a good location and ambush the patrol so that they wouldn't be disturbed for hours till another patrol was sent out to see why the others hadn't returned.

I must confess I'm in very poor spirits today. We have faced two disasters during the last week near Rustenberg, where we were ambushed by a group of Boers and we are left with only 30 men out of our original Devon's Squadron of 112. We are, therefore, waiting for reinforcements to come in.

One major mistake was made by General Roberts when the Boer Commandant Krause, their official in charge of Johannesburg, promised that the mines would not be damaged if the British would allow them one full day to withdraw their army intact from Pretoria and the surrounding area. General Roberts agreed to this. All next day, Louis Botha's army headed northwards, taking all the heavy guns and ammunition along with all the gold mined from the Rand—enough to pay for the war effort up to that point and still have over a million and a half pounds left to carry on the war from stronger positions in the north. In the north, they could carry on guerrilla warfare for another year and a half. All of this was moved during the victory celebrations that were going on all day and most of the night. From this mistake General Roberts soon found there was no such thing as a civilized war—all wars are barbarian games and final victory was a long way off.

Love,

Jack

Occupation of Johannesburg May 31, 1900

Krugerdorp
October 3rd, 1901

Dear Flora,
     Received your letter of September 1900 which finally caught up with me—which is not surprising as we have been moving quickly from one trouble area to another trying to get one jump ahead of the Boer commandoes. We kept moving north and are now in the Rustenburg area after leaving Kroonstad. We had no sooner got here when the Boers had slipped away and General Smuts came in behind and captured Modderfontein on the railway line south of Johannesburg—surprise to everyone, as it was considered a safe area. The Boers also captured a mail and supply train—no doubt with many of our long-awaited letters and parcels from home. We seem stalled due to horse sickness and we have only 16 sound horses left for the whole troop.

     I thought I should write as we never know where we will be tomorrow. We arrived late at night after a week of long days riding and after walking to help the horse. My job today will be to wash and trim horses' feet so they will be in good shape for a 20-mile ride into a Boer strong-point in a small valley with a narrow entrance. Water, as ever, is very scarce so I had to use my mess can to dip water from a tiny stream coming out of a spring. The stream is so small that it took over 10 minutes to fill the mess can. The cleanliness of the horses' feet comes ahead of us getting a wash. In fact, it's three days since I was able to get a good wash—so we look a dirty lot. The wind seems to blow day and night and picks up the sand which covers everything, leaving grimy mess on our clothes and everything else. I'm promising myself a wash and so intend using only half my mess tin to wash the horses' feet and half for myself.

     We arrived in our staging area at 6 p.m. after a 25-mile march. Once we arrived and had grazed our horses, we were served with one pound of flour (that had to last us for supper and all the next day). Puzzle 1: What to make? Puzzle 2: How to cook it? Puzzle 3: How to start a decent fire with perfectly green wood? We solved our problems by 11 p.m. As a result, we had some very passable pudding of flour

and water—boiled then fried the next day with a scrap of jam that had
been issued to each person. The buns you talked about in your letter
sounded good to me. However, I would rather you not talk about what
you had for dinner in your next letter as it makes me homesick. I'm not
grumbling about what we have to eat, but it was the silliness of serving
flour at that time of night, especially with reveille (wake-up call) at
3 a.m. the next morning. The following day we were served stewed
meat covered with one-eighth inch of dirt which the wind had blown in
while it was cooking and before it could be served. We tried to scrape
the dirt off the best we could without losing any food. The dust blew
into the tea which made it look like it had milk in it—the tea lost all its
glamour.

Moving out of captured town of Krugerdorp

We are supposed to have a good number of Boers penned up in a valley along with a convoy of supplies. We had hoped to have got them to surrender before we tried to force our way in. However, it's reported they are under the command of either De Wet or De la Rey, who are both such clever leaders and usually manage to slip away during the night—which they managed to do, much to our surprise. Before we leave here I want to tell you the items I want Mother to send me:

1. Always send a stamped addressed envelope, as the post offices here are not reliable.
2. Send two lots of saccharin in separate parcels, as often someone in the postal service will swipe anything that is sweet. They are sold for 3s 9d each—but are worth their weight in gold as there is little sugar to be found. (While we're on the move, it's next to impossible to find any.)
3. Slip in good pencils which are good to write home.
4. As we don't get paid while on the veldt and I don't have any since we left the ship, send me £1 in half sovereigns. We have all been talking about the best way to send things from home and have come to the decision it should be a small box about 8" x 4" x 4". Tack it down and sew all around with canvas and label it "Medical Supplies and Comforts." Then write the address on the canvas as well as the labels several times in case of damage. Also, number the package so I will know if one is missing. Put in some money (but not much at a time), fill the corners with chocolate (as that's nice to have after a long ride). I would also appreciate chocolate for making hot drinks—it may be a trouble getting it but one can will last for six months. Register all letters. As soon as they leave the civil authorities, the military is only a trap to catch all the goodies that are sent—as you would soon learn if you were here.

The last letter I sent from Wran Poort and we are now back again after a long night march back to camp. It's only possible to travel at night because of the numerous snipers up in the hills and other vantage points. Another column of men came in to relieve us after a long week. We started out in the evening and reached Oliphant's Nek by morning and we each picked up a bushel of oranges and tangerines. We left the following morning thinking we were in safe areas. However, it wasn't so safe, as there were snipers all the way and we lost quite a few of the men. I nearly got hurt when trying to get off my horse in a hurry when an explosive bullet went off just in front of my horse and it reared up. I got a foot caught in one of the stirrups and got dragged some distance before it came loose. Fortunately, one of the men managed to catch my horse and we got shelter behind a Kaffir hut.

The road from there was through a valley where only one column of our troops had been before. Had there been many enemy troops, we couldn't have got through. From there we marched from Rustenburg to Boshof Nek, which we held for several days till we were relieved. Fortunately, there are lots of oranges and other fruit, so we have had plenty to eat until we could get provisions from base camp (one issue of bread) and rejoined our column at Megattas Nek. Since then, we have made one-day journeys to Selon's Krall (Basuto), which is a village. I managed to get a good wash at Rustenburg next day— and even washed my shirt and repaired my pants that had got torn when I was dragged by my horse.

About the time we thought we had the Boer forces cornered, we heard the news that De Wet wasn't there at all—and all we had cornered was a rear guard left behind to keep us busy while De Wet had moved during long nights, riding quite a distance south within the next few days. For the first time, he carried out an invasion of the Cape Colony, which everyone in command thought was safe. Two of the heavy guns we captured recently were the same guns that the Boers had captured twice before. One gun had the names scratched on it of the British who had first used it. Later, the names of the Boers who had used it before we got it—our names came next and other names will come. Some of these guns pulled by horses are heavy 4.7" naval guns and can't be moved fast enough to the rear if a strong enemy force strikes suddenly and captures the guns. The Boers are so mobile that there is no point in taking prisoners, as they had no firm territory to keep them in. All they could do was take all the arms and ammunition they could use, together with the prisoner's jacket and pants, then blow up or burn what was left and let the prisoners walk away. So far, the only territory we control most of the time is the railway lines and the big towns; the smaller towns and villages change hands regularly.

As soon as we ride out to take another stronghold, they ride in and take the base we left which makes the moving of supplies exceedingly difficult. Many times, the Boers capture and eat our rations before they get to us. General French and his Cavalry were considered the most efficient fighting force the British had and many of us hoped we would be sent to join them rather than patrol railway lines and mop up small groups left as rear guard after the main Boer forces had left to strike in another vulnerable area miles away (to catch British forces off guard). Many of the Boers now dress in British khaki uniforms and use Lee Metford rifles, as their supply of Mauser ammunition is in short supply and they get lots of our ammunition by capturing a supply column or train. The only Mauser shells left seem to be the dum-dum, which is outlawed by the Geneva Convention because they blow such a hole in a person if hit. It's unfortunate it was outlawed but it has not yet ratified by all nations.

With love to all,

Jack

June 25th, 1901

D ear Percy,
    I was glad to get a letter from Mother and hear all is well at home. I gather she expects the war to be over any day now. It sure doesn't look that bright from here. We are back in Rustenburg again—safe and sound—with another convoy of supplies, but it gets more risky each time as we are now practically surrounded and can only move at night when you can see the flash of a gun or rifle firing on us and we can fire back and either kill or scare them out. This happens only for an hour or so before another bunch of snipers move in to different positions. We will be unable to leave here till reinforced from outside arrive, as the hills are choked with Boers and other columns can't move for want of stores as they can only come in by slow ox carts and mules—the railway line was blown out three nights ago not far from the supply base.

    Our only source of food is fruit when we can sneak out at night and pick a bucketful. The following day we went on picket only 1½ miles from camp—close to the main Kaffir positions. We can't use horses as they make too much noise when they walk. We have been busy building forts of rocks and stringing barbed wire for the last two days when we're not on watch. We all look forward to nightfall, as the snipers can't see what they are shooting at. In the daytime we have to be quick, looking over the rock walls to make sure no one is coming or you get shot. The Kaffir position is enormously strong. It is a ridge about two miles long, rising to a point in the centre which is entirely covered with walled rings of trenches that would hold 20,000 men easily and could not even, if defended by Natives, be taken without many heavy guns or being surrounded and starved out. I will be glad to get out of here, as we have lost a lot of men.

    It will be nice to get another letter and parcel from home—if they manage to get through! Add to my list of wants a waistcoat with lots of deep pockets to carry lots of ammunition and fruit to eat, as supplies getting through are very scarce and unreliable. I gather I lost two of your packages, as I got no. 1 and 3—and the next was no. 5. I'm afraid our friend General De Wet and his men enjoyed them, as they also have to scrounge for food a lot of the time. As soon as we take an area, the Boers come in behind and take that area over, cutting off supplies again.

Field dressing station

July 11th

Didn't have time to finish writing, as we've been under attack all the time since I started writing on June 25th. Have been spending most of our time working on forts built of trenches and rocks piled up around to shoot over, as the snipers seem to come from all sides. It's tough for those wounded as we can't get them out except occasionally in the dark—and only those who can still ride can be taken. Some have had to stay three or four days before they can be moved. There is absolutely nothing good can be said about wars as you look into the faces of the wounded and try to give them hope. When this is over, I'm going to travel as far as I can get away from all of this and try and get myself together—as most of us seem to be walking around in a daze and not sure what we are doing. I know that if I get hit I hope they do a good job of it, as I don't want to go through what some our fellows have gone through, waiting for days to be taken out or die before this happens.

July 20th

Finally, we got through the valley after days of fighting and are now in Terrust for a short stay. We will be able to get ourselves and our equipment back in good shape and have time to mend and wash clothes which are in bad shape. I still have needles and thread left from what you sent a short time ago. I've been using them even to sew up minor flesh and skin wounds, which certainly helps them to heal. I boil the thread and needle before I start. The doctors are all too busy back at Base Camp, tending the serious wounds and they can't get out to front-line positions. As you know, I've never had any training along this line in my life and started to sew up horses with success. Then a wounded friend of mine, who couldn't get back to Base Camp due to enemy action, asked me to sew up his minor wounds to help stop bleeding—which was successful. He was braver than I would be.

Today, when things got quiet we even had time to play football against some of the Boer prisoners we had taken during the fighting the day before in the valley. The Boers sure can shout when they get a goal and also a hug when the game was over. Some of them even asked if they could help to get the war over, as it had gone on too long and they didn't have a chance to win.

Monday, July 29th, 1901

I'll get this letter finished yet. We were called out suddenly last night when an attack started and have been on guard all day and helped pick up sick horses that had either been wounded by shell fire or that had bad feet—something like foot rot we get in England (mainly on cattle and sheep). The animals' feet have to be washed and treated, whenever possible. Thousands of horses and mules get killed as they can't hide behind a rock, like we can. One thing I soon found over here is that horses are more important than people. You can bring a lot of men on a ship but not many horses.

Yesterday I was sent out with four men to a fort which was used as an observation post to warn the main defence lines of danger approaching. Most of the day we watched through field glass, both the enemy and our own dispatch riders going back and forth with messages. We could also hear fighting over the hill—but couldn't see anything. Two of us kept busy by digging an outhouse and cutting a log for anyone to sit on. At night, we took it in turns to be on guard to make sure no one came close without us knowing. The Boers are very good and can travel at night better than we can. In the middle of the night when on guard I had to stop four patrols who had to give the password. One of them gave the word "Powell" when it was supposed to be "Pearl"—so all the guard was called out to stop them coming closer until the right password was clear.

It looks as if the war may soon come to an end, as more and more prisoners are being taken. All the prisoners we have taken lately have behaved well, even though they are all covered with sores after riding day and night trying to get away from us. No doubt we don't look that much better, as none of us have had a chance to wash up for well over 10 days.

I had the opportunity to talk to De la Rey's nephew yesterday at Buffles Vlec after he was taken prisoner. He talked freely about past events but nothing about present events. Because he is a medical man and De la Rey asked for him to be allowed to return and take care of the sick, he was escorted back to their lines without incident.

Other prisoners talk freely and say that the last three weeks have been hell on earth, as they have had no rest and haven't unsaddled their horses for over a week—so they could dash away as our troops approached. Most of the horses are covered with saddle sores and couldn't go much further, even if the Peace talks break down—and I'm sure most of our men couldn't find the strength to follow.

One thing for sure—I've learned a lot during my stay in the Army in South Africa—how to take care of a horse, mend my own clothes, and I've also learned how to live in the rough with little water, food or shelter. The next place I want to go will have big rivers, lakes, and plenty of fish and wildlife. I've also learned a lot about people and the tremendous size of the area we covered from Cape Town to the Orange Free State and the Transvaal—it will make England seem very small and rather dull.

While I'm lying awake at night trying to get to sleep with the shells bursting nearby, I often wonder whether I will want to stay in England or look for peace and quiet in America—possibly Alaska or northern Canada, where there are so many opportunities for someone with a little imagination and who is willing to work. I've met with several Canadians serving in South Africa, who I've got to know fairly well and they describe the life out there as so free and easy. People in Canada work together in small communities. They can obtain land as a preemption they claim and with hard work they can build a cabin of logs out of the forest, clear a few acres of land, and then get full title in a very short time. I fail to see how it will be possible for me to do this in England, where all the good land is owned by someone.

I have no firm plans at the present time, as I'm too busy staying alive. Providing all is well, I will return to England to see you all—so don't alarm Mother by telling her I could possibly move on after a while to seek a free environment in which to live. I may not even get rich; however, it should be better than the 2s 6d I get now. With my carpenter training, I should be able to make a fair living away from the hustle and bustle of city life, where I could never be able to own a section of land (640 acres) that my Canadian friends tell me about while we are lying behind a rock wall on a long night. This is when many good stories and dreams come out. I'm looking forward to the war ending, as the senseless killing seems to go on night and day.

Brother Jack

January 23rd, 1902

D ear Dad,
Hope you all had a good Xmas. For a while last summer I
thought I might be home. However, the peace process seems to be
pretty well at a stalemate, with neither side giving up much ground.
We seemed to spend months during the fall either trying to get supplies
of ammunition and horses to replace those we'd lost or else trying to
keep supply lines open to others who came in to relieve us in forward
positions. I lost my horse recently by shell fire, which I regret a great
deal as she was such a friendly, faithful horse. I have a new one but it's
not nearly as good as the last one.

A lot of hope was placed in the completion of the Kroonstad-
Lindley blockhouse line that has been built over many months. It was
built to try and stop the Boer forces from moving quickly from one
area to another to avoid capture. So far, it doesn't seem to have
achieved all that was expected. Our officers were confident in late
February that we had De la Rey's forces bottled up in a valley and that
they couldn't possibly get out. Yet after a week of heavy fighting with
rear guard forces, we found he had slipped away during a dark stormy
night. He captured Tweebosch a few nights later, which was nearly
75 miles away from where he was supposed to be. There were other
reverses during March, even though we were still taking more and
more prisoners who kept telling us the war was as good as over—even
though it didn't look like it from where we were under attack day after
day. Although the Peace talks going on, we hear little about the
progress.

May 31st, 1902

Just came back from a long night on patrol and thank God, I
can finish this letter as the war ended this morning and hope I can soon
get home to see you all and have a big celebration in Evenley.
Love to all.
Your son,

Jack

Army Form B. 2077.

Should this Parchment be lost or mislaid no duplicate of it can be obtained.

N.B.—Any person finding this Certificate is requested to forward it, in an unstamped envelope, addressed to the Adjutant-General, War Office, London, S.W.

PARCHMENT CERTIFICATE of Character on discharge, or transfer to Army Reserve, of No. *26623* (Rank) *Private*

(Name) *John Lee Shelford*

(Regiment) *7th Bn.*

27° (Devon) Squadron

His conduct and character while with the Colours have been, according to the Records :—

Very good

(Place) **ALDERSHOT**   Signature of Commanding Officer

(Date) *11th Aug. 1907*

Description of the above-named man :—

Age *21 yrs. 6 m.*   Height *5 ft 8½ in.*

Complexion *Fresh*   Eyes *Grey*

Hair *Dark Brown*   Trade *Carpenter*

Marks or Scars, whether on face or other parts of body   *nil*

H W V 50,000 5—02. Forms
7 22 12   B. 2077
      24.

Aldershot

August 11th, 1902

D ear Mum,
   It's been a long wait for ships to move a lot of us back to England—over 250,000 men anxious to get home. During the wait I did a lot of reading in the papers here about the tremendous loss on both sides during the war. We suffered over 100,000 casualties out of the 350,000 who were here. Over 22,000 are buried here. There were over 400,000 horses, mules and donkeys killed, as they couldn't hide behind rocks and ant hills like we could. They were out in the open at times, trying to get enough dry grass to eat in order to stay alive. I'm sure neither side can claim the war was won or lost by the other sides by brilliant or stupid strategy—but more so by who made the least mistakes. In one major battle the British lost trying to break the siege of Ladysmith, the Boer generals were very surprised as they thought they had lost till the British started to withdraw across the Tugela River. The journey back from Cape Town was pleasant but seemed to take a long time.

   I'll be back home at the end of the week once I get everything cleared with the Army. I got my discharge from the Army on August 11th, 1902 and once I get my big paycheque, which is around £65, I'll be back home for a while before moving on to America or Canada.

Jack

CHAPTER 2

LIVERPOOL TO AMERICA

The letters in Chapter 2 cover the trip from England over to New York. Dad then worked his way across the United States from New York to Buffalo, Hayse City, Kansas, San Francisco, and then up to Vancouver, British Columbia.

Buffalo
april 11

Dear Mam

I believe I told you we had a rough journey & that we did not get to N.Y. till sunday. Tis a pretty harbour numerous small islands covered with houses studded here & there, also a big statue of Liberty standing ~~out right~~ in the bay. all the streets except a few of the best are rough ~~~

New York
April 1st, 1903

D ear Mother,
We got away from Liverpool on time about 12:30 p.m. and moved very slowly for the first hour then picked up speed till we ran into strong winds as land was disappearing out of sight. I sat up on deck as long as I could till the waves started to splash up on the deck so the Captain ordered everyone down below for safety reasons. While up on top, I sat thinking what adventures lay ahead when I reached America. These thoughts were fine until I got below and the room seemed to start going around, which surprised me as I'd persuaded myself I'd not get sick no matter how hard the storm blew. All my good intentions soon disappeared and I was sick for the next two days.

During that time I didn't care if the ship sank as I felt so bad. On the third day, I decided I should try and eat something if I was going to last till I reached shore. While having a bowl of soup, some French girls came and sat down at the same table, so I thought I should show them how much French I had learned in school—which didn't seem to impress them very much, so they giggled for a while and flirted with everyone that came by. They tried hard to talk to me in English; however, their English was like my French so they never did get to know I was saying how lovely they looked.

It was unfortunate, as I'm sure they would have been a lot of fun during the trip over to New York. Fortunately, after they left a very nice Irish girl sat close by and we got talking about where we were going on reaching America. She was very nice and we had long discussions during the trip and I said I was going to Alaska for a few years to make a little money then start a homestead somewhere in western Canada or Alaska. She thought it was such an exciting idea and both of us were sorry when the voyage ended and we never saw each other again after relatives came to pick her up. She wanted to write once in a while; however, I had no address and didn't even know how far I would travel this year. As time went by, I wished I'd asked her to send letters to you in England till I settled down to work in one place where I would have an address.

On arrival in New York, I stood and looked at the Statue of Liberty that overlooks the harbour and carefully read *The New Colossus* (by Emma Lazarus) on the base:

Not like the brazen giant of Greek fame,
  With conquering limbs astride from land to land
  Here at our sea-washed, sunset gates shall stand
A mighty woman with a torch, whose flame
Is the imprisoned lightning, and her name
  Mother of Exiles. From her beacon-hand
  Glows world-wide welcome; her mild eyes command
The air-bridged harbor that twin cities frame.
"Keep ancient lands, your storied pomp!" cries she
  With silent lips. "Give me your tired, your poor,
Your huddled masses yearning to breathe free,
  The wretched refuse of your teeming shore.
Send these, the homeless, tempest-tost to me,
  I lift my lamp beside the golden door!"

(Source: *Encyclopedia Americana*, vol. 25, 1982, p. 637)

It made me feel good, as it gave me hope that there may still be something for someone like me who came here with nothing, except my carpentry tool kit—and still wearing my Army patched pants, shirt and tattered military hat.

I had no trouble to pass Customs; however, my carpenter boxes with tools did get knocked about on the ship in rough weather. When I move from here—wherever I go—I shall store one of them. Railway storage is exorbitant—25¢ if left for one day and 10¢ for each day after—so it soon runs you up a pretty big bill.

There is only one class on American railroads, except for colonists. If they book right through, they pay less. Work is not so plentiful as I had expected and I have only worked two days so far, which is just enough to keep me in food and shelter, if I'm careful. I've had time to walk around and see all I can before moving on. The harbour is very pretty, with the numerous islands covered with houses scattered here and there—also the big Statue of Liberty standing out right in the bay. All the streets, except a few of the best, are rough paving stones on edge, which are rough to walk on and dirty. They seldom seem to be swept. Nearly everybody here lives in rooms in small apartments that don't have cooking facilities. Meals are generally very good. the room and food cost me roughly $2.00 a week. No doubt, there are better places in town but around this area, most places seemed very dirty and a lot of the people don't speak much English. I've met people from nearly every country in Europe.

The skyscrapers are very big and you get a good look at them from a wonderful overhead railway and electric trams and Yankiemus, but they fail to impress you like London. It's very easy to get about the city as the streets start in the middle and go to the Thousandth Street or Avenue each way. I like the system where every 100 yards there is a shoe shine man with a comfortable chair wanting to shine your shoes—quite luxurious compared to London where you have to stand while getting your shoes shined and one person works on each shoe. My old brown shoes now shine like silver; they sure do an excellent job. I only wish my clothes looked as good.

I could see my face in the shoe when a little Italian had finished. He charged me 10¢. I was so pleased with it that I gave him another 5¢ as a tip. I didn't know till next day that the going price was 5¢ and he had already taken 5¢ as a tip.

I'm finding a few odd jobs building shelves and cupboards in a new restaurant which will open next week, as long as I get my work completed. The owners have treated me well and have brought my lunch and coffee so I don't lose any time and can work 12 hours a day.

There is no doubt if I wanted to stay for a while I could get plenty of work; however, I have my sights set on Alaska so I don't want to get held up on my way to the west coast then going north. I only intend to stay and work enough to carry me on to the next stopping place—so I will be moving on next week.

Love,

Jack

Buffalo, New York
April 16th, 1903

D ear Dad,
    I'm now in Buffalo and it's quite different. New York was easy
to get around, while in Buffalo it is rather hard. The city is more like a
circle and each big road leads to the centre—more like the spokes on a
wagon wheel—not so easy to find your way back if you walk too far.
There is still frost and snow here on April 16th and it looks like it will
stay for some time yet—but the lakes are open. Have not been to
Niagara yet, but electric cars run daily so shall go when I have time.
    Have done one day's work but not very satisfied. Pay alright
but people I have to work with are all Germans speaking pidgin
English, so there are dead-locks through misunderstanding. They seem
to think that *mit* stands for every English verb and I really believe they
think I don't speak English at all. Work is not as plentiful as I had
expected, owing to a strike at Toronto which has flooded this town
with carpenter/joiners.
    Do not yet know how I shall get on *mit* the Germans, so am not
sending address as yet. It is a very dirty town with no conveniences of
any kind whatsoever so that I am not keen about stopping here long but
shall for a short time in order to get into the life cycle of work which is
different over hear, with such a mix of foreign people and many
languages.
    While working the other day on a house the owner came by to
see what sort of a job I was doing on the cupboards I was making for
him. He was an English gentleman and thought it was a good job and
sat down to talk for a while. I told him I'd been out hunting last
weekend and enjoyed getting out of town. He got very interested and
asked if I'd like to go hunting next weekend as he was going up into
Canada for a couple of days. He gave me directions on how to get to
his farm early in the morning, which sounded like a lovely chance as I
had visions of getting a chance to try out my gun on something larger
than a jack rabbit.
    To my surprise, when I turned up at his farm early Saturday
morning he came out from the barn riding a lovely horse with another

one following behind, along with 14 hunting dogs. As soon as he saw me with the gun, he quickly told me I wouldn't need that and to leave it at the barn. I'd never been out on fox hunts in England but always wondered what they were like—so I went along for the ride.

We had a very enjoyable two days riding through some fairly open country. We never did see a fox but the dogs seemed more interested in rabbits—much to the annoyance of their master. He wanted me to stay for a while and do some more work around the farm, but I have decided to move on once I've completed my job, which will only take a week or so—then I will have plenty of money to move on to the next place.

Near the end of May I left Buffalo and started moving west and taking odd jobs as I went along—mainly working on farms building granaries to store grain. It seems they grow a lot of winter wheat in these parts and hope for a record crop, as prices have moved up during the last year. A lot of places we passed through looked like good farming areas; however, it seems most of the good land is already taken up.

At the moment I plan on staying in Kansas during the grain harvest, as I'm told there is always work at that time of the year for a good carpenter—as the farmers and grain companies always seem to run out of space as the harvest comes in.

In one granary I was working to build a chute which was over 100 feet long to carry the grain down to the railway boxcars down below. I was shocked at the filth of some of the people working with shovels to move the grain around so it would dry. If left in one place, it could mould and not be fit for sale—except for pigs. Some of those didn't give a damn for anything and even went to the bathroom in the grain, as they were too lazy to go outside. The first chance I got, I told the foreman to give me a hand for an hour and see for himself what was going on. It wasn't long till he was horrified at what he saw and fired all of them.

Will write again when I move on.

Jack

Hayse City, Kansas
December 9th, 1903

D ear Arthur,[1]
Received your letter some time ago but didn't have time to answer. You told me you had an exam in school; however, it seems other things were on your mind and you forgot to tell me if you passed—but I hope you did—so you will have to move to another school and get away from your charmer, Dorothy, who I fear is depriving you of all your boyish thoughts and amusements so early in your life.

Just remember—you're only 17 and I'm 23 and yet, unfortunately, untouched. Take an example from me—learn a lot first before you spring the trap. Even then, you may lose your trail in life. Of course, it's all very well fancying you are desperately in love and all that gives you something to think about—but before you make a complete ass of yourself, go away to school for a time and see how absence and other young ladies' charms act on your poor distracted heart. Just look at the common sense side of the question and then examine your own thoughts.

First of all, you live in Evenley, a beautiful sleepy little village with absolutely nothing to distract your thoughts from a certain subject when once fastened there.

Why—digressing a trifle—directly I stay in a place about two weeks the novelty is worn off, I have that peculiar itching sensation that can't be scratched clinging to my heart in huge clumps. Going a little further, I have been here so long that I have no heart left. It is divided into three equal parts: Love, Common Sense, and Travel—of which one at a time gains complete control over the others. It brings a case of seeing and being on guard. Directly I leave here I shall have all my heart again in full force.

Common sense will tell you how many young ladies—needless to say, nice—have you ever been at all intimate with. Thirdly, your

---

[1] Arthur was my Dad's younger brother. This letter was written when Arthur was 17 years old and in love for the first time.

age. You are very young, boyish, and she is older. Most always, a man picks one that is younger. Fancy tying yourself for life at your age—17—to age 67, I would say. Oh, Horrors! That is a long time. When half hooked to a girl you have only half a mind to do the right thing. Remember, once hooked, you cannot do as you please when someone else has more or less a veto power over you.

All I'm saying is, don't go too strong till you have been away for some time. I believe you have a fortnight's holiday where you can think and you can't do much damage waiting till after that is over. I hope you will excuse me giving you advice and hope **after** your holiday if you still think the same way, then go back and win the fair lady.

I have a good job right now, even though I had a tiff with my employer the other day and thought of quitting and moving on west. I managed to ease my feelings by asking for a 50¢ rise and to my surprise, I got it. So I shall stay a little longer if we can get along till after Xmas at any rate. I'm pretty flush with money so I don't care whether or not I get fired.

I bought a new gun, a repeating Winchester, which holds six shots—a beauty for looks but have not tested its shooting qualities yet—but will soon.

Your brother,

Jack

Hayse City, Kansas
January 10th, 1904

D ear Arthur,
It's been a long time since I got a letter from home and was lonely over Xmas. The weather is well below zero and dark skies. It's so dull that when I pick up my fiddle I practise an octave low and instead of playing "Home Sweet Home" and "Rule Britannia, Britannia Rules the Waves" I find myself playing funeral hymns and sad songs.

In fact, I felt real homesick for the first time. Once New Year came along, the sun came out and the world looked great again. In fact, it looked so good I thought I might stay awhile. I can't believe the change came about simply because I ended up the year with a rip-roaring party on New Year's Eve after meeting a group of young people and ended up at the Dutch Lassies Restaurant and Bar. There were six of us—three men and three young ladies. One of the girls was lovely and had a nice personality and kept us laughing half the night. For the first time, I realized how easy it was to lose your head over a pretty girl—so I should apologize for giving you a bad time in my last letter about falling head over heels in love with the lady in your life.

Towards morning, all were wondering what to do New Year's Day and someone suggested taking a long walk out of town. I said I didn't think I would go as I'd just bought a new gun and wanted to see how good it was for shooting jack rabbits. I got a surprise when the jolly little girl said, "I want to go. I've never even thought of the fun it would be chasing a jack rabbit around a bush. I've wasted my last two years trying to catch a man." We bought a pound of cheese for 10¢ and a loaf of bread for a nickel to keep us going till we got back.

We saw a lot of rabbits but had trouble getting a close shot at them, as each time I went to aim the girls would laugh and the rabbit would run. After several hours of flirting and shooting we were able to get three, which we took to one of the girls' homes and cooked them up in a big stew pot with a bunch of vegetables which was real good.

We spent a very enjoyable three days before we had to start work again. I think I will quit at the end of the month, even though I know I won't enjoy the next job as much as this one as I'm boss of the crew now and don't expect I will like being bossed at the next job. I've made good wages here and averaged nearly one dollar an hour, but if I'm going to see Denver and 'Frisco before spring I will have to make a move—even though I hate to leave my newfound friends because we have had a lot of fun together.

I've swallowed enough dust on the job here and enjoyed the fresh air while out in the country chasing rabbits. I think I would like to move on where I can get a job out in the clear air of possibly northern Canada or Alaska. It sounds by the newspapers here that the Japanese are going to fight sooner or later and if I get to 'Frisco in time, it will be a lively town as tons of contraband of war will be shipped from there.

Our weather continues grand, as we get perfect sunny days— just right for work—with ten degrees of frost each night. We have had continual skating but no snow, so the frozen ponds stay clear. When we do get some snow, I am going on an excursion to the Saline River to spear fish and shoot jack rabbits and quail, which seem plentiful. We have had below zero three times, but only for two or three days at a stretch. The natives say it is wonderfully mild for this time of the year. Back east and north of here, they have been registering as much as 40 below zero and I don't need that when we all go fishing through the ice.

Next morning we left at daylight and arrived at the river after a two-hour walk. We cut a hole in the ice on the river just below a riffle, where the fast water enters a pool below where the fish congregate and rest before going further upstream. The water is clear and it's easy to see them in three or four feet of water. We lit a fire on the shore close by and cut a log six or eight feet long to sit on to get warm once in a while. Once we caught a fish we split it down the middle and after taking the insides out, we threw them to the girls to toast them on a forked stick over the hot embers in the fire.

I think they enjoyed that more than sitting perfectly still on the ice to wait till a fish appeared to either gaff or spear it before it sees you and darts away. We make our gaff hook out of very small iron rods or heavy spring wire. They are placed in a camp fire till red hot, then we pound them into a big fish hook with a rock, then sharpen the point which is a big job and requires lots of patience to keep rubbing it with a sandstone rock till the point is sharp as a needle. Once this is completed, the test of your skill comes when you try to slowly put the hook over the fish, then give it a quick jerk and yank the fish out of the water so fast it won't fall off. Better still is to flip it over to the girls sitting by the fire to hear them yell if one lands on them. The spear is far more difficult to make and I do that at work, where we have an anvil for bending iron rods into the shape we want or for sharpening plough shares which are brought in by the farmers around the district—so I get fairly good at it. With the spear, I hammer out a sharp point on the end then take a sharp coal chisel to the red hot iron and cut a piece that acts as a barb, which will keep the fish from getting away once speared.

I'm getting fairly good in my spare time with the blacksmith forge, anvil and hammer to make horseshoes and sharpen tools of all kinds for farmers when they come to town. I thought it was a good thing to learn, for later if I settle in a remote area with no such services to do this type of work, I won't have any trouble doing it myself.

I was very sorry to get your letter and hear that John Taylor is very sick. I'm not surprised as he didn't look good when I came back from Africa. It will be a big blow for Percy and also Safie Mattinson, his bride-to-be; however, it's better for her if it happens now rather than after they were married. I'll have to write and cheer her up if I can, as we always got along well any time we met. It's wonderfully easy to be philosophical when oneself isn't directly concerned or affected. I notice it more each day I live that we can easily get detached from the goings-on in the world that doesn't affect us directly.

A few days later after the enjoyable fishing trip, I decided all good things must come to an end if I was to get out to the Pacific Coast before spring—so I left after many tears and a farewell party that lasted till 5:00 a.m. when the train was to leave and everyone came to the station to see me off. The train was over an hour late, so we spent the time dancing on the station platform and telling stories till the train arrived. I certainly shouldn't be giving you any more advice about your love life, as the jolly girl here in Kansas and the young group left my heart in a flutter for days. When I reach the West Coast, I hope to send you another letter and tell you all about the trip and what the West Coast looks like.

While on the journey from Kansas to 'Frisco, I got talking to a fellow that had been in town for some time, so I asked how he was making out. To my surprise, he said, "Just great. I started my life in America as a cowboy on a cattle drive from Arizona to Texas and in 12 short years I've worked my way up to be a taxi driver in 'Frisco."

Hope all is well in England.

Jack

San Francisco
March 2nd, 1904

To Brother Arthur,
    I'm not going to lecture you again about falling in love too fast at such a young age. This time, I'm going to console you with my thoughts, word and deed with your problem at school. Do I not remember the jealous nature of inspectors, if it were not for special traits of theirs, my lengthy review of what I wrote about the new Element called "A Short Treatise on Argon" would now be occupying a beacon place in the world of science—instead of being subjected to the same chemical process as that for which beacons are intended. But enough—let us instead of bawling like kids at their injustice, despise the originators of the insult to conquer them by again writing papers which even their ignorant, jealous and sordid minds dare not consign to ashes for fear that the light would still shine. By the way, I'm speaking of what you shall do, not what I did do.
    What did the Fair Dorothy do when you broke up? Did she faint, squeal, scream or throw fits, or did she take it like a heroine and say, "My Arthur, my onliest one! I grieve for you. I pity you and as I love you, here is a peanut and a periwinkle to make out for the disappointment." Here, of course, lies the only true solace for you. May she come nobly forward and give it—but who, except the devil himself, knows what a feminine will do? Surely not me. I have the greatest trouble in keeping track of my own mind, without trying to study the whims of half a dozen female hearts.
    I keep wondering how John Taylor is doing. The last time I heard from Mother he seems to be getting worse. I wrote to Safie to let her know of my concern, yet can't think of anything else I could do. I gather the wedding has been postponed to a later date. Mother said you weren't looking very extra brilliant. If I hear any more such reports, as your guardian (having legally adopted you at your birth), I shall have to issue a mandate that you study no longer and come with me to Klondike, where I can have you under my supervision—besides giving you in my own person a steady example to follow.

Mother's doubts, notwithstanding, I am so sorry that Dad didn't get his right choice of whisky. Quite a case of the old 'un taking his horns in. I feel sorry for him and hope it didn't bring extra pains. Just tell him I learned an excellent remedy for almost anything. It is whisky and water. The water should be either poured or rubbed in on the outside of the glass with judicious precautions against either heat or letting the water get inside the glass. The whisky is to be imbibed frequently—if necessary, forced down.

You will see by the address I'm in 'Frisco working, but am proceeding to Vancouver via Victoria by steamer on Sunday. Don't write till you get my new address. Many reasons (unnecessary to mention) make me determined to go on to B.C. without getting a steady job—even though there is plenty of it here with good money. It's not difficult to get $30 a month if you have any experience.

I came direct to 'Frisco rather than stopping off at Denver, as intended. I stayed longer than planned in Kansas with all the young friends I met, especially the pretty girls in the crowd. The season is getting on and I want to get north for the spring. 'Frisco—other than rain most of the time since I came—is jolly good. It is unique. It takes just the same position here as Capetown takes in South Africa—as a large shipping port and the tropical vegetation, polyglot population, even temperature, all kinds of cheap fruit which you can buy for next to nothing. It also has a land-locked harbour. It has a Chinatown that is the greatest feature to the visitor. You can get a good breakfast for 25¢ and lovely dinner for 50¢. There are reported to be 70,000 Mongolians all packed in a few streets covering about 26 acres, temples, theatres, joss houses, shops, opium dens—everything purely Chinese from ladies' slippers to old mandarins' pigtails.

I'm sorry to say that many of the old ladies with bunches of black hair and the reports that old Chinks being queer are false—such is human nature. They are very pleasant to get along with. I, of course, being interested in hair—with my own giving me a good deal of trouble—and there's not much left. Naturally wishing to get acquainted with beauty-making devices, I got behind a nice Chinese belle and examined her hair. Now I didn't know that, according to their custom, whether married or not so is their hair done. It appears she was married and, as I was about to stroke her hair, an extra big Chinese man grabbed her away and I was only able to notice that she had a bald spot and had tried to cover it with long black hair. From then on, I thought it better to shove my hands in my pockets before getting into real trouble. I had always the desire to pull pigtails and it might lead to rather serious consequences from a lot of the Chinese community.

I like to see them get about. You can't say they walk—they seem to quickly shuffle along, which looks as if they are afraid of jarring themselves. All wear slippers—men felt soles one inch thick; older women the same, except a heel on them; nice young belles wear heels with three inch soles. They are very pretty. The boys wear comfortable slippers and young girls anything that has a tendency to sprain ankles such as round bottomed slippers or an enormous heel stuck right in the centre of the foot. The little boys look nice with their white soled slippers; yellow wide breaches tied tightly at the bottom. They wear black loose coats and variegated coloured round hats and with gloves interlaced with double the amount of yellow and red.

The barber shops are good but a tedious process. They shave everything—eyes (except lashes), nose, ears, neck and forehead. It takes an hour to shave one ear. At the back of some of the barber shops is often an opium den. Just to further my education of culture, I decided to peep in the door and saw a couch filled with mainly Chinese people, where they were passing around two-foot bamboo sticks and inhaling till stupefied. Some were so stupefied, they listened to the horrible sounds which some villainous old Chinese is drawing forth from some pattern of violin made before Adam. I thought I would buy another violin to see if I could play it, so I opened the door and was going in when some half-drunk man gave forth such a shriek that I at once thought I didn't want that special violin anyhow and sorry to say, I hiked quickly as I hadn't got a gun with me or even a knife.

What a difference there is between the Japanese and the Chinese—in size especially. In the crowd, you seldom see a Japanese man over 5'3", while the average Chinese is 5'7" or 5'8". The Japanese are brown looking, while the Chinese are a pallid yellow and have strong muscles on their body.

I know Dad would have a lovely time here in San Francisco fishing—as you can catch 20- or 30-pound salmon right here in the harbour. I caught a 25-pound salmon yesterday and took it to a Chinese restaurant and traded it to the cook for free meals during my stay in town, which I thought was a good deal. They also have lovely parks, a zoo and museum, etc., which is an interesting place to spend a few days. The rain has been horrible. You seldom see the sunset over the Golden Gate Bridge more than once a month.

After living in the dry, clear Kansas air then coming here to the mild, damp air, I don't like it as I feel colder than I was in Kansas—where we saw the temperature go down to 30 below zero. I hope it will be better further north.

It is 850 miles to B.C. and I am looking forward to seeing it. Hope I don't get seasick, as the big waves roll across the Pacific and catch the ship broad side, which makes it roll around far more than if the ship is facing the waves or going with the waves.

Tell Mum not to take me seriously, as I'm not capable of it after coming out of Africa with all the death and destruction caused by war—where it seems that no one really wins when you see so many young men under 20 getting killed.

I must say goodbye for now, as I have to see my barber before leaving for Victoria.

Jack

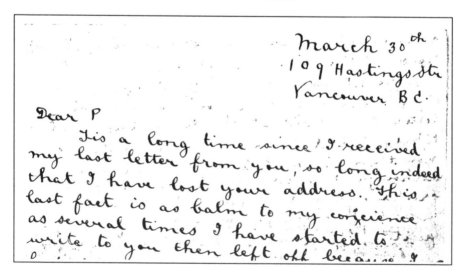

Vancouver, Canada
June 12th

D ear Flora,
We left San Francisco in the early morning—just before light
and the clouds cleared away and wind went down, which was a good
start on the way north. I could see land on the right, which looked like
lovely country from our view out at sea. At times I wondered whether I
was setting my sights too far north to Alaska and might be better to
settle in the vast areas of Oregon that are still mainly unsettled.
However, every time I went to sleep I would dream of the open spaces
up north where a person would be free to roam wherever he wanted
without being hindered by too many people trying to restrict your
freedom—as it was in England and would be the same some day in
Oregon and Washington. I always felt since I was 12 years old that it
was near impossible to own land in England unless you were born into
a wealthy family that owned large tracts of land and could hire people
to do the hard work. I fully realized this could not happen to me, as my
dad made so little as a school principal in Evenley.

It sounds by your letters that my two brothers and you are going
on in the educational field, which is great, as you will no doubt have
more security than I will ever see. I often take a look at myself in the
glass and it shocks me to see the view of a rather battered slouch hat,
not a very kindly face, collarless neck, an old Army jersey, shabby suit
and thick high boots that hold a certainly not lazy spirit but careless
and inconsistent, except for the urge to travel that will take me away
from the masses of people and wars that come all too often in the more
over-populated countries of the earth.

After thinking all of this, I made up my mind to do more to
improve my appearance in the eyes of those travelling on the same
ship—so I shaved and had a haircut and changed my shirt and pants.
Many on board are heading for the Klondike or the goldfields in the
Cariboo country of B.C. There are only a handful of women on board
and most of them are going to Victoria to meet their future husband.
Some of the people on board are those who made a few dollars in the
Klondike and returned to 'Frisco for some fun and to spend all their

money—which is easy if you go to the rough areas of town where fast girls and slow poker players are more than willing to take their money. Most end up with nothing and have to get money from a slippery con-man for a grub stake to get back.

We arrived in Victoria and only stayed overnight, so I walked around and stopped in two bars in order to hear what people were saying about the job possibility—which didn't sound too good. Many were talking about Nanaimo (70 or 80 miles up-Island), which seemed to have a better future than Victoria, as the coal mine up there was employing a lot of people. They ship between 150 and 300 tons a day, which mainly goes to San Francisco and other ports south. The coal is selling for $6 a ton at the mine or $12 a ton landed in San Francisco. They tell me that some is sold as far south as Mexico for even higher prices.

If Vancouver doesn't turn out good for me, I'll try Nanaimo; however, I don't want to work underground. I'm more interested in building houses for those that are willing to work underground. The main deposit is situated only a quarter mile from town and the coal reaches the dock, where the water is deep enough for large ships to dock. The principal shaft is over 1,200 feet long and goes to a depth of 270 feet from the surface. It seems a long way down to me, so I think I will move on to Vancouver.

Victoria and Vancouver Island are very pretty and I hope to get back before too long and take a good look to see if there is a good place to settle and build up a farm, as they tell me there is good soil in many areas—especially near Duncan, which is mainly a logging town and some farms which likely have a bright future in the long term. A boat leaves tomorrow morning, so it should be a nice trip across through the many islands in the Gulf of Georgia.

Jack

109 Hastings Street
Vancouver, B.C.
March 30th, 1904

D ear Percy,
You will note my new address is 109 Hastings Street in Vancouver.

Here I am in Vancouver as I didn't stay long in Victoria—as it didn't appear to be a very lively place for someone like me to stay. Another passenger on board told me I wouldn't have much trouble in finding a job here in Vancouver because when he left to go south to San Francisco there were a number of houses going up on Hastings Street, where finishing carpenters, like myself, could get a job easily. He also said that there is a lot of mud on Hastings Street and they were trying to build a plank sidewalk—as you would sink six or eight inches in the mud while walking at this time of the year—so this project will employ a lot of workers. The mud condition was caused by hauling logs down the street to a new sawmill at the foot of the street that had been built late last fall and opened in October. They were cutting logs further up Hastings Street, which is a little more than a trail—only good enough for oxen to skid logs down far enough where they could be loaded on to heavy wagons pulled by four oxen which brought them down to the sawmill. It's remarkable what four or six oxen can pull. Yesterday, I saw a load with five huge logs on their way down to the mill.

I quite like Vancouver, as it's so close to the forest where I can take my gun and hunt deer. Yesterday, I borrowed a little ten foot boat from another worker and paddled it across the harbour to North Vancouver, where there is only a few shacks with people living in them along the shore. Some of them are tied to large trees on the shore and they float up and down as the tide comes in and out. It's a good place for deer hunting as people seldom go over there and you can wander anywhere you like without disturbing anyone. I followed a stream about half a mile through thick brush, large trees and soon got a deer, which I dressed out and brought it back to hang in my landlady's shed at the back of her house—which was a very nice home with three bedrooms, kitchen and dining room. It is a good-sized house with 950 square feet, which is better than average size on this part of Hastings Street.

My landlady was pleased that I got a deer, as she has three boarders to feed. She tells me meat is expensive to buy and she has to pay up to 15¢ a pound, which she thinks is terrible. Most of the vegetables either come in by boat from Vancouver Island or from Chinese gardeners located near the mouth of the Fraser River, close to Ladner.

I received three letters from home today—from sister Flo and two from Arthur, who still seems to be back with Dorothy and enjoying his love life. It doesn't seem he took my advice I sent from Kansas that he was far too young to get serious. I was sorry to hear that John Taylor died, which I wasn't surprised about, as he looked so ill when I saw him just before I left home. It will leave a big hole in your little circle of friends and tell Mrs. Taylor how sorry I am. I will have to write Safie and try to cheer her up, as it came so close to the planned wedding of her and John.

You will be interested to know when I got here my landlady thought I looked so scruffy she showed me first a very dark room—so I told her I wasn't a bat and didn't like the dark—then she gave me a better room, even though she didn't seem impressed until I brought in my two boxes of luggage that had finally caught up with me. I thought she was throwing out a little, so I thought I would impress her m ore by displaying in my room the glass clock I got in Africa, my Japanese compass, Chinese vase, my gun and field glasses I got in Africa, and even collar boxes, etc., etc. She saw the room once and was suddenly very, very obliging and wanted to move me into the best room. She thought I must be an eccentric tourist, so I threw cold water on the deal as she wasn't my kind and told her I was just a carpenter. I locked up my little treasures and the landlady is now just obliging enough, although she still seems curious as to where all my letters come from.

I was pleased J. Judge and Miss Potts are getting married, as it's the wise thing to do when they plan to farm in B.C. In my opinion, the North West Territories are more the place to go from what I can observe here, although this new railroad across Canada could well make a boom for both mining and agriculture. The weather is so wet (and I can't work in the rain), so I'm only making enough to break even. I can't say I don't greatly love working here as a carpenter as things are so peculiar. Have already been sacked once—but it's very little trouble to get another job so I'm again working between showers. While off work for a day, I nearly bought a lot on a new area being developed on Granville Street near False Creek. They were selling for $19 a lot—which seems high—so I put the money back in the bank as Vancouver will likely not be much more than a fishing village for some time—but may take a look later on after being in Alaska for a year or so.

I bought a new .30-30 Winchester for $20, which I will need when I get to Alaska. My .22 rifle will be too small if I want to shoot a caribou or moose, as I hear there are a lot up there if you get in the right place. I don't know much about hunting and fishing other than what I learned from Dad and a few things I picked up in Kansas chasing jack rabbits.

This will be my last letter for a while as I'm heading north. I was going last Thursday but my employer begged me to stay and finish the house I'm building just one block from where I'm staying on Hastings Street. I also got a bad cold so I agreed to finish, which he was very happy about. I've already bought my one-way ticket, as I plan to stay in the north for some time as I heard from people coming off the last boat that there was no problem getting a job in Alaska or the Yukon.

Love,

Jack

109 Hastings Street
Vancouver, B.C.
June 12th, 1904

D ear Percy,
      Later in the week, I'm leaving on board the *Amur*, a C.P.R.
ship, that makes regular trips up to Skagway, then another smaller ship
that will take me to Nome and on to St. Michael on the mouth of the
giant Yukon River, where I will catch a river boat and hope to get to
Fairbanks before winter sets in. We will leave the Yukon at Fort
Gibbon and Tanana Village, close by, and go up the Tanana to
Fairbanks—which I plan to make my base for the winter. I'm confident
I can get a job there.
      Before I leave I have to get busy mending all my clothes and
darning my socks. I was happy to get from home a good supply of
needles and thread. I can only take the clothes I stand in and the rest of
my things have to be boxed and shipped by freighter which, hopefully,
will arrive in a week or so before the Tanana River freezes—which
normally can freeze before the main Yukon River. I have doubled all
my clothes on the inside—in places they wear a lot like the knees and
elbows. I still wear the old khaki breeches which are double bottomed
for cavalry use in South Africa—it's amazing how long they've lasted.
I'm getting better at patching—however, last night when I'd finished I
tried to put my pants on and found I'd sewed the pockets shut with one
of my patches, so had to start again. Darning my work socks I do fine,
except I seem to use my thumb as a pin cushion regularly. I have to do
a real nice bit of fancy sewing to get the right size button hole, as I lost
several buttons and had to use smaller ones that wouldn't fit the button
holes so I can keep my coat, pants and shirt done up—they keep
wearing larger all the time or get torn and have to be sewed again.
      I stayed a few extra days and spent four days hunting over in
North Vancouver. I paddled across Burrard Inlet and left my little boat
under a big tree and walked inland about three miles—mainly
following the Lynn River. I took a blanket and a lard pail which makes
a good tea pot or a pot to make rolled oat porridge or rice. You don't
have to carry much for only four days. I found a nice place to camp at

the fork of the Lynn and a small creek. There were a lot of nice big cedar trees from where I could watch up and down the creek in hopes a deer would come out. It was a comfortable place to camp, as it was dry under the trees and the cedar bark is an excellent starter for a fire. I was unlucky and didn't get a deer but sure enjoyed myself, as I didn't hear or see another person all the time—not even a human track in the sand along the river bank.

It was my very first time out in the woods at night and got one good scare. I'd seen a black bear track close to where I camped and was wondering if he might come around and try and take my small supply of food. I was fast asleep when I felt something sniffing the top of my head. I was sure it was Mr. Bear making himself free with my provisions then wondering whether he was thinking of something better under the blanket. Then he starts lightly scratching my hair which was far too much for me to stand, so I gave an awful yell, jumped up and got my rifle to my shoulder and pulled back the trigger ready to fire—when all of a sudden, I turned and saw by the pale moonlight a nasty little squirrel whisking up the nearest tree. I felt so foolish when I realized all he was wanting was a little of my hair to make a nice comfortable nest for his mate. It was a good lesson for me in the years ahead: Try not to panic until you are sure what is disturbing your sleep.

On the fourth day, I decided to cross the Lynn—a mountain stream that looked so easy to cross. I pulled off my shoes and socks, rolled up my breeches and waded across. Everything went just fine—I came out the other side with a sprained ankle with three bruises on the other, along with two sore feet covered in sand. I was told by a good friend that the only way to get rid of the sand and mud on your feet is to walk out on a log that has fallen into the river and wash your feet in the clean water or the sand will irritate your feet if you put your socks and shoes on with the sand still on your feet. I thought to myself, "That makes a lot of logic"—so I walked about 20 feet so I could sit in comfort and wash my feet. It felt so nice to have my sore feet in the cold water that I stayed for some time until I thought I heard footsteps in the gravel on the shore. I looked up and there was a nice buck deer standing beside a bush where I had leaned my rifle when I came out to wash my feet. I jumped up and thought I could reach my rifle before the deer got too far away. Unfortunately, I slipped on the log that had a patch of loose bark and ended in the river—up to my neck. Needless to say, the deer took one look and bounced away into the heavy brush—never to be seen again.

With clothes and matches all wet, the only thing was to wade back across the river. Fortunately I'd done something right—I'd left three matches in a notch of the tree where I'd made camp. So after the fire was going, I peeled off all my clothes and sat for two hours drying it all out before going back to the boat to paddle back to Vancouver and walk back to 109 Hastings Street where I boarded.

This experience certainly taught me a few thing about hunting. It also made me realize two things: (1) always carry a few matches in a water-tight container, especially when walking close to water—where you can slip and fall in; and (2) also, beware of wet bark on a log over a river—it's just like stepping on glare ice as the bark slides off the wet wood underneath.

Once I get on the boat going north to Alaska I'm going to grow a beard again to look as if I belong in the north. However, if you could see my patched clothes they may think I'm just a bum from down south. I'm sure if I walked across the village green in Evenley the whole town would turn out to see just who it was. My landlady is quite concerned that I'm going to Alaska tomorrow without knowing where I'm going to stay. She also insisted I send her my address when I get to Fairbanks, so she can forward my mail when it comes in.

Love to all,

Jack

CHAPTER 3

NORTHWEST TO ALASKA

The letters in Chapter 3 describe the trip up the Coast from Vancouver to Nome, Alaska, visiting several places up the coast of British Columbia and Alaska. Dad then travelled over to Hamilton on the mouth of the Yukon River by freight boat, then by riverboat up the Yukon River to Tanana, where the forks of the rivers (Yukon and Tanana) meet. The chapter concludes with Dad's travels up the Tanana River, then some 250 miles to Fairbanks.

1904

D ear Mother,
       The trip up the coast from Vancouver was very interesting—with the high mountains and forests, except in areas that have been burned over by forest fires that covered huge areas and left the area black (from recent fires). It seems to take two years before they are green again. Most of these fires were caused by lightning and Indians burning off old growth in order to have new thriving forests in which to hunt. Once the willow, alder and many other bushes come back, the animals and birds flock to the area for feed and the area is ideal for the Indians to hunt deer, grouse and other species for food. After the fire in high altitudes, the mountain sheep and goats move in to feed, especially if it's close to high rocks for protection from wolves that have difficulty in travelling under those conditions. They come out to feed in the early morning and evening—and the rest of the day and night they stay up in the shade of the rocks and on a narrow ledge where they can see if danger is approaching.
       We stopped at the little Indian village of Bella Coola, where I talked to a few Indians and they told me about the lovely open rolling

country over the mountains—with miles and miles of gentle rolling hills that stretch as far as the horizon. There are hundreds of lakes where fish were plentiful, as well as huge rivers draining to the coast— some of them are over half a mile across and most of them in the interior are navigable with river boats during the summer months.

There was a lot of talk about opportunities on the Queen Charlotte Islands for prospecting and farming, as the snow seldom lasts for long and the rivers don't seem to freeze more than for a short time, so prospecting is possible most of the year and vegetables of most kinds are possible to grow and sell to prospectors. It is stated that the Hudson's Bay Company found the Haida Indians on the Island are using golden bullets rather than leaden ones, as it is easier to find gold than lead. Some of the passengers were going to get off at Port Edward and hope to make their way to the Queen Charlottes and spend the winter there before going on to Alaska or the Yukon.

Our next stop was at Port Edward, near the mouth of the Skeena River, where they let off a few passengers and freight. There were a lot of fishermen (both white and native) who set their nets along the river where thousands of salmon travel on their way to spawning grounds up the Skeena and many tributaries that join the main Skeena—which goes inland for over 400 miles.

I haven't been able to find many people I met who knew anything about the interior—excepting a few Indians who travel the river—which is the only means of transport (except walking over the high mountain passes). By the view from out at sea, these mountains appear to be a formidable barrier for travel into the interior. Naturally, most of the Indians stay close to the rivers and lakes and seldom go more than five or six miles from the shore—except while trapping in the winter when they will travel further following the smaller creeks and lakes to catch as much fur as they can to sell to the travelling fur buyers—mainly from the Hudson's Bay Company, but also from several small independent buyers who are reported to be mainly shady characters that they will give you a bad deal if you don't watch out.

I got off the boat for an hour or two and looked around to see what was going on. I enjoyed very much watching a gathering of Indians talking to an English fur buyer who wanted them to go back up river and trap all winter and sell him all their fur next spring when he would come back. Naturally, the Indians wanted to know the approximate price they would get for marten, beaver, muskrat, lynx, mink, fox, wolf and otter. He talked to the Indians for over an hour about the up and down cycles of world trade in fur prices; however, he made it very clear how much he liked the Indian trappers and there was no way he would give them a bad deal after them working so hard all winter tramping through the deep snow and bitter cold for months. After he slowed down for a minute, a big Indian from Hazelton walked up to him with some eagle feathers and gave a short speech on how much the Indians liked him and they were going to bestow on him the valued title of "Walking Eagle." His chest came out and with a big smile, he finally asked—after making a long thank-you speech—what did the "Walking Eagle" title mean, as he wanted to tell his friends back in England all about it. The Chief answered by saying, "It means if an eagle eats too much he is so full of shit he can't fly and has to walk and you, my friend, are the best bull-shitting son of a bitch we have seen for many a moon and we think you deserve this honour." One thing that was clear—it ended the fur buying for at least one day till another bunch of trappers came along that had a better image of the fur buyers.

On leaving Port Edward, we boarded an American ship that made many stops on the way up to Nome—which made for an interesting trip. We got reasonably good meals; however, most of us had to spread our blanket on the deck to sleep at night as there wasn't much room elsewhere. Fortunately, the weather treated us kindly. We could see the large glacier at Juneau—which made the air cool at night even in the summer time, so no one took their clothes off to go to bed.

Our next stop was at Sitka, which was the capital of Russian America and formerly known as New Archangel and the major town in the country at that time. It was exclusively the headquarters of the Russian America Fur Company, which is as large and aggressive as the Hudson's Bay Company. The island on which Sitka is located is on a group or archipelago discovered in the early years of the Russian discovery. The island where Sitka is located was named after Baranoff, the real founder of the settlement of New Archangel who, for a long period, managed the affairs of the Russian American Trading Company in the days of its early history—a troubled and eventful time. Baranoff was chosen because he was a successful merchant in Siberia, was well educated, had superior attainments, and was recognized for his great courage and perseverance.

In the neighbourhood of Sitka there are extensive fisheries and up to 150,000 salmon are annually exported to the south and islands in the Pacific. As soon as a boat-load of fish arrived at the wharf, a number of women (mainly Indian) arranged themselves in two lines and very quickly cleaned and gutted the salmon—something I watched with care as I thought I might want to do it later on. They would throw a few buckets of water over the heap of fish, then place them in vats and put them in brine for shipment. Each woman took her share as wages—which was one large fish weighing 20-30 pounds—worth little to her except to eat.

We were invited to a reception while the ship was loading supplies at Sitka. They served raw vodka—usually half a tumbler full which they encouraged you to drink right down. The local name for it was "Chain Lightning." Most of the older people—mainly of Russian descent—talked of the good old days when Alaska belonged to Russia and there were 180 church holidays in a year. Now they are confined to Christmas, New Year's, Washington's Birthday and the 4th of July— but if the enlightened citizens of the country choose to avail themselves of the privilege, they can enjoy two Sundays in a week owing to the fact that the Russians come from the east and we come from the west. There is a day's difference where the two meet and their Sunday in Sitka falls on our Saturday. Business people don't like it, as often stores are closed for both Sundays.

One of the best businesses in Alaska is St. Paul's, Kodiak Island, where they cut ice from artificial lakes which were made for this purpose. Each one is 40 acres. They can make a lot of ice during their five months of cold weather—not like the interior where the winters are nearly eight months long. All of this ice is shipped south where there is great demand in the hotels in San Francisco and Mexico.

Kodiak was included in the sale of Alaska by the Russians. The company didn't like the sale, as they thought they might lose the ice trade. When the formal transfer of Russia America to the United States was made on October 18th, 1867, the Russian flag showed great reluctance to come down and the cord stuck on the yard arm. A man had to climb the flag pole in a hurry to get the rope free. Unfortunately, the flag then fell on the heads of the Russian soldiers—much to the dismay of the crowd that watched.

The Bering Sea is very shallow and ships can anchor nearly anywhere—but seemed so large to us that we thought we would never get to Nome. To pass the time I did a lot of reading about the early years in Alaska. There were several good books on board the ship and better still, there was a nice little library in Nome.

The town seemed quite busy when we arrived on July 26th, 1904. The trip took nearly three weeks. It seems Nome is one of the main supply bases for inland Alaska and the Yukon until the river freezes solid and stays closed all winter till the ice on the river goes out in late May or early June. Many ships from ports in Siberia call at Nome for trade with Alaska, as the Russian American Trading Company is still very active buying fur at several points in Alaska. Quite a lot of Indian trappers and some white come down the rivers after break-up to sell their furs—as they think they get a better deal than from American fur buyers.

I found many of the crew on these ships are Indians from Siberia—and they look quite a bit like the northern Mongolians I saw in San Francisco. Many of them spoke highly of the Alaskan Indians as being honest, hard-working people and were proud of how successful their North American relatives were making out in such a harsh climate. It's not surprising; they could well be from the same race a long way back.

Yours,

Jack

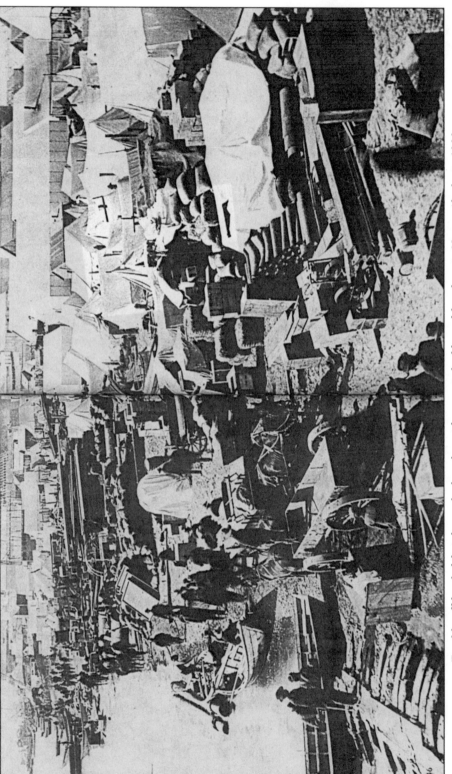

Freshly off-loaded freight on the beach amid tents pitched by gold seekers in Nome, Alaska in 1900

146

Nome, Alaska
September 1904

D ear Dad,
    As a teacher in Evenley, you might be interested in a small bit
of history I've picked up reading here in Nome. The Russians had to
fight their way across many areas of Siberia—especially in the eastern
parts. They used the hardy Cossacks from the Siberian Steppes to lead
the advance to the Pacific shores. They soon captured the Kamchatka
Peninsula in 1725 and areas north in 1728, where large amounts of
ivory were found in the northern arm of Asia called the Chuckchi
country. They also found many large strange trees washed up on the
shores—trees not found in Siberia. In 1830 and 1831, they made
several attempts to find land across the sea—but failed. Their boats
were too small to carry enough supplies to travel far. These boats were
made out of crude wooden planks sawed from timber in the area. The
early Aleut hunters from the Aleutian Islands had a name for the
continental mainland of Alaska—which was called the "Great Land."
    In the closing chapter of Russian expansion east, Vitun Bering
(who was actually Danish by birth and employed by the Imperial
Russian Navy because of his past bravery) led an expedition in 1741 to
try to discover a continent believed to be between Siberia and the
Americas. He had two ships—one called the *St. Peter* and the other,
the *St. Paul.* They set out from Petropaulovsk to try to find the riches
they thought lay to the west. The sea was covered much of the time by
fog, which they found when approaching the Aleutian Islands. The two
ships got separated and never regained contact again during the
voyage. For several weeks, Bering couldn't get clear of the fog and
finally when it cleared he could see a high mountain in Alaska—later
to become known as Mount Elisa. Bering and his men went ashore, but
made no contact with any inhabitants although they found signs of a
primitive civilization that had left pieces of arrowheads and spear
tips—which were well made and had sharp points like a needle. The
men found these things very interesting, as they were similar to those
found embedded in whales and walruses that had been washed up on
the shores of Siberia at least 20 or 30 years before the expedition.

There was no contact made with any natives. On the way home, they were hit by a huge storm and the ship was broken up on an island; however, most of the crew managed to reach shore. They managed to live all winter on the island by collecting sea life on the shore and meat from seals they caught and from dead whales that washed up on the shore. Bering died on December 8th, which was a shock to the remainder of the crew as they trusted him to save them. Once the shock was over, they proceeded to collect parts of the wrecked ship and make two open boats which they were then able to sail and paddle back to Petropaulovsk in Siberia in the spring of 1742. The men brought with them many sea otter skins that they had caught during the long winter. This was the start of the fur trade in Russian America.

In 1778, Captain Cook led an extensive exploration of the west coast of North America to try to find the North West Passage which others had searched and failed to find. When he reached Cape Elizabeth, Captain Cook took possession of the land for England. Later he proceeded on his voyage to the mouth of the Kuskakwim and on through the Bering Straits as far as Ice Cape to the north. He was very optimistic that he had found the North West Passage or the mouth of a huge river.

Later, in 1791, Captain Vancouver carried out extensive investigation of the coast and made a report in 1793 that there was no such passage and corrected Cook's report. These two formed the basis for England's claim to northwestern America. Spain was the third nation to claim the northwest. All these claims came to nothing when Russia sold Alaska to the U.S.A. in 1867.

The Russian American Fur Company was established as the first trading company in Alaska on Kodiak Island in 1784. The first schoolhouse was opened in 1788 at Sitka. At the same time, other countries were trying to move in, so the Russian settlement asked the Russian Navy for protection from rival trading companies and were turned down. It was a wonder there wasn't a fully fledged war over the ownership of the west coast; however, cool heads on behalf of the four interested parties mainly prevailed.

When I arrived in Nome and an old prospector told me that Attu Island in Alaska was further west from San Francisco than San

Francisco is west of Eastport, Maine. I found that hard to believe! He had to show me on a map of North America before I would accept what he was telling me. Alaska was bought from Russia in 1867 for $7,200,000, which amounts to only two cents an acre. It doesn't sound much when you hear about the vast amounts of gold shipped out of Alaska in one year. It's reported that in 1903, $10,796,000 worth of gold was taken out of Alaska. It was likely the best buy in modern history. So far, the United States has mainly ignored Alaska as the popular saying goes, "Never a law of God or man runs north of the 53rd parallel."

When we arrived people came down to meet the ship to see if they could get anyone to stay and work before heading up the river to the goldfields. Not many ever stopped to listen as they were in a hurry to catch the first boat leaving Nome to take them across to Kolik or Old Hamilton, where they could get onto a paddle steamer. An old Indian came down to see the ship that we had come in on, as the captain was showing interested people what it looked like and the Indian wanted to see what made it move without paddles. After taking a long look in the engine room, the Indian shook his head and said, "Too much wheels make man too much think."

Gold miners' shelters at Nome, Alaska

One fellow asked me what I'd worked at and offered me $5 a day as a carpenter—which I thought sounded good. Another reason I took the job was to learn all about how people performed their job in

Alaska, as I'd heard it was quite different from where I had worked in the U.S. I also wanted to talk to travellers to find out where the best opportunities were so that I would have some idea about where I should get off the river boat. Most seemed to think Fairbanks was a better opportunity than going right through to Dawson City.

While I was in Nome I helped build a little shop and warehouse to keep supplies dry till they were shipped up river. I also got to know a few trappers who told me there was more money to be made trapping in the winter and cutting wood for the river boats in the summer than digging for gold. Having heard about this, I went out and bought four dozen No. 1 traps at $1.50 a dozen to catch marten, muskrats, weasel and mink along with three dozen traps for larger animals such as lynx, fisher, fox, otter, and beaver. I also bought a supply of 500 rounds of ammunition for my .22 and .30-30 rifles, as well as snare wire which I could make into snares to catch foxes, wolves, or lynx. I thought it would be cheaper if I got these supplies here rather than up river— which proved to be true.

I worked in Nome for the best part of two months—10 hours a day. That gave me a good grub stake for the winter as I was fairly certain the first winter would be a challenge as I got to know my way around. I'm hoping to get a job in Fairbanks and in my spare time I would explore the different side rivers to find out what they had to offer in the way of fur animals, fish in the streams and game animals in the area. I know so little about these things I have to learn fast if I am to survive in the north—which I plan to do for several years if all goes well.

Will write later.

Jack

FROM NOME TO FAIRBANKS

Fairbanks, Alaska
September 25th, 1904

D ear Mother,
I left my little 10 foot by 10 foot room in Nome and caught a freight boat that needed men to load supplies in Nome and to unload and transfer the supplies to a river boat in Hamilton. This worked very well for me, as I got a free ride and had plenty of room for my newly acquired supply of things I had bought in Nome. I was tempted to stay in Nome all winter and leave as soon as the ice went out on the Yukon and Tanana in the spring. However, I decided to make the move in the fall to get an early start in the spring because I wanted to make a few dollars to give me a start in my new life in Alaska. I don't expect it to be easy, as I have no experience about their way of life and living by myself in such a large wilderness area where anyone can travel for hundreds of miles without seeing one person. This life will be a tremendous challenge.

I was determined not to get too entrenched in one place like so many in England, where they stay in the same village or town all their lives without knowing what other parts of the world looked like. The fellow that ran the small freight ship wanted me to stay with him and help run coastal supply trips during the winter; however, I decided to keep moving.

Once the supplies were loaded aboard the paddle steamer, I waved good-bye to my new-found friend who assured me, "If you ever come back, be sure and see me as you can have a job any day you like. There will always be a need for men like you."

Once the paddle boat was loaded with people, freight and mail we left for the long trip up to Fairbanks—over 700 miles up river. It was expected to be one of the last runs before freeze-up, which can come early with a quick cold spell in the fall. Most of the people on board are mainly headed for Fairbanks or Dawson City, then on to the numerous gold fields—many of which would be two or three hundred miles up numerous rivers or over mountain passes. Most of them are prepared to stay the winter, as travel is impossible during the winter months unless they have a dog team and could move down the rivers on the ice. Otherwise they would have to stick it out until late May or early June before they could float down—either on a raft made of six to eight logs nailed together or in a small boat if they had one.

It seemed there was little concern about getting sick or injured, as they knew when they went in there was no turning back. The food supply, therefore, had to be planned with care and they also should have known beforehand whether there was any game or fish they could get during the winter to help out if they ran short. This is no easy task for a greenhorn. Quite a number made the fatal mistake of not taking enough food to keep them going till spring and for them, they never did live to see the green grass come up in the spring.

The first two days going up river in the paddle steamer was great, with bright sunny days and cool nights. We had all paid our fare and were content with everything—even though we only had our blanket to throw over us at night, which is great in nice weather but not so good when the weather gets cold and wet.

On the fourth day after we passed Koserefsky (Holy Cross), we were told by the captain that the wood cutters were on strike and we would have to cut the wood every day to keep the boilers fired up in order to keep the steamer moving. Our spokesman told the captain that we had paid our fare and that we didn't have to cut wood and that we, too, were on strike as of that moment. The captain said quietly, "That's OK, fellows, we will pull into those big trees on the bank and tie up." He then went on to say, "Make yourselves comfortable because if you don't want to cut wood, we will be here for a long time as the ice doesn't normally go out till May and I hear from people coming down from the interior that the ice is now starting to form in sheltered bays and along the shore of the river." The thought of a long cold winter and having to build shelter for the winter out of trees soon put an end to the shortest strike on record.

We spent the rest of the day cutting wood to keep the steam engines running for another day. So from there on till we reached Fairbanks we started out each morning at daybreak, stopping for the night at 3 o'clock to give us time to cut enough wood before dark to run the boilers for another day.

The captain turned out to be a nice fellow. He even helped pack wood up the gang plank and pile it up on deck. In some ways, it turned out well for me as one of the crew was good at sharpening and setting crosscut saw teeth. On the second day, he cut his hand quite badly and couldn't file any more. The saws got so dull that we could hardly cut without a lot of hard work, so he spent an hour showing me how to sharpen a saw (which will be very valuable later on).

Having to stop early each day, it took a long time to reach Fairbanks. The days were getting shorter and on dull days it started to get dark soon after 4 o'clock. I thought we would never get to Fairbanks. Lodging was scarce when we arrived in Fairbanks, as there seem to be several gold claims that are causing a lot of excitement and people are coming in from Dawson City and other places as they think the next big strike will be around this area.

I had no choice but to go and buy myself a 10 foot by 12 foot tent and a small collapsible stove with eight feet of stove pipe and go and set it up outside of town. I got it all set up and was feeling proud of myself—until I cut a tree down for firewood. I mistakenly thought all trees were good to burn—like the cedar I had used on my first camping trip to North Vancouver. I cut it up into small pieces to get my supper cooked and keep me warm all night. I was struggling along with little luck when an old Indian by the name of Sam came by to see what all the smoke was about and who his new neighbour was. He took one look at what I was trying to do, then looked me right in the eye and said, "Him wood just as green as white man. You come with me, I show you old tree. Him dead and dry up, him make good fire." He stayed close by for three weeks, then he went up river to his trap line. It was lucky for me that he had shown me how to find good trees for firewood. Many Indians started a little forest fire each fall to ensure that he had plenty of good wood for the next year. It takes one full year to dry the trees for use after they have been burned. The commercial wood cutters that supplied wood for the paddle steamers and firewood for those living in town followed that example.

People who had lived in Alaska during the early gold rushes told me that the rivers are the main means of transportation during the summer; however, the average summer is only four or five months, so transportation the other eight months is mainly by dog sleigh and snowshoes. Horse travel is more limited, except close in to a town or mining camp where people use the horse to ride to town for supplies or to spend a night in the bar.

The Yukon and Tanana Rivers are very wide in many areas— which make it difficult to travel and find the right channel which is navigable. The Yukon is navigable, when open, for over 1,200 miles. The records show that during a 6-year period the date for the first boat to arrive in the spring between Dawson City and Whitehorse was approximately four months and nineteen days from between June 4th and October 23rd. Occasionally, steamboats have carried supplies up the Tanana to the Delta River—one even reached the junction of the Nebesna River, which is nearly 450 miles from the mouth of the Tanana. Light draft boats can go even further up the Kantishna branch, as well as the Chena, Tolovana and the lower Volkmar. The latter are also used to get supplies into other remote areas during the summer months and by dog teams during the winter. It's fortunate there are so many rivers and smaller streams that can be used like roads into the vast unexplored regions of Alaska and the Yukon.

Having listened to many old-timers, I got such a feeling of excitement that I can hardly wait to get started on my life in Alaska.

Jack

CHAPTER 4

FAIRBANKS, ALASKA

The letters in Chapter 4 describe life in Alaska for a green Englishman trying to learn the ways of survival in a vast country. You either adapted to a new life by trapping, hunting and fishing—or perished during the first winter (which many did) when out on the trap line between the end of October and the end of May—often without seeing another human being during this time.

april 6th o 5 .
Box 741 Fair Banks
Alaska

Dear mam

my hand is stiff it won't hold a
pen good but hope you'll be able to
decipher this. I have just got in from
a 6 weeks trip of about an hour agone
to be after having dinner have sitten
down to write to you. I have been
up Clear Creek trapping marten got on
very well for an amateur I got 54

October 29th, 1904

D ear Dad,
     I've got my camp comfortable and everything in place that I
need for the winter—even though I don't expect to be here all the time,
as I plan to scout out some of the small rivers and creeks that drain into
the Tanana. Yesterday, I started looking to see what there was around
Fairbanks, where I might work. By chance, I passed by a fellow who
was measuring up a building lot near the edge of town, so I stopped to
give him a hand as all he had to measure with was a piece of string
with a knot tied for every foot. When I told him I had a proper
measuring tape over in my tent, he was quite impressed and said, "You
seem to know what you are doing, how would you like to build the
house for me? It will give you a chance to get your feet on the ground."
This sounded like a good idea to me.
     We soon got the house marked and a peg in each corner—once
I had my tape to do the job. The plan would give him a home of
890 sq.ft., which was larger than most houses being built at this time.
From there, we went over to a little restaurant for lunch and I was
surprised with the quality of the food they were serving—certainly
better than what I would do back in my camp. The rest of the day we
spent looking for some good spruce trees out in the forest and in an
area where a team of horses could skid them out and load them on a
stone boat—which is made of two logs with a platform on top. The
house logs are rolled on top, then the horses can pull them to the house
site. It also works well to move eight good sized rocks to the building
site, where they will be dug into the ground and levelled out on a solid
base to hold the bottom logs off the ground—otherwise they will rot in
less than five years. Finding the right sized rocks that two people could
roll onto the stone boat proved far more difficult than finding the right
trees. It took over three days to find them and get them in place.
     The following day we found the right sized logs for the beams
for the floor. Once this was completed, he said, "From here in, it's all
yours to complete. Take care of the horses, as you have close to a two-

mile haul for the logs. They should be able to pull one round of logs at a time and try to get all the logs about the same size so they will go together better. Even then you will find it takes a lot of axe work before they will fit properly to keep out the cold wind during the winter. You will find lots of good moss in the beaver swamp we passed while looking for the timber."

Before he left he stopped to say that he wanted the house finished by the end of January, as he was the foreman out at the mine and he wouldn't be of much help except for an hour or so any time he came to town. I'm sure he knew I was pretty green about the north country and before he left he had to tell me a story about the young Englishman who came to Alaska and asked an old prospector what he could do if he came across a grizzly bear while walking in the woods. The Old Timer said, "Don't worry. They seldom attack and if you do exactly what the bear does you will find nothing will happen to you. A week later, the young fellow was taking a walk when he came past some big trees and there was a big grizzly bear right in front of him. The bear stopped to look at him so he stopped. The bear took three steps forward so he took three steps forward. The bear stepped back so he stepped back. The bear sat down so he sat down. The bear stood up and went "Woof" so he said "Woof." The bear proceeded to take a shit and the young fellow said, "Ha, ha, I beat you this time—I did that when you went 'Woof'."

His wife was coming in from Dawson City by dog team as soon as the weather was fit to travel. They say that January and February can be tough weather for travel in this part of the country, with temperatures going down to -30 or even as low as -50 during some of the worst spells. The short route from Dawson City to Fairbanks is over some pretty rough country with part of it around timber line on the mountains with little cover in case of a sudden storm—which can come up in a matter of hours in areas like these. Once this happens, there are only two choices—try to get down to shelter below the timber line or dig under a deep snow drift with the entrance facing away from the direction of the wind and you hope that the drifting snow will soon cover the entrance to help keep it warm inside until the storm blows over and it's fit to travel again.

You certainly have to have admiration for some of the women in the north who appear not to be afraid to start out on a journey such as this, even with young children. The easy route is by following the frozen river, which is at least three times as far. Even this can be very treacherous if heavy snow comes and the weight of the snow pushes the ice down and the water comes through and leaves up to a foot of water mixed with snow on top of the ice. It is very easy to get into before you realize the danger. If this happens, the women have to carry the load through the snow and water, and find a big tree where they can get a campfire burning and set the sleigh on end near the fire to melt it off—before you can get going again.

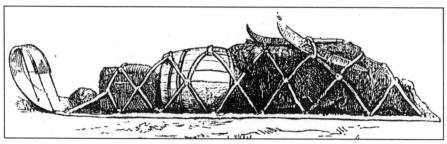

Fort Yukon Sledge (loaded)
When I built my sleigh I tried to build a copy of this.

My job building the house at $5.00 a day certainly kept me busy—trying to blaze the logs with a hand axe so they would fit tightly on top of the other, which takes less caulking to keep the house warm during the cold spells. It took days to get the first two rounds up and it looked as if spring would arrive before I got finished. I wanted to get the roof on and make the door and windows before the cold weather hit, so all I had to do was put the glass in and set up the stove so I could work in comfort building the cupboards, finishing the inside work and making a table, rough chairs and bunk beds. Fortunately, luck came my way or I couldn't have got it finished by the end of January as planned.

I was making coffee on the campfire when a Norwegian fellow from the mine came by and looked at my efforts. Then he asked, "What on earth are you trying to do using a small Hudson's Bay axe to flatten the logs? Your work looks more like an old beaver has been chewing away and didn't know what he was trying to do to those poor logs." Fortunately, after a cup of coffee I felt a little better when he said he was staying in town for the weekend and would show me how it was supposed to be done. In an hour, he was back with a broad axe he had borrowed from a friend. The axe was as sharp as a razor blade—and he had four logs blazed in a very short time and they were so smooth it looked like it had been planed.

We had all four logs in place so quickly I could hardly believe it. I wanted him to stay, but he refused and handed me the broad axe and told me to try standing on the log and be careful not to cut my foot off while blazing the log. He took a string and rubbed it in the fire coals, then he tied it at each end of the log and pulled it as tight as a fiddle string then he lifted it in the middle and let it snap back on the log—which made a black straight line. As he left, he said, "Now you can get to work and learn a lot about log buildings if you can follow the straight line without cutting the string." This proved to be more difficult than it looked, so I kept trying till dark and after I'd ruined six nice logs I finally got the knack of doing it and got the logs so they would fit—and all went well. In less than two weeks I had all the logs up to a normal height of six feet.

The next step was to get the roof on. There was a small sawmill in town so the owner was able to get some rough lumber for the roof and floor, which I put on quite quickly. The weather was starting to get cold and snow was falling nearly every day—so it was nice to have the roof on and a fire going inside. The owner was so happy to see floor and roof on the next time he came to town that he sent word back to the mine there was going to be a big party as there was a lot of space in the house before the partitions were in place.

I played the violin and another fellow had a mandolin and people danced till five o'clock next morning. Some even danced outside around the fire when there wasn't room inside. Unfortunately, there is a shortage of women—nearly 10 to one—so the ladies hardly sat down all night. There was a tub of water on the stove for anyone wanting a hot rum. Before morning people were gathered in circles trying to convince someone else to build another house so they could have another party.

Once the house was completed by January 15th, 1905 his wife came in from Dawson City over the top by dog sleigh. The weather remained nice for this time of year and several other dog teams travelled with her and they had quite a pleasant experience travelling under such ideal weather conditions. She was happy to see a nice big fire in the stove so they could get warm again after the long trip of close to 300 miles by dog sleigh. The two children enjoyed the trip so much that they asked their mother when they could go back and do it again!

The gold mine is in a muddle as 3,000 men are on strike for an 8-hour day and $6.00/day pay in place of the 10 hours/day and $5.00/day they now get. In my opinion, they certainly deserve it—but doubt they can get it. There are too many people coming from Dawson City and elsewhere looking for work to get a grub stake during the winter so they can spend the next summer looking for the big strike of gold they are sure they will find. These miners work dreadfully hard and very few can stand it for long. Last week more than 150 of the poor devils had to leave as they were pushed too hard and couldn't take it any more. It's terrible to see some of these people taken out as some can't even walk.

It's not easy to find other work at this time of the year as too many are not trained to do anything else except swing a pick and use a shove. Even if they make it to Whitehorse, they couldn't afford a ticket to Skagway and back down the coast to either Vancouver or San Francisco.

I've never had to work in the drift tunnels and don't intend to start as long as I can find work as a carpenter—which should be easy because there isn't any doubt that there will never be too many carpenters in this north country. Even if this were to happen, I still wouldn't go into a mine as long as I could set a trap, go out and shoot a moose or caribou, or set a net for fish to sell in town or out at the mine.

After finishing the house I had a few days to myself, so I spent my time looking around town for people coming in with different types of sleighs and dog teams. Some used seven dogs, others five—and some even chose three for light loads. I decided the 5-dog sleigh was what I'd try first and see if they could haul all I needed. The first thing to do was to find a small birch, which is tough wood once dry. I found lots of birch trees but looked for two days before I found two that had a bend for a turn-up on front which would be great for the job. Once I got the sleigh finished and ready to go I decided to try another type that had no runners—only a board that could be turned up in front. All I needed was to whipsaw a plank less than an inch thick and 10-12 feet long depending on the number of dogs I intend to buy. In order to get a turn-up in front that will glide over the snow, I had to put one end in boiling water for an hour then strap the board to a solid log so that only a foot could move to bend the front of the board up by exerting steady pressure on the front with a small winch. It takes a lot of patience, as it takes a long time and the wood must remain in the hot water all the time. The bottom side of the board is planed smooth and waxed or treated with hot seal oil which penetrates and keeps the wood from getting wet—which could make it twice as heavy while travelling in mild weather. This is the same method used in making snowshoes when one wants a turn-up on the front in order to clear the snow while walking. If the snow is hard after warm weather, most people use the small Bear Paw snowshoe, which has no turn-up and is only half the length of a regular snowshoe. The latter is normally five and a half feet, depending on the weight of the person. Some of the Russians and Scandinavian people prefer them even longer.

Once I got two sleighs built and two pairs of snowshoes, I was sure I was ready to go trapping. (A large sleigh and 5-7 dogs can carry close to 400 pounds.) I bought myself three dogs which I thought with my help we could take a run up the river 20 or 30 miles to see if everything worked. Everything was going well until I saw up ahead a dark patch of snow. I took no notice of it until I got into it—it being a slush patch which I should have tried to get around but with no experience, I got right in to over a foot of water in the snow and the sleigh got clogged up till the dogs couldn't move it. I had to unhook the dogs and splash through the cold water and snow pulling the sleigh two or three feet at a time. The dogs had the good sense to splash their way to the river bank and lie down under a big tree and try to dry themselves off. Finally after nearly an hour's work, I got the sleigh to shore. By this time it was getting colder as the sun had gone down and

I could hardly lift the sleigh in order to stand it on end in front of the fire I built. Once I got it warm enough to melt all the ice and snow frozen to the sleigh, I then set it in the snow and tied on our few belongings, hitched the dogs to the sleigh and thought I could reach camp before it was too late and dark when the moon went down.

The dogs and I tried hard to move the sleigh and couldn't budge it an inch and soon found I'd made the fatal mistake of setting the sleigh into the snow before it was cold—something I'd been told never to do. Again, the fire had to be stoked up and the sleigh set close to melt all the frozen snow off ready to try again. However, it was already too late and getting dark and cold, so the dogs and I spent the night sitting by the camp fire. The dogs did better than me, as they lay in the snow nearby and their fur kept them warm. All we had to eat was a can of beans. One thing though—it was a good lesson which I will never forget and likely saved me a lot of hard work over the years.

Best wishes to all.

Jack

Box 741
Fairbanks, Alaska
November 27th, 1905

Dear Mum,
    Received your letter—the first since I left Vancouver. It was nice to get all the news from home. I'm sure it's been here for some time and the folks at the Post Office only condescended to get it to me today. From now on, please get all the family to address letters to me at Box 741, Fairbanks, Alaska. I have to pay 16 shillings in your money for the letter box for one year, which should make it better.

    I've been taking it easy after spending the summer mainly learning how to fish and hunt with the help of my Indian friend who still thinks all white men are stupid and won't survive up here too long—but I must say I enjoy his company and advice which has helped a lot. So far I can't seem to get him to talk about old times before the white man came in. He would look at my letters and say, "Indian no write um."

    My partner and I are trying trapping up in the Delta Lake country, which is about a 100 miles up river and looks like a good place to trap for the winter. We took one load up by boat which went very well and got camp set up for the winter, then we decided to leave the boat here to use coming out in the spring when the ice is clear on the river—which will be close to the end of May. We decided not to walk back to Fairbanks, so set to work building a nice little raft made of dry logs for the two of us to float back down to Fairbanks and return with the dogs with the second load of supplies. We thought we could float back down in four or five days, so didn't take many supplies of food for the trip—but enough for only five days! Everything went well the first day so we travelled till dark and stayed for the night. When we awoke the next morning it was snowing hard and it seemed much colder than when we had left camp. It was, therefore, miserable travelling in the snowstorm but we thought the storm would soon blow over with the colder weather coming in. All went well until around noon when we reached a stretch of the river where there was little current to keep it from freezing and there was a skim of ice which slowed us down, as one had to break the ice while the other pushed with a pole as there was not enough current to float us downstream. The snow kept coming and the ice got stronger as we slowly moved downstream. We kept trying till after dark as we kept thinking we would reach fast water, where we could get a good start the next morning.

By the time we realized the ice was getting thicker, we had decided to camp for the night. But it took us ages to get the raft to shore as there was already close to an inch of ice and the snow was starting to lie on top of the ice. When daylight came, the storm was still bad—we could only see a few yards down the river, the wind was blowing at gale force and it was still getting colder. We found we could now walk on the ice, so we decided to stay the day and put up a shelter with whatever we could find. We spent the night with a big fire from wood we had gathered before dark, we managed to keep ourselves fairly comfortable all night. By morning, the storm had let up with only a very fine snow and no wind. We, therefore, decided to start to walk out even though there was already over a foot of snow on the ice, making it difficult walking. We had to keep testing the ice to make sure it was safe to walk on and we kept fairly close to shore in case we hit poor ice—which we did a little before noon when we got careless as the ice seemed good—and both of us fell through the ice. Luckily, we carried a 10-foot pole and were able to get out.

When we got out of the water, our wet clothes started to freeze—making it difficult to walk. Therefore, as soon as we could see a good place to camp, we went on shore and fortunately we both had a waterproof match case, so were able to get a fire started to dry off all our clothing. We took off all the outer clothes and hung them on a pole above the fire and stood close to the fire to dry our heavy underwear—which took some time. It was too late to start out again once we were dry, so we decided to spend the night getting all the clothes dry and ready to travel next day.

The next day the sun managed to come out for a while, which made it better to travel in most stretches of the river. However, the weight of the snow had started to push the ice down and slush started to show through which created a foot of snow and water—something which was almost impossible to walk through without getting wet nearly up to the knees. We found it better to stay right on the shore line, where the shore kept the ice solid with little or no slush. This was fine and we made good time walking, except that it was more than twice as far following the shore than it would have been cutting across the bays in the river. Several times we tried but found deep slush in the way and we had to go back to shore.

We were still making poor time and the food was getting scarce, so we had to make do for eight days on a conglomeration of wet flour, corned meal, a little oatmeal for breakfasts, no baking powder, and only six frozen onions. Every day we looked out for ptarmigan or willow grouse in the river willow patches—but with no luck. It seemed that everything but us had moved into the heavy timber during the storm and nothing was moving. On the seventh day, we camped early and I took a walk back into the spruce forest and luckily found three spruce hens which made a meal fit for a king after being toasted over the camp fire.

By the time we got to town there was snow three feet deep. Fortunately, the river blew clear of snow in some areas which helped a lot. It took us a little over eight days to walk out. It was nice to get back to my tent—which, unfortunately, had been flattened by the weight of the snow. We, therefore, spent some time digging it out and setting it up again. I thought, "If it quits snowing, we will wait two days then try to break a trail through with the dogs along the side of the river. We will only be able to go a few miles with a light pack then come back for the night and try to go further the next day when the trail is frozen solid and we can make good time."

I had ordered several hundred dollars worth of supplies from Chicago—mostly clothing, traps and light, dried edibles (such as dried apples, figs, prunes), and a new tent. However, the latter's failed to arrive. It's gotten stuck at either Dawson City or Skagway, so I'm having to buy things at these high prices in Fairbanks. It's a pity, but it can't be helped. It will do for next winter. I also had 30 pounds of sweets coming in, so that's another case of mouth watering like the Xmas pudding you sent last year and which didn't get here till spring (after it had all been spoiled).

Hope Brother Art doesn't get too serious with Dorothy, as the reaction might spread to the Arctic Circle and make me take a squaw as a wife. There is a very pretty one around here who looks better every time I come down the river.

November 28th

I'd better finish the letter or it will be here till spring, as we decided to start tomorrow because the weather has improved. The river has frozen hard so it should be safe to travel on. I will write again if I happen to see someone travelling the river—that could mail the letter for me. I expect to be in here for at least three months and if trapping is good, I'll stay till spring and until after the ice goes out when I can bring the boat back.

Hope you enjoy a good Xmas and wish I could be there for a few days and see you all again.

Love,

Jack

Box 741
Fairbanks, Alaska
April 6th, 1906

Dear Mum,
I've been up-river since November and expected to stay till May. However, real warm weather came early so I decided to get out of here and go back later to get my boat—or I may leave it there and build a new one a little larger than my little 14' riverboat, which has a flat bottom in order to enable me to travel over real shallow water. I couldn't do such a thing with a "deep-V" boat. I plan on building a 23' boat with a nice sized tree with not many knot holes in it (knots can weaken the boards). I spotted a few good looking trees up-river, which I can fall right alongside the river and just roll—in and float down to my tent. Then I can build a platform about 10' high and get my partner, Bull James, to help me get a log on top and whipsaw enough lumber for a boat of this size. It takes only four good boards for each side and another four or five for the bottom and the 3" strips around the top make it strong so that you can set heavy things on it when loading the boat. The lumber has to be well dried first then planed by hand—something that could take two or three days with a first-class plane like the one I brought out from England.

For an amateur, I did very well trapping marten (54) and 15 mink. The prices of them vary a great deal, according to size, colour and quality of fur. Some are worth $10, while others are worth only $2 or $3.

I haven't seen my partner since he left in November to go back to Fairbanks, but I hope he is still okay as we plan to haul a lot of our traps and supplies up the Chena River to try again next winter. I like to get as far away from the main river as I can in order to keep away from the Indian trappers—the latter seldom get far from the river. The Indians concentrate trapping mainly for otter, beaver, mink and muskrats—which seems to keep them busy and they don't have to get far from their boats before freeze-up and with their dogs when this happens.

The snow sure went fast when the warm weather hit five days ago. I was a little frightened as I'd pretty well cleaned up on most of my grub (except for six pounds of flour and some tea), so I made tracks for Fairbanks. I had to come some 25 miles down the creek. The creek was in overflow water on top of the main ice for about 12 miles. I had to wade up to my knees with the sleigh—sometimes floating, sometimes running on the ice—and my dogs following on the bank. These creeks and rivers are about the only roads we have—and bad ones they make at this time of the year. Most of them are about as crooked as a lawyer, so that to go 10 miles you journey at least 20!

Every five or six miles I meet slush (the water running over the ice) of various depths from one inch to two feet. Unless the weather turns real cold again and freezes the water solid enough to walk on, a person has to get up on the bank and cut a trail to try and get by the bad stretches. These continued overflows make the ice of enormous thickness of 4-6'. Generally, you can reckon to reach solid ice—even if there is a foot of water on top. In these areas, you can't drag a heavy load and blankets have to stay on your back to keep them dry—you can't afford to let them get wet or else you won't survive long in a harsh climates like this.

My food supply was getting short, so I couldn't waste any more time chopping a trail through the trees on the side of the river. Also because the weather was warm, I splashed through the slush patches—stopping only to eat a bit of bannock and dry out a little when too cold.

This certainly is a young man's country. The worst travelling were the six miles from Fairbanks when I crossed a patch of nigger heads, where the grass from the last year is free of snow and leaves a hump a foot high with 10" holes between them, which makes for terrible walking. I pulled, sweated and swore my way through. I even packed half the load half a mile at a time then came back for the rest of the load. Finally, I had to make two trips with my supplies and a third to get the sleigh before I eventually reached the Alaska trail which went into Fairbanks.

I arrived in the dark, tired and hungry—so I lit a big fire and peeled off all my wet clothes, wrapped a blanket around me, and cooked up the last of my flour into a type of a bannock. Sitting around

Sales slip for purchase of cabin; shopping list; and recipe for bread
1905 or 1906

the camp fire, I thought of what you told me—the old saying, "Towards spring a young girl's thoughts turn to love." And looking at my family, it looks like towards spring a young man's thoughts turn to fishing. No doubt Dad likes his fishing and that is what I will do for the summer to make a few dollars.

I haven't seen my partner as yet, but I think we will try our hand at fishing and try to take an easy summer. My partner is good at getting out and selling things but he spends more time running around from one place to another and doesn't always have time to work.

Can't think of more news, so will close and try and get to the Post Office in order to get the letter away and see if any mail came in for me during the last five months when I've been up river trapping. I find it strange since I came back and I have to watch myself as I got into the habit of talking to my dogs as if they were people—and people look at me and wonder whether I've gone a little queer. I have to take something to read next time but can't carry enough when your only transportation is what you can pack on your back and whatever the dogs can pull on a sleigh—which is not much for four or five months.

I found myself reading, morning and night, the printing on the Carnation milk can just to have something to read. The Carnation milk is thick and very sweet—nearly like candy. I always try to take a bag of hard candy which lasts a long time in your mouth. Most of the time in camp I'm kept busy cooking my meals or skinning and stretching the fur I catch so it will dry and keep for the winter. This can be a real big job, especially with otter, muskrat, and mink which often have a lot of fat on the inside of the hide that has to be scraped with a sharp tablespoon, which works well. I can do a hide in 10 minutes or less. With a beaver, you must cut the fat off with a very sharp knife—something that's not easy to do without cutting the hide, thereby greatly decreasing the value when it's sold.

I was having so much difficulty trying to scrape clean a big beaver that I thought I should go and talk to my Indian friend Sam, who often came to see me when I came to Fairbanks. When I got there he was sitting on a stump drinking tea that I'd given him on my last trip. His wife was trying to feed a new baby and at the same time, pulling in the fish net and taking the fish out and resetting it again, then cleaning the fish and splitting them to hang on the branches of a tree to dry. While doing all this, she seemed to have time to run out in the forest to collect firewood to cook meals over the campfire. While drinking our tea, I asked him to show me how to scrape a beaver hide. He surprised me when he said, very indignantly, "I **don't** do that kind of work—that is squaw work. Men don't do that kind of work. You need to get squaw. I go find one for you." I thanked him for the offer but didn't think I would get one for a while. He asked his wife to tell me how to clean a beaver hide, but she couldn't talk any English at all (which is very common with most of the Native women). However with sign language, she did show me a few good pointers that helped me to cut down the time to do one beaver from two hours down to one—and in time, I got much better. However, I couldn't match her speed. She could do one in 15 minutes without any trouble—and do a lovely job and never make a nick in the hide.

All of the fat collected—whether it came from a beaver, moose, caribou, wild geese or anything else—was stored with care out in the cold. The fat is used for light in a tent and even heat. Daylight is short and you can't sleep all the time when it's dark, so you need a light to do something. I spend a lot of my time making fish nets. All you have to do to get a light is put a heavy piece of string in a small can with the top cut out, then heat up the fat and pour it into the can while keeping the string in the centre, and then let it cool. It's just like a candle and burns for hours. This device throughout the north is called a "Bitch." I didn't know what people were talking about when I first came up here. I was talking to an old prospector when suddenly he got up and said, "I've got to go out and make a bitch before it gets dark or I won't be able to see."

Choosing needed supplies to take for a long stay in the woods for a winter is a very difficult task and you have to think about it for a few days before making the big decision. You know you have to take flour, rice, rolled oats, corn meal, dry beans, baking powder, salt, pepper, matches, dried fruit, ammunition for the guns (a .22 rifle to shoot ducks, geese, rabbits, grouse, ptarmigan, squirrels and other small animals; also a .30-30 to shoot caribou, goat, deer, moose or bear if you find a den). All of these you have to rely on completely for your meat supply for yourself and the dogs. Once you have these and think you and the dogs can pull or carry a little more, then you can drop in a few luxuries such as a bag of hard candy, Carnation milk, sugar, bacon, onions, carrots, turnips (which can be kept fresh if you get in before cold weather and you can put them in a hemp sack with a small rock to make them sink; you then tie them to a pole and let the ice freeze over the top and they are safe for the winter. The best place is a small pond or lake that won't freeze solid to the bottom of the lake. Once the lake freezes, all you have to do to get some for dinner is cut a hole in the ice and pull the bag up, take out what you want, and then drop the sack back down again. Always be careful not to cut the rope where it goes down through the ice—you should chop with care or you can lose your winter's supply! It's best to heap snow on the hole in the ice, then it doesn't freeze down so much. Without doing this, the ice on the hole can be 5" thick during a cold night. This idea doesn't work well on a river or creek, as they overflow at least twice during a winter and you can end up with 5'-6' of ice—and you don't want to cut through this thickness every time you want something out of the sack.

I talk to everyone I know who stays out for long periods—and even the real old prospectors admit they always do forget something. I'm sure this happens to most of us—even those with experience! I like vegetables; however, it's not common practice to take raw products as they are too heavy unless you can take horses or a boat into your base camp in the late summer or early fall before the snow gets too deep for the horses to travel. Dried fruit and vegetables are frequently used. Bears are also a problem when you take supplies in early and leave them till you go back later in the fall to trap. The only way I've found to beat the bears is to tie a rope between two trees that are about 20' apart with a loop in the middle that holds another rope—used to lift your supplies up and down with as needed. I tried putting a log across between trees with the rope in the middle to pull up and down. Unfortunately, an old bear climbed one of the trees and walked along the pole and managed to reach the supplies. In this case, I got my money out of him—when I came back to camp, he came for more— and I was able to shoot him (which was great). The weather turned cold before much snow came and the meat froze and stayed frozen, which was excellent. It lasted me much of the winter, together with the very tasty ptarmigan (which were plentiful in the short willow areas in swamps and marshes).

The bears, grouse and all kinds of birds know where they can find berries—mainly in the recently burned over areas. They also know where the best vegetation can be found in the early spring, where recent slides have taken place and where the vegetation, especially the fireweed, comes up with a new vigour a year or so after the slide. Slides happen regularly after heavy rains or snow slides in mountainous areas or along creek or river banks. The old bear must have a marvellous ability to smell out the salmon streams during spawning season where they will come for miles so they can gorge on the salmon and put on fat to carry them through the long winters. This is before they find a den in a good cave or dig a hole under a big tree which will keep them dry so they can conserve energy by sleeping most of the winter. During the winter the bears live off the fat they've stored up during the summer and fall when food is plentiful. Occasionally, they will come out of their den during a warm spell in March or April and look around and then go back in.

Grizzly bears don't hibernate as long as black bears, and I've seen their tracks in the snow in December. Grizzlies will often follow the rivers and lakeshores looking for moose or caribou that have drowned in the early winter before the ice gets thick enough to hold them. The shore ice freezes solid before the centre of the river freezes over, and a lot of the larger animals perish in the rivers and lakes. I've watched grizzly bears spend hours digging a big moose out of the ice. They seem to have the good sense to scratch the ice all around the animal and when they get enough uncovered they have a good feed of frozen meat. Then they go and lie down nearby for a day or so.

It's a good idea to stay away from an area where you know a kill has taken place, as the bears guard their kill jealously against anything that comes close—whether it be a human, another bear, or even a moose or caribou. A grizzly bear will stay out of hibernation until all the food supply is gone. Black bears seem to prepare their den in October, even if there are plenty of berries. However, black bears may not go into the den until the first snow comes. On one occasion, I came over a small hill when there were two feet of snow on the ground and saw where two big grizzly bears had come together and had had a big fight. I could tell this because the snow was trampled down for over an acre with blood stains over most of that area. I kept my rifle ready as I made every step—just in case one came out after me. All I found was the skull of one of them, which was very large and, by the size of their tracks in the snow, the bears too must have been pretty well matched. It was obvious the one finally killed the other and stayed in the area until he had finished eating the other before leaving. I was glad I hadn't come along a day earlier while he was still guarding his kill. I was glad too that I had my rifle handy, as most days on the trap line I travelled with only the .22 rifle or nothing at all—especially if I have too much to pack with either traps or fur I caught that I would leave my gun back in the cabin or tent.

I have a good contract with the local barber, who buys the bear fat for 25¢/pound. Bear fat is a soft fat. When rendered down, it is liquid. The barber then makes the fat into hair dressing by adding a little of various perfumes and selling it to his lady customers as a hair tonic of various types and fragrances.

The only other way to ensure the bears and wolverine don't get into your food cache is to cut off four trees 10'-14' up from the ground (depending on the snow fall), as the wolverine don't hibernate like the bears. One then builds a platform out of split logs, after which you build a log wall about 8' square (or whatever size you think you need to hold your supplies) with a small door on one side. A split log roof is best as the water will run off. The most important thing of all is to wrap tin around the posts holding up the cache so that animals of all kinds can't climb up. Even squirrels, marten, mink, fisher and especially wolverine can make a terrible mess if they can get in.

One time I left the ladder leaning against the door. I hadn't been gone for more than a few hours when an old wolverine came along and got the door open and make a terrible mess. From then on I always was careful to take the ladder away. As an old trapper said to me, "If we don't get that old wolverine, he will get us. He is so smart."

With love,

Jack

Meat cache to keep bears and other animals out

September 28th, 1906

D ear Dad,
    I've had a good summer after such a slow start when finishing
trapping early in April. I completed a few carpentry jobs up at the mine
and some in town. None of them was big, but good enough to buy food
and three 60' fish nets for catching salmon as they came up the rivers. I
also helped my new partner Mike cut firewood to sell in town;
however, our best sales are to the river boats as they take a lot of wood.
One advantage I have over my partner (who is good with horses) is to
sharpen saws of all kinds. My carpenter training in England sure
comes in handy here in Alaska. All our wood is cut up with a cross-cut
saw and if your saw is good and sharp with the proper set on it, we can
cut a lot of wood in a day. The worst problem is finding good trees
close to the river and also a good location where the paddle steamers
can come in and pick up the wood. If you can find a curve in the river
or eddy where there is sufficient depth of water where the steamer can
tie up to a tree on shore, which is usually the best location.
    Most of the trees close to the river were cut for firewood some
time before I came up here. The banks of the river are as bare as a
pasture in England. We found a good location further back and many
good dry trees. With horses and a heavy two-bunk sleigh, we can move
a lot of wood down to the river's edge in a week. The best time for this
is early winter before the snow gets too deep and again, in the early
spring before all the snow goes. In a light snow winter, we can haul all
winter.
    They don't get the real deep snow like I get up river on the trap
line. I made the heavy two-bob sleigh when things were quiet before
the fish came in last spring. I managed to find flat iron strips two
inches wide and one-third of an inch thick, which will last a long time.
All I had to do was to cut them with a hack saw into the right lengths
for each runner. The right wood is far more difficult to find, as I
wanted birch which is a hard wood once dried. It's difficult to find a
tree that has the right bend to make the turn-up at the front.
    After much searching, we did find four trees that would do.
They have to be strong to carry a heavy load of wood over rough

ground. I also make all our own single trees, double trees, neck yokes, and axe handles. They are stronger than anything you can buy in a store. In good conditions, we can haul two and a half cords on one trip if there are no steep hills to climb (we try to avoid such hills). When we get the logs to the riverbank, we cut them into the right length needed to stoke the boilers on the paddle steamers.

Last fall, before leaving for the trap lines, we built a long chute down to the shore—where rather than packing the wood by hand we could set it on the chute and it would slide right down to the paddle steamer. The captain was very impressed, as it cut loading time by more than one-half. The wood we cut for home use in town had to be cut into much shorter lengths to fit in home fires, which come in various sizes.

Our greatest problem was finding dry wood, as the area had been burned over by forest fires some 70 or 80 years before so there wasn't much natural dead wood from old growth. We try to find as much as we can or else we cut green trees in the winter when the sap is down then let it dry for a year—a system which ties up a lot of our money. You can't cut trees when the sap is up, as they don't dry properly. There is so much moisture in the wood that it seems to ferment and the wood goes sour and won't burn properly.

One good thing about the wood cutting was that it was my good fortune to find three good spruce trees which were clear of limbs that made excellent boards for building boats. We cut the logs the right length for the boat I built (24' long). We then whipsawed the lumber in early April. The wood soon dried with the sun and spring winds. I was able to plane it by the first of May and got the boat built in my spare time on weekends—and it was ready when the first run of King salmon came up the rivers. I did a lot of scouting around to find the best streams off the main river where other fishermen didn't seem to go. I carried my rifle along with me and managed to get two moose and a nice bull caribou—which sold really well in town where miners were hungry for meat. They are so anxious to find gold they won't even stop to shoot a moose.

I find it surprising how few really do find gold in much quantity. Most lose every penny they had when they came in—with nothing left to pay their fare home. Most of them have to seek work from a big company that has more money for equipment and know-how to find better prospects. The bigger companies can also get down deep enough to find gold. Most individuals don't have that ability, knowledge or capital to achieve this. There are some rare occasions when some do; however, I doubt it is more than one in a thousand.

In my travels, I find people living in tents miles from town. They spend their winters cutting wood to build fires in the hole they've dug to thaw the permafrost in order to get down to bedrock where they hope to find gold. They build the fire in the evening and let it burn most of the night in order to thaw enough in the bottom of the hole to keep them busy digging the next day. Most times, they can get down another foot or 18", depending on the soil or sand. This routine goes on day after day all winter. Occasionally, someone gets buried in the hole if the sides happen to cave in before they get the cribbing in place to keep the walls of the hole from sliding. Some of them just never turn up in the spring; others have a friend who might come looking for them later on. I don't envy them at all. I'd rather go out and trap, catch fish, shoot moose or caribou, or just cut wood for the steamboats rather than spend my life digging for gold. Fortunately, there aren't many people like me who are content to do this. Most of the others want to try the big gamble and find their fortune in **GOLD**.

Gold on platform ready for shipment on river boat.

Fishing went very well once I had learned which rivers and streams were good on different days, weeks, or even months and had made good contacts for selling them after I'd caught them. I soon found the three nets I'd bought weren't enough and I'll certainly get more for next season. I spent much of my spare time mending fish nets, as some of the big King salmon can make a big hole in the net and a river otter can do even worse. I had to make a fish net needle, which is made out of wood. You thread it back and forth to carry the mending thread. In order to make one mesh you have to thread through and tie three times to gain four square inches if you are catching big fish. If catching small salmon, then you use three inch also for grayling—a freshwater game fish of the trout family. Grayling has a larger dorsal fin of a bright colour and is found in the area stretching from the United States to Alaska. Grayling is a good eating fish and is very popular with the buyers, who pay more for them. Also, they can be caught all year round—unlike the salmon, which only can be caught when they come back to spawn during the summer and fall. I've even been lucky in catching grayling through the ice in the winter. They sure go down well after eating bannock and beans!

To net grayling, it requires a 2½-3" net, depending on the size of fish in the area. I went up a side stream and caught a boat load with a hook and line and a small net. I cleaned out the insides of the fish and paddled all night to get them to Fairbanks before they spoiled in the sun the next day. I also did well with the salmon if I could keep my nets in good shape.

It's often hard to get good nets for this kind of work. It seems the thread isn't strong enough to last any length of time. The thread I buy is much stronger, so my next winter's project will be to make nets by hand. I find that if all goes well I can make two feet a night. The nets I like are 60 feet long and four or five feet deep, depending on the depth of the river you are fishing in. If I want it longer, I tie two together.

As you can see by the number of letters I write, I don't have many days in a year with nothing to do. I shot another bear that had lived on the dead, rotten salmon lying on the sandbars for too long. When I took the bear fat to my friend the barber, he told me to get the hell out as it smelled just like a rotten salmon and no one would buy it for perfume—no matter what he added! I guess I'd been living along the river too long and got immune from the smell of it. I'd better watch from now on. I should only take a bear if it has lived on vegetation or berries for some time—when they are really good to eat—or else get the fat for cooking. Most people up here try to get bear fat for making pies or anything else that requires lard. I tried smoked bear meat when I went to dinner with an Indian friend recently—and it was real good. I'll have to try doing it myself. I'm also going to try to smoke some moose or caribou meat to take on the trapline. The Indians smoke and hang the meat on a tree branch to dry. This will keep for months as long as it's kept dry. They call it "Jerky." It's light to pack. Instead of lunch, you can shove some in a pocket or in the packboard with the traps and snares you carry while on the trapline. You can chew on it all day—a little like chewing gum, except it keeps its taste better and gives you a little nourishment as you walk along the trapline.

Hope all is well.

Jack

January 20th, 1907

Dear Art,
As usual, I'm behind time for writing by over a month—but delays will happen somehow up here and the winter is very queer, to say the least. Xmas day I sat in a tent in my shirt sleeves with the flap on the tent tied up because it was so hot—two above freezing! Three weeks before and after, the thermometer was jumping from two above freezing to below zero—it's been beastly weather for the last five days. It's been from 40-50 below zero and today, it's back up to zero. It's not good trapping weather. I like it when it stays around five below and not too much snow.

I took out 270 traps and got about 200 of them set when the weather changed and it started to snow—as it's been doing ever since. I cleared the darn things of snow three times, which is no light job when you pull out 200 traps from a foot of snow three times in succession and reset them, hoping the storm will break. It's also hard work breaking the trail with snowshoes. I had to use my big snowshoes, as the light ones are no good till the snow pack settles and you can walk along on top, making travelling easier. Right now, there is over four feet of loose snow, where even with the big snowshoes I sink down over a foot every step. I can't go many miles in a day before I have to turn back.

I was provisioned up until New Year, as I thought travel would be good by then. I have sat here every night gazing at an abnormally empty flour sack for the last two weeks, while the dogs thought I was experimenting to see how little they could live on. The snow is such that the dogs can't get around. If they try, they go down so deep in the loose snow you can hardly see them. Fortunately, I saw a big buck caribou not more than two miles from the tent and was able to shoot it. The snow conditions were so bad I couldn't use the dogs to pull it back on the sled, so had to pack it myself one quarter at a time. Every day I went out to clear traps I brought a quarter back with me.

I don't like living on straight meat, so once the weather settled down I packed up and left for town early in the morning and kept moving till dark. Then I would camp for the night in order to get a good bit of sleep so I could get an early start next morning. For the first 40 miles I had to break trail with snowshoes for the dogs to come behind pulling the near-empty sleigh. It only contained a hind quarter of caribou, three pounds of flour, 28 marten, an ounce of salt, and a few rolled oats—all that was left at camp. The only reason I brought the whole hind quarter of the caribou was as a bit of insurance in case I ran into difficulties on the trail condition (e.g., slush on the ice)—something that can slow you down to only a few miles a day. Fortunately, I hit the snowshoe trail where others had broken the trail, so I made good time the rest of the way.

Luckily, the marten are a good price right now—otherwise my expedition would have been a total failure. Very little fur was travelling with the light fluffy snow. They just couldn't get around. At least with the high prices, I made just over $4 a day. I shouldn't grumble, however. I did better than anyone else in this section and no one can buck Dame Nature when she decides to enter the picture with wrathful anger.

I arrived in town after five days' travelling. It was sure nice to see a few lights in windows—which I hadn't seen for nearly four months. Today is wash day for my clothes. It's nice to have warm water on the stove, which makes life easy.

As soon as I can, I will get this letter in the mail—hopefully, it will get to you before spring. With the steamers not running in the winter, it will have to go out by Dawson City, Skagway and down to Vancouver. I plan to hit the trail back for another three months tomorrow. My partner Mike is doing well cutting and hauling wood to the river but, unlike me, he has a long list of grievances against his dogs (I'm very pleased with mine). Buster is a fine, sturdy dog and pulls well. Betsy has far more sense than most humans, while my yellow dog, Nugget, pulls so much he makes himself nervous and makes so much noise barking all the time that I may get rid of him. Good dogs save you a lot of work.

I'll write again in the spring and hope all is well with you and the love of your life, Dorothy.

                                              Brother Jack

March 1907

D ear Arthur,
We made good time on the trip back—with no snow on the trail
we had made coming out and good weather all the way. The going was
so good I even got lazy and let the dogs pull the sleigh and supplies for
much of the way—and I just walked behind with my pack. Once back
to my tent I spent several full days rebaiting my traps and getting them
all in good condition. The bait I use is mainly beaver castor, fish oil (if
I have it), grouse insides, head and feathers. I still had 73 traps I hadn't
got set in the first part of the winter, so I set out at daybreak scouting
out a new area to find marten tracks and signs of other fur animals. It
was a dull day and all conditions against me when I started—except
for my trusted compass. I walked for hours with a slight wind in my
face, so I thought it was easy to get back to camp keeping the wind to
my back. I found no tracks of anything so decided to make a detour
and return to my tent and try a new direction the next day. The wind
suddenly went down and there were no hills or sun to guide me. I
guided myself with the compass for a few miles , then I did what the
Indians call "Come my tracks again"—that is, when I came across my
own trail and realized I was travelling in a circle! I examined the
compass and found that with a little persuasion it would point north in
any old direction and couldn't be relied upon at all.

It was getting late and no grub, no bed, and nothing to guide
me—except myself. I had to think it over about whether I should stop
and light a fire and spend most of the night in misery or whether I
should try to follow the tracks I had made coming in, or whether I
should strike out in the direction I thought I should go. Before I
moved, I happened to see a small whiff of snow blow from a tall tree
and observed where it landed. I thought I would try and spot the
direction of the wind again and keep my back to it. I didn't see any
more wind blow from a tree, so I tried hitting a tree with the back of
my axe (in order to shake off the snow), and was pleased to see the
snow blow in the direction I was going. I kept doing this every
100 yards and eventually did reach the trapping trail I had been on the

day before. It was easy to follow in the dark to the nice warm tent once the stove was lit.

This experience should help you to make a decision about whether you want to move from England and come to Alaska. Big decisions are never easy—but don't be afraid of making a mistake. We all make them in life. If we don't want to make mistakes, we shouldn't get up in the morning. I don't want to offer you any more advice, but if you quit the Postal Service, make a complete break and come out regardless. Fortunes aren't made in a day, but moderate comfort is easily attainable. Take no notice of what people say about how tough it's going to be. Just go ahead and blaze your own trail. You know the goal you are after and the direction you want to steer. You will soon find that many lines lead to the same mark and you can draw these lines as well as anyone else. There are more opportunities in northwest Canada or Alaska than anywhere that I know of. Always remember, there are other jobs besides farm labour everywhere, but any job eases your mind while looking for another. I, myself, have never been in any place yet where sober, industrious men were easy to find. Everybody is looking for such men. I wish I had known before that you were considering coming over and I wouldn't have got tied up with my partner Mike and could have joined forces with you—as we could have made a good team. Right now, that would be impossible as it would cripple both of us trying to untangle our business. Having said that, it won't hurt you any to paddle your own boat and if you can't handle it very well at first you will feel prouder later on as you shoot safely over the rapids of life afterwards. I've found everything I've done has been exciting and plan on doing many other things before I get too old. I still have the notion of leaving behind my life in tents, trapping, fishing, etc. and finding some land I can call my own—where I can raise a family in peace and quiet (somewhere in northern Canada or Alaska).

The rest of the winter was good trapping after a warm wind came in for two days and the snow crusted so I could go anywhere I wanted on my light snowshoes and the fur animals started to travel when they could skip along on top of the crust without any trouble. As there are also lots of ptarmigan in the open meadows and plenty of fool hen (Franklin grouse) in the timber areas. I had no trouble keeping myself supplied with meat.

Hope to hear from you soon.

Jack

October 3rd, 1907

D ear Dad,
    I've had a very good summer, working hard fishing and cutting wood. If we can sell the wood, we will have a few dollars in our pockets. No doubt, I won't get another letter out of here before Xmas—so have a real good time and I hope that all will be in good health. I plan to make two trips into my base camp with my brand new boat. I can carry over a ton in it if going down river; however, it's slow going if I have to pole it upstream. The Tanana is a very wide and shallow river much of the year, so I have a 14' dry pole to push myself upstream—which can be very slow going if there is much current in the river. Some days, with tough going, I only get six or eight miles.

    Coming down, I paddle and let the current do most of the work for me. With the flat bottom on the boat I can go over shallow riffles with only four inches of water. Most of the Indians come to look at the boat and want me to build one for them. I've told them I'll show them how to build one for themselves. So far, I haven't had any come for lessons. The Indians use mainly dugout or birch-bark canoes. The dugout in this area is made from a huge cottonwood log. It must be a big job making one—I haven't tried to do it yet—and I likely won't.

    I had no sooner got the boat unloaded and all my winter supplies stacked safely under two nice spruce trees when the storm hit and started with heavy wind and rain. Later, it turned to snow during the night, so I had to stay up most of the night in order to keep my food supplies dry and watch that the canvas was in place as I didn't want wet flour, rolled oats and rice for the next six months.

    My little tent (10' x 12') kept the storm out pretty well, and only my pillow got wet. I decided that morning I wasn't going to do this all winter—and that I'd build myself a small cabin as my base camp and use my tent as an overnight camp on one of my branch lines. So, I sat down for breakfast at daylight and sharpened my axe so that I could go out and cut enough logs to build a cabin.

    One thing—there were plenty of trees about 10" to 12" in diameter, which was just the right size to build a cabin 10' x 12'. I could get two nice logs out of most of the trees. Fortunately, there were enough trees close to the cabin site and I could fall them over the building, cut them the right length and swing them into place without much lifting. I cut enough for four rounds by 2:00 p.m. After lunch, I went out into the swamp and gathered enough moss to put between the logs to keep the cabin nearly air tight for warmth in the winter. The next few days were spent putting the logs in place to build the walls—just over 5' high. Next came the roof which would bring the height of the cabin up to 8'. I made this by splitting logs about 6" in diameter. The logs were then placed flat side up supported by the ridge pole which sat on top of a 6" x 3' upright log. The second layer of split poles is then placed flat side down to cover the cracks between the first layer. To my surprise, it kept the rain and snow out very well! The door was made out of split wood about 1½" thick with strips over the cracks between the boards. I made the hinges on the door out of strips of moose hide from a moose I'd got on my first trip. The windows were more difficult—all I had was a piece of glass 2' square that I'd happened to put over my food boxes to keep things dry.

The weather was miserable most of the week, so the cabin seemed like a palace when I moved in and got the fire started. It takes a few days with a good hot fire to dry the cabin out, especially when you use green logs. Most of us carry small collapsible light tin stoves for use in tents or cabins. They can be carried in a small space and assembled quickly. They seldom last more than one season and after they are used they soon rust out, especially if not in use for a month or two.

Once the cabin was up, the weather settled down with only a few inches of snow—it was perfect weather to travel and set the traps out. I set out four trap lines—one in each direction from the cabin. The first two, up and down the river, were set for mink, otter, weasel and some marten, fisher or wolverine that happened to cross. The other two lines, which went away from the river in both directions up to higher country, were set mainly for marten, fisher, lynx and fox. These branch lines are between eight and ten miles long, depending on the country for travel (if the terrain was very steep, they would be less). These lines were over night ones and on these I built a lean-to which is made by nailing or tying a pole with moose or caribou hide between two trees eight feet apart. There are small poles leaned against it, which hold the spruce or balsam boughs up which will then keep the snow or rain out. In order to get a good cover, you have to start at the bottom and work up to the top, which makes an overlap of branches all the way so that the rain runs off. It's surprising that water or snow seldom come through if you take pains to do it right.

The boughs for a good job should be no more than a foot or 18" long. One end is covered the same way, facing the prevailing winds. The place for the fire is built three feet outside the open end so that the heat of the fire reflects inside the shelter. If you make up the fire with three or four big round logs, the fire will stay alight all night and keep the chill down to a reasonable level, especially if you use good-sized rocks, if available, to pile up behind the fire which reflect the heat back into the shelter all night—even after the fire goes out.

My dogs have settled in pretty well and were great to carry traps, bait and supplies. Once the lines were laid out and the traps set, I often left the dogs back at the main cabin—or I took just one to pack. I brought a fair amount of dried salmon that I'd caught on my first trip with other supplies. I was concerned, however, that I might not have enough for the winter if I couldn't get a moose or caribou while up here. Most of the moose move downriver into the willow flats for the winter if the snow gets too deep. The caribou only cross once or twice in a winter in order to move from one feeding area to another, if they're disturbed by wolves. However, some winters you may not see any.

Luck was with me this winter when, in late November, the river still had some open areas over swift water. I went downriver on my trap line and only a mile below my cabin, a pack of seven wolves had chased a small herd of 15 caribou across the river and the caribou ran onto poor ice in the middle of the river, where they broke through and couldn't get out again—the ice kept breaking as they tried to get out and once exhausted, they soon drowned. The wolves had killed three others that had got across the river. After the wolves had had a good feed, they never came back again. Only two caribou survived as I circled the area for tracks in the snow. I thought I might get a few wolves but never did. I sat on a ridge overlooking the river at dusk and dawn, hoping to shoot one or two—but they never did return. All was not lost, however, as I took the dogs and sleigh down and cut three of the caribou out of the ice and brought them home to feed the dogs. When I had skinned and cut the caribou up the meat looked so good that I hung the hind quarters up for myself—it was very good and we did very well all winter.

Any time I ran short I'd bring another caribou back as the meat kept frozen in the ice. It would take an hour or more to cut one out of the ice. The weather stayed cold enough to be able to keep the meat frozen until late in April. Soon after I moved into the cabin, a squirrel soon found a nice and warm place up in the roof between the poles to make a nest. He loved to sit on one end of the cabin and tease the dogs. They would try and try to jump up and get him—but never would quite make it that high. He would also jump across to small trees and come down close to the ground and chatter at the dogs to see them try and jump through the deep snow to try and catch him. Once the dogs had a trail through the snow and could travel faster, the squirrel was smart enough to go to another tree where the dogs couldn't move so fast. The dogs never did give up, trying week after week to catch the squirrel. The latter got so friendly with me that he would come down and take a piece of bannock or some other goodie out of my fingers—and even off my plate if I wasn't watching! He was good company for me all winter and I spent many hours talking to him. It sometimes seemed that he understood what I was saying, as he would tilt his head from side to side as I talked. He stayed close all winter until the beginning of April when a girlfriend came to visit and the sun started to give some warmth so they spent most of the time up in a tall tree chattering to each other and sitting in the sun on a nice day. In bad weather, they would come down into the roof of the cabin and chatter at me, especially at day-break. He still comes down to get handouts, but his friend is shy and will stay five or six feet away and hope that I will throw her something. They would also go out and eat on the frozen caribou along with the camp robbers who spend a lot of their time there. They tried to stop the chickadees and the Downy Woodpecker from getting their turn for a little fat. Even in the very cold weather (i.e., weather well below zero), they would come and peck away. I'll never know how they keep their feet warm when I have to walk around with two or three pairs of wool socks on!

During the winter I also had a very scary experience in the middle of January. I was skinning a mink out on one of my branch lines and cut my finger—but didn't think much of it as I'd done it many times before and the cuts had healed up quickly. However, this time it was different—within two days it had developed into blood poisoning. A thick, red streak ran right up my arm to my armpits, which scared the hell out of me. Travel was impossible, being over 200 miles out of Fairbanks. I quickly decided to do what the Army told me while I was in South Africa if you have a bullet wound when you're surrounded by the enemy and can't get back for medical treatment. The best thing to do is to heat water then add salt if you have it. After this, dip the wound in hot water (if it's your arm or leg). If the wound is elsewhere, apply a hot sponge made of cloth or wool clothing or moss from a swamp (which is excellent as a sponge as it keeps the heat in for a long time). Keep the sponge on until it gets cool, then dip into the hot water and start again.

You must—or I must—be mistaken in what we were saying about salmon, as one of us was wrong. You cannot catch these northern salmon with hook and line after they leave the sea. They don't eat at all. I didn't have the right lure these days. However, I've heard the Puget Sound fishermen say that sometimes one will take a spoon bait in the tidal waters. That's right because I caught one in San Francisco Bay. On the rivers, I have gutted thousands (no exaggeration) and cannot see any semblance of food in their stomach or entrails. Indians from Holy Cross Mission at the Yukon mouth that I asked say that the salmon are much more oily there than up here. That means that they subsist on that oil on their journey.

Three weeks ago, when the fall Chinook salmon started to run, I caught from 20 to 40 a day in the fish wheel and after they were split and hung up for three days, oil would ooze out and fall to the ground. Now the wheel only catches about 30 a day and a big proportion of these are scabby, wormy, blind, deformed fellows. Being hindered by one or more of these reasons, it has taken them longer to make the trip and they have consumed all their oil. When they are split and hung up, not a drop of oil comes out. Even the dogs turn up their noses before eating one, so I quit catching them and will know better next year— and I won't try to catch them so late in the year.

Early in the summer (in the females), the spawn gets so large that it seems to me that it fills up to the detriment of all other organs— in fact, every little space inside the fish is filled, even reaching as it does right up to the throat and weighing up to 1½ pounds.

October 20th

Didn't get my letter finished because I was too busy cleaning up fish and splitting them down the middle from the head and leaving the tail held together with a little bit of skin. After this, I put them in a salt brine for a day and a half. Then, the fish can be hung up on a line with the skin inward—or if no line, then the branches of a tree will do till they dry and cure. This takes four or five days, depending on the weather. Once this is complete, they will keep for months providing they are kept dry.

The Indians, no doubt, have done this for centuries for a food supply to last the winter. When I take supplies to my trapping ground, I'll take a good number that I can hang up in a big tree by the cabin for myself and the dogs. No doubt, the camp robbers (Grey Jay) and Chickadees will be pecking away on some, but I certainly don't discourage them as they are like my dogs and are good companions to talk to. They get real tame and come to take handouts right by the tent. I've even had them come inside if I leave the flap of the tent open on warm days. They are by far the very best companions a trapper or prospector can get.

As I sit by the river at night, I noticed at last that the moon varies with the sun the further the sun rise to the south; in a like proportion, does the moon rise to the north and as one arc declines, so does the other grow larger. On a clear night, you can see thousands of stars. I spend a lot of hours watching the Northern Lights dance all over the sky. Sometimes, they look just like a huge curtain opening and closing. Some nights, you can hear them crackle and rapidly change into hundreds of colours and shades.

In your last letter you asked about the wild bird visitors we get up here in Alaska. There are quite a few in the summer—the House and Sand Martins, but few swallows in this area. There are numerous Tomtits (Chickadees), which stay all winter. Our real migrants are American birds, such as the big robin (far larger than the one in England), various songbirds, fly catchers, the Kingfisher, and all kinds of ducks. I'm happy to see ducks in order to make a good dinner once in a while. There are the yellow-brown willow wrens that are so common at home. They seem to stay only about three months, then they head south again. They are all gone now, except the winter birds—the camp robber, ravens, several species of owls, Bald Eagles and Golden Eagles, Ospreys, Gyrfalcons and Peregrine Falcons which stay closer to the coast or river if there's open water, numerous hawks, and three types of grouse (the Blue mainly in high ground in the hills or mountains, the Fool Hen or Spruce Hen and the Willow Grouse). In addition, there are the geese, ducks, swans and cranes come in by the thousands to nest over wide areas of the north. They raise their young in the forests, swamps and river valleys that supply an abundant quantity of food of all kinds that ensures rapid growth which is essential for them to mature in such a short season and enable them to make their way south before winter returns. Fly catchers of many species have an easy life with such a plentiful supply of flies. I only wish there were more birds to eat up all the mosquitoes, black flies, deer flies, and no-see-ums that pester us all spring, summer and early fall.

It's always amazing to me how many different species of sparrows (like the White-Crowned and Yellow-Crowned Sparrow), ducks and fly catchers that look alike, except for different shades of colour, and that they all mate with their own and don't cross. I've never seen evidence of voluntary cross-breeding among birds and animals of the wilds. This is a biological question the human animals might well consider before polluting the race bloodstreams. In my opinion, diversity of races makes the world an interesting place in which to live. They all have different approaches to life. If all continue to mix the way they are now, the world will be a much duller place to live in when all look alike.

The birds in the spring come in such large numbers that it would be nice to know where they all come from. The area where I camped during the summer was burned over by a huge forest fire that covered hundreds of miles. This brought an unusually large number of birds and animals. The fresh vegetation was springing up all over the burned area. It appears the fire loosened the soil for all kinds of plants to grow and seed last fall, which the seed-eating birds can scratch up and eat once the snow goes. The fire also allowed many berries to take hold in the loosened soil. Many of the seeds are carried in by the birds and animals and the seeds take root quickly including raspberries, black currants, cranberries, huckleberries, blueberries, wild strawberries, soapberries and bearberries, as well as dozens of other types. This abundance of seeds and berries brings in many birds and animals that eat on the fruit during the spring and fall (e.g., the grouse and ptarmigan, as well as both the black and grizzly bears). In many cases, the robins and hundreds of other smaller birds stay in these burned areas until the snow comes. Once the brush and grass appear in the second year after a burn, the moose, deer and caribou move in to enjoy their tender shoots. Even the mountain goats and sheep will feed in burn areas close to high cliffs, where they can run for protection from the predators—mainly wolves, bears, wolverines, coyotes and lynx. The predator birds (e.g., eagles, ravens) will take very young goats and sheep. The hawks, owls, falcons, etc. feast on the abundant supply of grouse and other birds that come in for the berries following a fire. Even the wolf, coyote and fox will mainly live on berries in the late summer and fall when these are plentiful following fires.

The new supply of fireweed, seeds and berries brings with it a rapid increase of rabbits, mice, chipmunks, groundhogs and lemmings. All of these things follow the fire. It would make you think this is nature's subtle way of using forest fires (normally caused by lightning) to clear out the tangles of old growth that have lost their usefulness in order to make room for a new generation of plant life that's worthy of providing an abundance of food for the wild life dependent upon it for their existence. There is no question that nature is wonderful to watch during the changing seasons and how it supplies food for the many living things on this earth—everything from bugs, birds and fish to large animals—yet it also shows its cruel side when a fire sweeps through an old, decaying forest that is a home to certain types of birds (e.g., the many types of woodpecker, nuthatches, tree creepers, etc.) that live on the bugs in decaying forests. The majority of these get burned up when the fire sweeps through, destroying many other birds and animals that choose to nest and sleep in sheltered forests close to their feeding areas in new growth areas. With a strong wind, these fires travel at a speed of between five and 10 miles a day—and even more, in very dry seasons. Also, in bug-killed forests, which are very dry, the sparks from the fire can be carried in the wind right across a valley and start the fire going on the other side.

When a fire got started in the hills many miles away, I was camped on a small island half a mile from shore, and I could see the smoke billowing into the sky in the late afternoon. Because I could see very little smoke the next morning, I didn't think it was anything to worry about. I'd seen several in the distance over the last three years and thought it would burn till the snow came and create good feeding areas for the game animals. I even drove stakes pointing in the direction of the smoke so I could take the dog team and try and find an easy route, by river if possible, that I could take the boat next summer and get to a good hunting area.

To my surprise, one morning I looked out and saw lots of smoke in the sky—just like a thunder cloud along with a strong wind blowing from that direction. I climbed up the highest tree on a hill and could see it was less than 20 miles away. I, therefore, kept myself busy cleaning fish I'd caught in the nets during the night—not thinking there was anything to worry about. That was until late in the afternoon— when I saw several moose and caribou running at full speed when they came out of the brush on a large open meadow just up-river from me. During the evening I saw many more before it got dark. The sky in the direction of the fire stayed light all night—and I knew the fire couldn't be more than 10 miles away, which gave me a very uncomfortable feeling. I wondered whether sparks might reach my island if the fire kept coming in the same direction.

In the morning, at daylight, more and more animals were in panic crossing the river—some even came to my island. Then, after a short rest, the animals would quickly move on. Most of the caribou were near exhaustion when they reached the river, with their tongues hanging out as they ran. Several calves never reached the far shore. When I climbed the tree on the island I could see the flames from the fire not more than two miles away, as it crowned the tall trees. By nine in the morning, the wind got up. The fire itself, when moving fast, creates its own wind and moves even faster. It was unbelievable how fast the fire travelled from tree top to tree top, while the fire down on the ground was half a mile behind the fire in the tree tops. Sparks and small branches covered with flames blew right across the river and started the fire quickly on the other side. I ran around with a bucket of water and put out sparks that landed. One landed on my tent and burned a hole you could put your fist through before I saw it and put out the fire with water.

I was lucky, as the centre of the fire passed by a mile up the river; however, the total size of the fire was tremendous and advanced on a front of over 30 miles and destroyed everything in its path. Some days it slowed down if the wind changed and blew the flames back from where they had come. However, once a strong wind came up it would be away again—but not with the same speed as the day it crossed the river.

The loss of wildlife must have been tremendous. I saw birds trying to fly with feathers burning. Moose, caribou, black and grizzly bears were running for the river with patches of burning areas smoking where live sparks had landed on them. Many managed to cross the river but got caught in the fire that jumped the river from the fire in the tree tops (which advanced more quickly than that on the ground). Some of the animals would turn and run back across the river and run straight into the fire advancing on the ground.

It's an experience I never want to see again—it nearly scared the life out of me. Many moments I was wishing I'd got in my boat and left my fish and nets as soon as I saw the fire a day or so before it reached the river. I never thought it could travel that fast. It certainly travelled more than 10 miles the day it crossed the river. Some time during that hour the fires crossed. It got so hot on the island that I had to retreat to the water. Then I would run out and throw water on the sparks that landed. I was very concerned about whether I would get out alive, as it was hard to breathe. I also wondered whether the fire would suck all the oxygen out of the air. No doubt, the fast-running river helped a great deal to keep things cooler than what it would have been a mile back from the river.

A week after the fire passed I packed up and left the area, as it looked so black with few areas still green. I thought there would be no wildlife for years to come. I was soon proved wrong, and at the end of the next summer all the willows and alder along the riverbanks were growing like mad, together with fireweed which was growing all over the area. It was remarkable how quickly the area greened up and the moose, caribou, bears and other wild life moved in from outside the area to browse on the luscious new growth. Even the birds came back to feed on all the berries that grew up in the burned area.

Once again, it convinced me that it's Nature's way of cleansing out the old decaying forest by eliminating all the spruce bugs and other diseases and replacing it with a brand new start which will grow and thrive for another 100 years, thus becoming home to most species of wildlife. There were the Ruffle Grouse, which likes the willow and brush areas along streams and lower areas, and the Fool Hen (Spruce Grouse), the friend of all trappers, prospectors, etc. who stay out in the woods most of the year. It's possible (with great care) to get these birds without a gun—either with a rock or picture wire snare on the end of a pole, the stick part of which you have to point well above the bird before lowering the snare extremely slowly over the bird's head. After this, you pull the pole quickly and you have a dinner! The main thing to do is to take lots of time—never rush or the bird will fly away. Also we have the Willow Ptarmigan and Rock Ptarmigan, which turn white in the winter and brown in the summer. They are hard to see. As they blend so perfectly in the summer and winter with their habitat, it takes a trained eye to see them. Many of these are also reasonably tame and will run ahead of you and will stay 15-20 yards in front. If you take a circle and set a dozen wire snares in between bushes that are close together, you can then go back and try to chase the birds into the snares. Like the Fool Hen, you have to move slowly, otherwise they will fly away. I've caught many good dinners by this method.

Pretty cold tonight. It's four sock weather—the colder it gets the more socks you put on. This cold makes the dogs curl up tight, but they won't retire to their house yet. They won't do that until they nearly freeze once and then they go in a shed so tight together that if you want to hitch them up you have to go and rout them out with a switch. It's about time I got them working. They are so sleek and fat with their long idleness and full stomachs. They've enjoyed all summer where they had nothing to do.

They are saucy and woe betide the poor devil of a dog that gets down amongst them in a friendly scrap. If the affair was allowed to end in a perfectly natural way, we would be minus a $50 dog about every few minutes till there was only one left—and he most likely would run away looking for more trouble. Luckily for them however, the affair doesn't end naturally. The instant we hear a scrap—no matter where or when—off we go—not with a whip or small stick but with a club—and get in the free fight, if you like. It's easy to get hurt yourself, if you're not careful. The fracas generally ends with at least one dog being knocked out completely with a sore nose—but it doesn't seem to teach them a lesson. They join in the next scrap—that is, all except Betsy. Betsy causes more scraps than all the rest combined. Once started, she moves out of danger and sits down and enjoys every minute of the action.

My faithful dog, Betsy

Unfortunately, I lost my favourite dog, poor old Betsy. I left her at home one day and came back late at night and found her dead. She tried to have pups and something went wrong—and she bled to death. She will be hard to replace in the fall, so I'm left with only Buster and Nugget now (Mike has borrowed two of my dogs), but he's a dandy and can pull more than I can. I'll have to get another two in the fall and train them to pull. Buster or Betsy were both good lead dogs and the others soon learned to follow. It's no wonder they liked the lead position, simply because when following behind the scenery ahead is not all that inspiring.

I got to be quite a moose hunter at last—but there are lots of tricks to be learned at that game. Moose are as wary as eagles and cunning as Jews. The Indian who taught me some of the tricks of hunting said, "You savvy (know) too much—pretty soon you catchum more moose than me." I could see he was a little upset, so I gave him my yellow dog and that appeased his wrath, as he had great admiration for Nugget who, he said, was like a squaw—"could pull good and talk all the time." He could certainly pull but his talking powers were too much for this child. He got me so mad once when he scared a big moose away that I took my rifle off the sleigh to shoot him. However, just in time, I remembered the trails were so bad this winter that it made me think I might have to pull double his load and mine. I paused and let him live till spring—for which I was thankful, especially when I came back with a heavy load and bad snow conditions. Some people shoot their dogs in the spring, as they can buy another one in the fall cheaper than the cost of feed for the summer. I don't like this practice as, to me, the dogs are just part of me. With me fishing in the summer, it doesn't cost me anything to keep them for the summer—except a bit of trouble when they jump out of the boat if they see a rabbit or something else to chase.

The rabbits are quite scarce this year, so it's not so easy to get one for dinner. I like them nearly as much as grouse. If there are many around, I set snares for them on the rabbit runs (they use their trails so often that they leave easy-to-see, trampled trails in the moss, leaves or snow in the winter). Two years ago there were so many they were peeling all the little trees coming up in the burned-over areas or those logged for firewood. I sold quite a lot to a Chinese friend who had a restaurant. A lot of people liked rabbit better than moose meat and would ask me to drop off half a dozen when I came to town. I catch most of them with picture wire snares which I attach to a spring pole— that is, an 8' pole placed in the crotch of a tree that is heavier on one end than the other and which is then attached to a small notch. When the rabbit gets in the snare he pulls it out from the notch and the heavy end of the pole goes down and takes the rabbit up two feet from the ground. This way, the rabbits die quickly and don't bruise themselves—bruising spoils them for market.

The Old Timers tell me that the rabbits go in cycles about every seven years. When the rabbits are thick, the owls and hawks multiply fast along with the lynx, foxes and other fur-bearing animals. Once the rabbits get so thick they die of disease and most of the predators die off from starvation and disease—then the next cycle starts.

By Jove, I've laughed at your guesses about the composition of those things I sent—the smoked meat and neck piece. Not one of your guesses was right. You evidently haven't had much fur around your neck, otherwise you surely would not class moose meat and sable in the same guess. The fur that looked like sable was from the underside of the Reindeer—so was the smoked meat, which came from the hind quarter of the Reindeer. You may have heard that the US Government and some individuals brought over from Siberia several hundred Reindeer, complete with Lapland herders, to test which part of Alaska suited them. They also taught the Eskimos how to handle the Reindeer. It was no good trying them around Fairbanks, as there is none of the peculiar food—the white moss, except in spots on the white hills. However, on the coast, from the mouth of the Kuskakwim north round the Arctic, embracing St. Michaels, Nome and all the Keewalik country, there is food in plenty and the animals do well. Any Eskimos wishing to own animals go to the mission, where they are taught how to care for and handle the Reindeer. When the Eskimos have completed the course, they would get six Reindeer the first year, eight the second, and 10 the third. Restrictions are placed on the Eskimos, otherwise some would drive the little herd to his tribe and have one grand Potlatch—which would be the end of the Reindeer. The Eskimo must keep the herd intact but he can kill and sell the rest of the offspring as he wishes. He cannot kill or sell the cow Reindeer without permission. This last embargo is laid on him in order to keep the business entirely in the hands of the Eskimos. In this way, they will not be a burden on the US Government. The latter have a commitment to pay the huge sum of 3¢ day for each Native or Eskimo towards education and relief, if they're destitute.

This all started in 1889 when Dr. Sheldon Jackson studied ways to help the starving Eskimos and Natives, who had lost their food supply of seals, walruses, and other animals due to the overharvesting by settlers coming in from outside. Dr. Jackson learned from Captain Healy of the Revenue Service that Siberian Arctic tribes lived comfortably on their herds of tame Reindeer. They made a proposal to the US Congress in 1890, which was turned down because they thought the plan was ridiculous. Sheldon Jackson refused to give up and raised $2,100 from public donations. The animals could only be bought by barter. Jackson and Healy went to Siberia and bartered for 16 Reindeer in 1891 and 171 in 1892. Once the importation was proved successful, Congress in 1893 made small appropriation for Reindeer Services. Imports continued until 1902 when the Russian Government forbade further exportations. By this time, 1,280 Reindeer had been brought to Alaska. The herds had been built up to 400,000 and over 100,000 were killed for food, clothing and making souvenirs for export and sale to travellers. Rarely in history have the efforts of one man brought more benefits to starving people. Laplanders, who were familiar with Reindeer, were brought in by the Interior Department to educate the Eskimo.

The projects seems to have been a great success. In one generation, the Eskimo has advanced from the primitive and nomadic hunter to a civilization of men and women who have had the opportunity to acquire wealth in order to be able to purchase goods for a better way of life. It was the earliest—and perhaps only—Government action that introduced a new industry with practical vocational training that taught them how to adapt to local community needs and that resulted in training a primitive race towards independence and responsiveness.

It wasn't much later before another Government report claimed credit for the whole program and said that rarely in history have the efforts of starting an enterprise so small wrought equal benefits to an ignorant and starving people. I must say I took offence at such a statement, because I thought they were smarter than I was (if they were ignorant, what did that make me?)—because they were able to survive in such a harsh climate with no rifles, fish nets or a store within reach to buy food and clothes. It certainly makes my lifestyle look easy— when all I have to do is hitch up the dogs and in a few days I could go and buy nearly everything I wanted if I had the money.

A transplanted herd of Siberian reindeer blankets the Alaskan tundra

In my short experience, I have found the Eskimo to be generally a peaceful and docile person. Nearly 4,000 of them live in the delta of the Kuskakwim.

Another thing the Government report did not say—the reason why they were starving was because of the large number of hunters who came up in the better weather during the summer and fall to overharvest the seals, walruses, and other game populations. To the Eskimo, the spotted deer is a priceless treasure. What maiden could help being jealous when she sees her best friend arrayed in a spotted deer parka trimmed with wolverine and with a nose guard of long wolf hair all matched with trim, together with mukluks of spotted deer tops—what could be a nicer present to a bashful maiden?

I'm sure if brother Art reads this he will want one of these glorious skins to give fair Dorothy, telling her at the same time that ordinary mouse-coloured parkas were not for such as she. No other lad would have a chance.

Love to all and have a good Xmas.

Jack

Tanana Crossing, Alaska
May 29th, 1908

D ear Mum,
       I expect you were wondering where my letters are. Haven't
written any very lately or received any. The mail service seems to be
held up. The paddle steamers have been back on the river since the ice
went out. The mail routes seem to have changed. The winter mail now
goes via Valdez and this will go by the summer route via Dawson City.
You will note my address has changed to Tanana Crossing as I thought
I would try fishing down here for a change. This means I will have to
build a new fish wheel and a few nets because the latter don't last long.
I made two during the winter when travel was bad, and they will last a
lot longer as the thread is much better than the nets I buy. I still have to
get those types of supplies out of Chicago, as their price and quality is
far better.
       I finished trapped in April but didn't do well—even thought I
did better than anyone else in the district, according to the local paper.
Fur was awfully scarce, except lynx—and I don't like to catch them as
they are so hard to handle and cheap besides. (I got 26 of them in
total.) The hide is so thin that it's difficult to handle. After we skin the
lynx, we put them on a stretcher with the fur inside so that the skin will
dry. After one day they are ready to turn—which takes a little skill as
it's so easy to tear the hide while doing this. Even though the price has
doubled, lynx still aren't worth too much (only $6½ a hide). Marten
prices were way up from last year. I got $12 each compared to $3.50
two years ago and $7.50 last year. In total, I got $700 for the winter's
work. I also got several moose and two caribou late last fall which I
brought to town and sold to the miners. I averaged 20¢ a pound lower
than last year due to a plentiful supply and a lot of miners not working.

June 2nd, 1908

       I'd better get this letter mailed before it gets too dirty to read! I
started to write 60 miles up the river where I was fishing for grayling
and got a boat load, which I sold yesterday for a poor price. I couldn't

keep them as they would go rotten if I held out for a better price. Too many people are short of money being as the mine is not doing well. I will go up for one more load before I leave here. I plan on going with my outfit for a year 400 miles up the Tanana to try out a new area.

I'm not sure yet on where I will get my letters, but there is a small post office and small store at Tananka Crossing, so I will write the Post Master in Fairbanks and tell him to send my letters there—I could go and pick them up from there during a good spell of weather. I expect to spend the winter only a little more than 100 miles from there, so it shouldn't be any trouble providing the dogs are in good shape to go and pick up my mail at least once during the winter.

I will take a lot of my gear, like traps and a supply of food that will keep such as 300 pounds each of flour, beans and rolled oats, as well as some dried apples and dried vegetables which I can store till I come back in the fall.

I received your letter containing Lucy's picture. She sure looks good but tell her I nailed the picture up on the tent pole when it was dark and, unfortunately, put the nail through her head. I certainly hope it doesn't hurt her any, as she is so nice. Many times I wonder what I'm doing spending my time out here in the wilderness with no one to talk to other than my dogs, the camp robber, and the squirrels. I may even go back to England for a month or two and see if I can cheer Safie up, as she seems down since John died.

The mosquitoes—here are very bad. They come out of the grass in the millions as soon as you sit down. If it's possible to get wet clay from the riverbank or in a swamp, I mix some with water till it's wet enough to stick on the face and hands which helps to keep the mosquitoes away. If you mix it either too thick or too thin, it will either fall off or run off. If you do a good job, it will keep the mosquitoes away for several hours. The only problem with this is you often get an itch and want to scratch it. However, you have to resist the temptation or you leave a target for the mosquitoes, black flies and deer flies. I dislike the black flies the most, as they are so sneaky they like to crawl in your ears, nose, and eyelids without you feeling them—but they bite out a little piece of skin to get blood and after they leave, a little blood runs out. At least the mosquito bites and leaves with no mark on most people.

What I dislike most with mosquitoes is that several will sneak into the tent when you get in. You try to catch them all before going to sleep by leaving one arm out of the covers and hope they will land and start biting so you can catch them all and get some sleep. All too often, there is a smart one who will wait till all is still then come humming by your nose and you wait for him to land so you can get him. Quite often this will happen five or six times before you either get to sleep and don't feel it or you finally get it. A black fly at least doesn't make any noise and you don't know anything till morning when you find spots of dried blood in your ear, eye or nose. At times, we get the tiny sand fly—or commonly known as "no-see-um"—who can come through the mosquito net with no trouble at all. They come later in the summer after the mosquitoes have gone for the year. The idea of covering my face and hands with clay came to me one evening as I was sitting by the camp fire in the smoke to keep the flies away. Suddenly, a young caribou bounced out of the willows with thousands of deer flies all over it and literally, dived into the mud in shallow water with just his nose out long enough to get a breath once in a while. The young caribou stayed like this for close to an hour when it got up and started to feed along the meadow. It was covered with mud and clay—and not a fly was bothering it. I got thinking that if it was good enough for a caribou it's good enough for me. Later on, I noticed other animals (bears, moose and even foxes and wolves) will do the same thing. A moose that gets frantic with flies will run at top speed to shake off as many as it can, then run right into a lake or river and go right under the water to get rid of flies.

There are many people who go mad with flies and run till they drop if they have no means of lighting a fire. After lighting a fire, you put green branches on it to make lots of smoke—or else you get up to higher ground where there is wind which keeps most of the flies away. I can quite understand how it could drive people and animals crazy. I was out not long ago and fell off a log while crossing a small river and got my matches wet and couldn't get a fire started. I was crossing a wide delta area several miles across which was covered with willow and other low brush that kept the wind away. For several hours I tried to keep the millions of flies away by purposely walking through thick branches to get rid of them—but with little success. Eventually, I reached higher ground that looked like a good place to spend the night, as I knew I couldn't get to base camp to get dry matches. I tried laying the wet matches in the hot sun, hoping they would dry and enable me to get a fire going. Before the sun went down it was plain to see this wouldn't work and the flies kept getting worse as evening approached. I got desperate and pried the bullet out of two .30-30 shells and scattered the black powder on a waterlily pad and put dry twigs over it—with a little bit of pitch I had found on a tree. Then I put the other shell with no bullet in the gun and fired the gun at close range, which made a flash and started the fire immediately. Without this, I'm sure the flies would have driven me mad. It certainly scared me and from then on I was far more careful to keep my matches in a small, water-tight pepper can everywhere I went.

Matches are more valuable than gold in this country, if you live long enough to learn. Things we take for granted back home are so important in a harsh country like Alaska or the Yukon. The hardy and those fortunate enough to get out in time are the only ones who survive for long. Mike had a rough time this spring during the break-up on the Tanana as the ice went out—and was lucky to survive and save the wood he had cut during the winter. He had his cabin a little too close to the river, as there was no level ground above the river where it was safe to build—so he took a chance too close for comfort. During the late winter he tried to train the dogs to run up on the roof of the cabin from a runway he had built from the bank, but they didn't like scenery and chose the bank of the river as being far more interesting. Luckily, he was prepared by leaving the wood up on the bank held by three good sized trees. He left them that way so that when the river freed of ice he could securely tie the three with ropes 30' up, then cut the trees nearly through at the bottom. Once clear, he cut the ropes and the weight of the logs above would break the wood left in the cut. All the logs would then slide in the river to be caught in a boom at locations where needed by the riverboats and domestic users.

This year there was heavy rain and very warm weather, which brought the river up more than eight feet in less than a week. This brought all the ice down nearly at the same time. One day there was a big ice jam a mile or so up-river. Once it broke loose and released a lot of water suddenly, the level of the river rose over 14 feet in two minutes. This meant sweeping everything ahead of it—trees, logs and everything (including the dogs which were down by the river when the flood waters hit). The dogs were swept off their feet and were down the river a few yards before they managed to reach the shore and scamper up the runway to the roof of the cabin to safety. (The roof was only inches above the flood water.) The dogs were horribly frightened but safe, as the cabin held in place as the water rushed down. The flood caused by the ice jam receded in less than an hour, but the dogs absolutely refused to budge from the roof for three days. It will be a long time before they trust rivers again.

Mike was smart and lucky to save all his logs; however, there were six other wood-cutters who lost their entire winter's supply in less than two minutes. Fortunately for us, our wood brought in a better price due to less wood being available to the wood-buyers.

Break-up on the river is always a mess and this year it came early (on the 9th of May)—the same time as the mosquitoes, swallows and geese come in on the first flight of the year. The river rose 15 feet above its winter level. Some of the smaller rivers coming into the Yukon brought down trees and bits of wood from mudslides that happen often over the years, especially in hilly country. Channels also change every few years. The water in the river stays dirty for weeks on end and is as dirty as the Thames River in London. The only way to get clean water during this period is to get it from the small streams.

One wood-cutter collected enough trees floating down the river to keep him busy for the rest of the summer supplying wood to the paddle steamers. He managed to catch the trees in a big eddy where the current swirled around before going on down the river again. It is quite dangerous work and it's not uncommon to lose someone every year if a big piece of ice catches them off guard. Some of the ice chunks floating down are as big as a house and 5-7' thick.

Break-up is an exciting time for those who live close to one of the large rivers—but it can also be a scary time when huge chunks of ice clog up in narrow parts of the river and tons of ice pile up behind. This pile-up brings the level of the river up quickly till the force of the water finally breaks the ice dam—that sounds like a clap of thunder as the build-up of water floods away downstream, tearing out trees and river banks as it goes down. This can happen many times before it reaches the sea.

A lot of money is made and lost each year in Fairbanks, as people bet on the time and date when the Chena Bridge will be washed out. Nearly all the people in town line up for hours at a vantage point from which they can see the bridge so that they can collect their money if they win before the other fellow leaves town. The 9th of May break-up is very early and the person who won collected over $12,000 on a 5:1 bet. Many over the years have collected far more than this. (The newspaper picture of 30th of April, 1907 describes this event very well.)

Hope next year I will be the winner and will make a trip home.

Jack

The ice going out on the Chena River, carrying away the Tanana Bridge

CHAPTER 5

KUSKAKWIM AND KAYUKUK RIVERS

The letters in Chapter 5 describe the trip up the Kayukuk River to the height of land overlooking the Arctic Drainage System and then moving over to the Kuskakwim River for a winter's trapping. The letters also describe the method by which an old prospector made a set of dentures out of a hard burl from a swamp spruce and the front teeth from a mountain sheep. (The molars were made from the back teeth of a bear.)

1908

Dear Percy,
   Received your letter with many thanks. It was nice to hear all is well at home. It's great to have a sister and mother who keep me supplied with needles, thread and patching material for my pants, shirt, coat, etc. I came in from winter trapping on June 5th when the Tanana was clear of ice—so the welcome letter was waiting for me in my mail box.

   I did very well trapping this winter but may try another river and area next fall as I intend to scout around during the summer after the first run of salmon is finished and before the later runs start. I hope to get two weeks when everything is quiet and go north of the Arctic Circle to see what the country looks like and what the prospects for trapping seem to be. I don't expect to find many Indians trapping that far from the main river system.

   Since I started to write last spring, I've seen a lot of new country so I'd better get busy and tell you all about it or all of you will think I got lost. During the summer I spent most of my time fishing on the lower reaches of the Koyukuk River, which is a branch off the Yukon River that drains from the north above the Arctic Circle. I found the area quite different from the Tanana/Chena Rivers and branch rivers where I fished and trapped during the last few years. I decided to move as markets were slow in the Fairbanks area, where I sold most of my fish.

The reason for this was that several medium sized prospects didn't pan out as well as expected and were closed down. Many of the people working there moved down to the Kayukuk River area, where good showings were reported on some of the branch creeks—so I guess I got the gold fever like the rest of them and decided to move and take my boat, supplies and dogs with me to set up camp close enough to supply the miners with fish and meat.

Method of drying the salmon catch on the Yukon River (Cann photo)

The fish going up the Yukon and its many tributaries would be in better shape closer to the ocean than further up-stream, where they lose weight fighting their way against the current. I find it wonderful that these fish can find their way back three or four years later to where they were hatched—in some cases, over 2,000 miles from where they leave the ocean.

On the way down-river, for nearly 400 miles, I kept close to shore so the dogs would follow me down. They had a great time chasing rabbits, moose or anything else that happened to be near the river bank—they even managed to scare a young bull moose out into the river which I was able to shoot and tow to shore where I could skin it and cut it into quarters, so that I could lift them into the boat. I was lucky because I was able to sell all of it to a group of prospectors who were prospecting for gold in one of the small creeks that come into the river not far about Mubato and the Kayukuk River, which is 550 miles up the Yukon River. This area was where I expected to spend most of the summer until the late runs of salmon up the Yukon were finished. Then, I would move on for the winter.

I spent several days finding a good camping area where there was a shelter for the boat, lots of dry firewood and overlooking a big meadow where moose or caribou would come out in the early morning or late at night—there seems to be a good market for both fish and meat in this area. It seems to be far enough up-river so that many of the travellers are getting short of supplies and are looking for fish and meat that will keep them going for another 100 miles or so (before they run out again). Many of the miners are in such a hurry to get to the mine fields that they don't have time to stop and fish or hunt. Some of them only stop long enough to eat then keep going till it's too dark to see. If there is a moon out, many will keep moving till two or three o'clock in the morning—then start out again at daylight. Many going far up the river go on the paddle steamers, but others—with little money and those who want to prospect along the way—do it the hard way and pole or paddle their way up-stream.

It's surprising to see some of them manage to find a little gold in small streams along the way. If so, they will stay the winter and try to make their fortune in any open water they can find. Others will try to dig for gold on higher ground where water won't come in to fill the hole. Some of these people come from many different countries, especially Australia and the U.S. They search till their money and supplies run out, then either go and work in a mine at poor wages so they can prospect again next summer or catch a ship back to the U.S., where they can make a few dollars to come back and try again. These people never seem to lose hope. Others try to find someone with money who will give them a grub stake and take a share of what they find. There is no doubt that very few hit it big and even those who do, go out and spend it on a good time till they are broke. There are always a lot of shysters meeting the ships in San Francisco or elsewhere who come to convince some unwary soul that they are your friends and they just happen to know where to find strong whisky, sloe gin and fast women for a good time.

FRAME WORK OF TCHUKTCHI HOUSE.

Eskimo shelter made from a frame of whale and walrus bones
covered with either seal or caribou hide

A shabby summer wickiup of canvas offers scant shelter to a
group of Copper River Athabascans

I soon found another good camping spot not far up the Kayukuk River where a small stream came in—just what I wanted. The next week I searched for a nice area where I could set my nets and build fish traps or a fish wheel, which generally work better on the smaller rivers once you find which ones the salmon like to spawn in. A good eddy in the main river is nice, as there are fish moving up-stream most of the summer—unfortunately, these are hard to find. As for the smaller streams, they are good for a week or so, then nothing till another run comes in. The big King salmon seem to come in first, followed by the Humpback (pink) or the Sockeye (red); the Coho come later. Some of them keep coming until late in the fall—it is good to have them when all the other runs are over.

I plan on making two **fykes**—a big box 8' long, 4' wide and 6' high. They are made of willows threaded together and not more than one inch apart—partly depending on the size of the fish you want to catch. They must be firmly tied at the corners so they won't slip and leave holes for the fish to get out. There have to be firm upright spacers every foot in order to hold the sides and end firm. There is a lid on the top with a catch that can be undone so you can take the fish out. The front of the **fyke** is made like a funnel with the small end inside the box so that it guides the fish through into the box near the top. The fish seldom find their way out, as they keep trying to get out close to the bottom of the box. You place big rocks in each corner to keep the box firm on the bottom of the river. Once this is in place, you drive stakes close together in a V-shape to guide the fish coming up-stream into the fyke. I find that a well-made fyke is better than a fish wheel, as the fish caught stay alive and fresh for days—or even weeks. Most fish caught in wheels generally die quickly so you have to stay close all the time and clean them as they come in—unless you build a well-made pond from them to fall into. Another advantage of a well-made fyke is that you only take the species of fish you want (that is, those that are saleable)—and let the others go. I mainly use twine to keep the willow bars firmly in place. However, if I have time I prefer to use moose or caribou hide cut the thickness of a good shoe lace, which holds even better if the leather is good and wet and well stretched before you use it. Many of the Indian people still use either strips of willow or cedar bark, depending on where they live and which trees are available.

*A fyke, a very effective fish trap which was widely used
by Indians, Eskimos and Whites*

Fykes work best in a moderate current where the water goes through without putting too much pressure on the cage. With a fast current, it is difficult to keep the box in place—especially if a drift log comes down at high speed, which can take it right out or destroy it. I even use fykes in lakes with some success—especially if there is a narrow channel on each side of an island. It takes a long time to make a good water wheel and in order to work well, the wheel needs an excellent location. In the same way as you use a fyke, a wheel is used to guide the fish coming up-stream into a narrow space the width of your wheel. Unlike the fyke, there must be a good current in order to turn the paddles reasonably fast so the fish won't jump out before reaching the top.

The fish wheels I make are cedar planks for the paddles which are 5' long and 16-18" wide with a 3" strip nailed on the front of the plank to help slide the fish in as one of the paddles comes up out of the water. The whole thing stands over 15' high. The outside of the wheel is like giant wagon wheels which hold the paddles between them. The paddles are set with a slight slope to one side so that when the paddle gets to the top it passes an open space in the wheel where the fish slide out and down a chute into a box or pool of water, depending on the way the wheel is made. The force of the water hits the up-stream paddle, which lifts the opposite paddle out of the water and keeps going around. These wheels are a lot of work to make.

The first one I built took me the better part of a month. I had no problem if I needed help to get it set up in the river, as most of the Indians from a small village nearby stood around for days watching the crazy white man trying to catch fish with something they had never seen. I spent a lot of time with the Indians, as I wanted to know where they fished and trapped so that I wouldn't cause a conflict by going into an area they used from time to time. Very few of the Indians had permanent dwellings and moved during the season several times. In the spring, many of the them moved and set up camp on a lake where they could catch freshwater species that spawned in the early spring—especially where a creek came into the lake or the creek left the lake, depending where the best spawning ground was. More often, the creeks coming into the lake are the best as the lakes seem to be better stocked with fish. This is due to the fact that more of the little fish hatched wash down to the lake whereas, if it's in a creek leaving the lake, a very high percentage of the fish are washed down to the main river and never get back to the lake. Many of these smaller creeks dry up early in the summer—particularly, if it happens to be a dry summer.

When dealing with nature, there is nothing 100% right. For example, in some cases where the spawning area is above the lake, so many little fish survive and with limited feed in the lake this means small fish. People living in these areas soon get to know where they can rely on a good food supply. When catching fish in the early spring and throwing the insides in a pit, it soon attracts the bears that have recently come out of hibernation and are looking for food. They come to these areas and are easily caught in traps, snares or shot when they come out in the evening or early morning. A bit of fresh meat at that time of the year looks pretty good. I try and get a two-year-old that I smoke and cure for winter use.

In the summer, the Indians move to a salmon stream and often stay the winter if they catch enough fish. They also pick lots of berries for the winter. Some have to move in the fall for a month or two, so that they can get more berries to eat and dry for the winter before they move back to where they dried lots of salmon. Most of the Indians seem to spend a very carefree life. However, a very large percentage die at a very early age—in their early 40's or 50's. There are also some who go on to live to a very old age. I enjoyed sitting around a campfire listening to those who spoke English. They spoke about their early life before they had guns and modern fish nets. Before this, most of their fish were caught in fykes and fish traps, by spears, or else the fish were guided into small ponds where they could be speared or clubbed.

Fish traps are very effective on streams where the fish are going down-stream to spawn. They put a big log across the stream and drive stakes behind and in front of it. Then they use big meadow peat sods to stop the water running through, so that it all has to run over the top. Once this is achieved, they tie small poles close together and pointed down-stream with the other end out of the water so that the fish slide down between the poles and then the water runs through—leaving the fish high and dry so they wiggle their way down and into a basket made of willows. This is where the big kids stand by the side and throw the fish out on the shore, where the women stand and clean them ready to eat or ready to be hung up to dry. In many cases, the men go up-stream and hit big paddles on the water to scare the fish down-stream to get in the trap. It's quite an efficient operation to watch on a good fish stream.

Another thing they showed me was the caribou corrals they built in a narrow gorge or small pass in a mountain on a main caribou trail. This was built of upright stakes dug into the ground and spaced 6" apart so that the caribou couldn't get through. Then the Indians put a number of posts spaced around the corral two feet from the inside of the fence and tied snares on each of them so that when they chased the caribou around the corral they would run around the side of the fence and get caught in the snare loop—then they could spear the caribou to finish them off. Some of the corrals were fairly large—up to three or four acres. In these, they would build snowhouses so that a man could stand inside and spear the caribou as they ran past. Once guns came in, the Indians used guns rather than spears. If they could get a herd running in the right direction down the trail, they could get the whole herd in the corral and have more than enough meat to last them and their dogs through the winter.

A Co-Yukon Deer Corral

I was surprised to see when the sun was bright that the Indians wore wood goggles with small slits to keep the glare of the sun out of the hunters' eyes. Once the Russians brought in sunglasses as items to trade, the Indians soon changed to the improved glasses. The boys were trained to shoot or throw a spear by the age of 10. They weren't accepted as being ready to marry until they had killed their first deer, caribou or walrus, single handed.

The Russians still play a major role in the trade life of Alaska, as it's only about 37 years since the Russians sold Alaska to the Americans. They brought in what they call "burning glasses"—which are very common—and I bought one as soon as I could as they are very useful to light a fire if the sun is strong. You hold the glasses to reflect the sun's rays onto a dry piece of lichen or dry twigs. They seem to be one of the best trading items—together with guns, gunpowder, caps, flints, bullets and axes. Trinkets and beads are okay for the women, but very few of them speak any English. The Indians here have a good laugh trying to tell me I need a squaw to make me clothes, darn my socks, dry my salmon, cook my meals and keep me warm during the long, cold Alaskan winters. They would point at a young girl (15-17 years old) and say something in Indian, which I couldn't understand. The girls were so embarrassed that they ran away and hid—much to the amusement of all around the campfire.

The Indians down-river make their snowshoes the same way as the Russians do—and not at all like the snowshoes made in the Tanana-Yukon areas. They take one long stick and bend it right around and turn up the front to clear the snow as you walk. Up-river, they mainly use two sticks and turn the toes of the snowshoes up, except for hard snow and trails where they make small and light snowshoes about 3' long with no turn-up on the front. The rawhide web in the centre part of the snowshoe is made from moose hide cut half an inch wide and wound round in bars—four across and two up and down. The front and back are laced with thin deer or caribou hide. Birch is the favourite wood in all areas (if it's available), but swamp spruce is nearly as good. There are two strong wooden bars across the snowshoe to keep the sides apart, which have a lot of strain on them.

When I first started to walk on snowshoes, the Indians had a good laugh as I kept stepping on the toe of the other shoe and falling on my face in the snow. When I finally picked myself up, they asked if I had webbed feet as I walked like a duck and told me that all I had to do was learn how to quack like a duck. They couldn't believe a man of my age hadn't learned to snowshoe long before then.

Most of the them have a good sense of humour and like to play tricks on each other in order to have a good laugh. Quite a few of those I got to know who live in the lower Yukon travel back and forth to Siberia and those from northern Siberia who come to Nome looked just like the Indians here. Even the Eskimos on both sides of the

Bering Straits look the same—which leads many of us to believe they came from Asia in the first place. Yet we will likely never know, as there is no written history to go back to and little seems to have been passed on from generation to generation, except the most important things like how to survive by finding food and storing food to keep them going through the long winters—which is more than the average white person could do with the limited tools at his disposal. It's taken the white races several thousand years to get to where we are today.

In many areas of Alaska, where it is mainly Tundra and no trees, many of the shelters are dug into the ground with a small doorway to get in through and covered with hides (mainly caribou or seal). They have a small hole through the top to let the smoke out. There isn't much smoke, as the heating is either whale, seal or walrus oil and the only light is like a candle with a wick of some kind in a can or the centre of a leg bone after the marrow has been taken out and the bone cut in half and the leg joint bone holds the oil in place. During the night they turn the heat off and stuff a piece of hide in the air hole—thus keeping it warmer inside.

There are also a few more permanent homes, which are very small but cleverly constructed. Because there is no wood to use for 2'x4' studs, they make the frame with walrus and whale bones tied firmly with strips of hide. They then cover the structure with walrus, caribou or moose hides—depending on what they can get. If there is a window, it will be small and covered with clear gut from the fur seals or walruses.

Clothing is generally made from fur seals with the fur side in. If made from caribou hides, they prefer to use the fawns as the skin is lighter so the coat won't be so heavy and thus easier to sew. With caribou, they generally leave the fur side out as the caribou hair is so thick that it keeps the wind out. Wind is the killer up here—far worse than the cold. Trims on coats and hats are often made from unborn caribou. They get these by either killing the mother a month before the fawn is born or chase the mother till she is totally exhausted and aborts the young. The hair of the fawn is so pretty and soft they are the dream of all the young maidens in the area. I don't think we should be critical of this practice, as they had no silk or cotton to use like many other races of people have.

The process for tanning the leather is very interesting and makes some people nearly sick to watch. It's made of human urine mixed with seal or walrus oil and left for several days till the hide starts to decay. The hide is subsequently rubbed with a fairly sharp rock or rib bone till the hide is flexible. Some of these people are expert in this procedure and most of this work is done by women.

Most of their boats made in areas where there is no timber are made of wet seal or walrus hides being stretched over a frame of walrus or whale bones lashed together using mainly the rib bones. It's quite an art to watch, as it's far more difficult than making a wood boat like I do.

Their diet is mainly fish or meat of various kinds from seals, walruses, whales, caribou, moose, beavers, bears, lynx, ducks, geese, swans and cranes, depending on the area in which they live. There is a great deal of difference in the diet of people living on the coast from that of the Interior. Those on the coast have a far easier living than those in the Interior. On the coast, they can get many kinds of sealife like clams, crabs, and many kinds of seaweeds. In the Interior, they have to live mainly on fish, meat, berries and some edible plants which are all covered up for nearly eight months of the year. Reindeer fat is considered a luxury to chew on while walking.

The safe storage of food can make the difference between starvation and survival. Each small band is nearly an empire unto itself and trade with others is nearly non-existent—except some during the short summer. Nearly all are located on rivers and lakes, which are the only sure sources of food supply. Many who either get careless or unlucky in storing enough food for the winter perish during the winter. The life of nearly all in Alaska is the survival of the fittest. When travelling the rivers as soon as the ice goes out, there are many sad stories to tell of people (both White and Indian) who were found starved to death during the winter. The reason for this was because the game animals failed to come through during the winter, due mainly to either wolves or heavy snowfall that changed the travel pattern of the animals.

I had a really good year fishing and hunting with the sale of fish and moose meat being excellent. However, I had one disaster with over two tons of salt fish. During the summer I was so busy I got a fellow who needed a few dollars to buy his food for the winter after he travelled from Dawson City to Fairbanks. I had him build wooden barrels that would hold 500 pounds each of salt fish. It seemed he had made a good job so I soon filled the barrels with a layer of fish, then scattered a fair amount of salt, then another layer of fish till the barrels were full. They were kept in the shade ready for market early in the fall when buyers from Fairbanks would come down-river to stock up before freeze-up and ship back by riverboat to Fairbanks—and even Dawson City, if need be. When I went to move the barrels to the riverbank for loading, I found—to my horror—that the barrels hadn't been made strong enough and sprung a leak, which let the salt brine run out, thereby allowing the fish to rot—they stunk like a polecat. I lost the whole lot, which cut my profit for the year substantially.

In late September, I took all my fish traps and fish wheel out of the river and stored them above the high-water mark for use next summer. During slow periods of fish runs up the river this summer, I explored for a new area to trap. My first trip was a quick one over to the Kuskakwim. A few miles below Holy Cross on the Yukon, it's only 50 miles over to the Kuskakwim so I blazed a trail I could follow with my dogs and limited supplies when trapping time started in the fall. My second trip was up the Kayukuk River where I worked on a small freight boat, helping them deliver supplies up-river as far as they could get—took me up to Beetles, which was a supply centre. After helping to unload all the supplies needed, I asked if I could get a ride back in two weeks if I helped them to load and unload at different points of call—either a few miners who needed supplies or a load of wood to feed the steam engine that keeps the riverboat going. The company were happy to have me along when they didn't have to pay me.

During the two weeks I made my way up the North Fork into the Endicott Range. All I took was a small amount of beans, rice, rolled oats and some flour. I also had one dog to help pack and my small .22 rifle to shoot grouse, ptarmigan, and anything else I might see that could be cooked into a good dinner.

From a high point, I was able to see into the Arctic Drainage. I enjoyed the trip very much, as the weather was nice and ptarmigan were very plentiful—I had no problem with food or shelter. As for trapping, it didn't look as good as what I saw over on the Kuskakwim, so decided not to come back and spend the winter—partly because I was at least 100 miles north of the Arctic Circle and the days would be quite a bit shorter than up the Tanana, where I'd spent the last few winters. Many of the rivers are closed with ice during eight months of the year, making travel more difficult. Some of the rivers in Alaska turn and change direction so gently that you can get turned around without knowing it on a dull day with no sun.

I met one party heading north. They came across a river heading in the right direction, so they built a nice raft of dry logs and proceeded on their way, happy about how much time they would save and not checking their compass. They didn't realize the river was slowly turning south and brought then back three days later on the Yukon River—not far from where they started heading north on foot. The last I saw of the party they were heading north with their compass in their hand to make sure they didn't come back to the same place again. Unless I'm very sure of my directions, I like to make a small blaze on a tree as I go by in order to make sure I can get back and if I find a better route, I make big blazes so I know which is the best.

On the 29th of September, I left the Yukon and followed the blazed trail that I made during the summer back to the Kuskakwim with very limited supplies of food, traps, two blankets, as well as my .22 rifle, an axe, and a small whipsaw, which one man can use to cut a few boards for building a boat or other small jobs like building a table or a bench to sit on. I made good time and arrived in only four days, which I thought was good. I followed the river up a few miles till I found a good patch of trees which looked suitable for making a small riverboat that would take me further up the river.

Before I got started next morning, a small supply boat came by and someone asked if I wanted to work my way up-river as far as McGrath, a small supply landing for miners seeking to find gold in nearby creeks. I was more than willing to go along, which saved me at least two weeks. Once we reached our destination, they found out I was a carpenter—so they hired me to build a small dock on the river to make it easier to unload supplies. This was just great, as in my spare time I was able to locate a good tree which would provide me with a 20' log to make my riverboat. They even helped me to get it up on a stand, where I could cut the boards needed. I was also assured of a ride down-river next spring after the ice went out. When they pulled out next morning, which was the last run for the season, I felt lonely for a day or two and started thinking I should change my way of life and try to find some land where I could build a house and raise a family.

For the next eight months I had lots of time to think about it— and finally decided I would write a letter to Safie in England during the winter and mail it in the spring to ask her whether she had ever thought of coming over to Canada to see what the country looked like. If she wanted to come, I would meet her either in Vancouver or Montreal. The letter was never mailed, as later on in the winter I thought if I had a good year trapping and fishing it might be better if I went back to England in the fall for a visit and talk it over. After a good night's sleep, I got my mind back to trapping and finding another good tree with few knots and a little over a foot in diameter which would make boards 8" wide and 1" thick to complete my boat (the other log didn't make enough).

If everything went well, I could cut three boards a day and I needed about 12 boards which were 20' long to make the boat—in addition to 2" pieces in which to make the ribs which should be not more than 16" apart so that the boat is strong enough for some fast-flowing water. Once I'd got four boards cut, I could build ribs which were not such hard work—and I could make them while taking a breather from cutting each board. I must say I never found an easy way to make a boat, but each time I got a little better.

Once the boat was completed I loaded my supplies for the winter, which I mainly bought at McGrath and slowly made my way up the river. There were several places where the water was so fast that I had to pack the supplies around the fast water and pull the empty boat up with a rope, then load everything up to start again. The weather was starting to get cold by mid-October, so I was anxious to get up as far as I could. Therefore, I used to pull the boat as far as I could between daylight and dark every day for well over two weeks. Once I had turned up the North Fork, I started to look for a nice location which was flat enough to build a cabin and far enough above the river in case of ice jams that could dam up the river for an hour or so before breaking under pressure. This is something you have to watch on all rivers in the north.

I finally found a good location that wasn't too far from the foothills of the big mountain I could see on a clear day, which I thought must be Mt. McKinley. An old prospector had told me that there were lots of mountain sheep, which if lucky can be found all winter in areas that blow clear of snow most of the winter. This was partly true but I had to walk a long way to find them, as the sheep didn't always come down into the foothills. Fortunately, I managed to get two caribou, which the dogs and I were able to bring to the cabin site.

After getting my meat supply for the winter, I took it easy building a cabin as there were plenty of trees nearby which made it easy. I was also lucky as there had been a small fire caused by a lightning strike about two years before—resulting in lots of dry trees being left for firewood. There seemed to be a lot of fur around, especially marten and fox up in the high country.

While looking for new areas to trap, I came across a prospector who had found a good cave in the river bank which he was using to make his home for the winter, as well as trying to find pay dirt along the steep river bank where the snow slid off. When I came along he couldn't believe his eyes—he didn't think there was anyone closer than 200 miles. It also made me feel better to know I had a neighbour less than 20 miles away. He had made a nice shelter by piling up logs, then heaping up snow to keep the storms out and leaving only a small hole for a doorway to get in. He insisted I stay the night—but wouldn't tell me his name, except just call me "Slim" (as he was a tall, gangly fellow but strong as an ox). Inside, he had a little stove and a can of fat with a wick in it for light. Its common name was a "Bitch." It would burn a long time on a can of fat, which he had got from a very fat caribou early in the fall. He went outside and came back with two big steaks—and I sat trying to figure out what animal they had come from, while they thawed close to the stove and I listened to the whole story before dinner was served.

Apparently "Slim" had left San Francisco two years before after having his last teeth taken out and having no money to get false teeth from the dentist. Since coming to Alaska, he had finally got tired of having to cut his meat up really fine as he couldn't chew up a nice big steak of moose or caribou. He decided to do something about it. So he found a small hard burl from a black spruce growing in a swamp nearby and cut it in half. After this he cut a slice just under an inch thick and kept scraping the edges with a sharp knife—process that lasted for over two months. At the end of the process, it fitted comfortably in his mouth. However, this was only the beginning!

Subsequently, he started scraping the inside of the plate so that it would fit his gums. He had nothing but flour to put inside his mouthto see where the high spots were. After this, he would scrape these areas and start the process again. This process lasted, with only his dim light to work by, during the long evenings of winter when it's dark for over 18 hours a day—so he had lots of time over the following three and and a half months when he wasn't sleeping.

When it was daylight Slim spent his time digging for gold, which so far was little better than good colours from four holes he had dug to a depth of 12-16 feet—or wherever he hit bedrock where the gold was supposed to be. Time and comfort meant nothing to people like this and slowly scraping his dentures was one way of passing the time when alone for seven or eight months.

All the time he was scraping his dental plate, he never stopped talking for hours about what he would do after he hit the mother load of gold, which he knew was down somewhere in this little stream and he would find it before the ice went out on the Kuskakwim in May. After he got the plate to fit his mouth, he started boring holes with the small blade of a tiny pocket knife. He had broken the point off, then sharpened the end, which he kept twisting to make a hole large enough to fit a tooth. He took the molars from a black bear and the front teeth from a mountain goat. The glue he used to stick them in with he had made by boiling caribou bones for hours. Eventually all the liquid had boiled away so that it was so thick it wouldn't run—this seemed to hold the tooth in the perfectly sized hole that Slim had bored with the little knife. I must say I was very impressed with both the job he had done—but even more so with the patience over the long months.

After the long story, Slim proceeded to cook the steaks in the frying pan and cooked up some rice in a 5-pound lard pail. A lard pail, together with coffee cans, was a very common cooking pot in trapping and mining cabins or tents. Once dinner was on the plates, he said with a laugh: "Now I can chew up this old bear steak with his own teeth that I put in my dental plate."

Next morning, I left at daylight to go back to my cabin and get the traps set out for another season. Because there were so many foxes around the timber line, I spent many days up on the lower levels of Mt. McKinley. On nice days it was lovely up there in the clear, crisp air. But in bad weather it is a good place to stay away from, as the storms can hit very suddenly and with the snow drifting and blowing it can cover your snowshoe tracks in a matter of minutes. I never did try to get up to the top—which looks a long way away and looks as if you should be prepared to spend at least three or four nights up there and even more if a big storm hits.

I don't think I have the equipment or the experience to try it and I certainly wouldn't be much for trapping, except at the lower levels near the timber line. On one trip I made up my fox line I spotted a small herd of moutain sheep. After hours of stalking them, I managed to come close behind some big rocks and shot two young rams—they made a nice change for my dinners. I took half of one over to my friend Slim, where we had Christmas dinner and both of us thought it was a real treat. Of course, it would have been much better with a bottle of wine. In the evening there was the most magnificent display of Northern Lights. They moved across the sky changing colours every few minutes. At times, it seemed like huge curtains being drawn as the colours behind changed colour. Much of the time there was a crackling sound as the colours danced in the sky. We watched on and off for hours—only going in to get warm then coming out again.

Fortunately, the weather hasn't been really cold so far this winter and it's nice to travel. The snowshoe trails stay open so you don't have to break trail every time you go to look at the traps. I've done really well so far and have already got over 60 marten and 26 fox of various colours. The silver foxes are the best price, but most of mine are crosses or red foxes, which are not worth as much. I also have 14 lynx, eight mink and 24 weasel which, so far, has been one of my best years.

On May 8th the ice went out on the main river. Therefore, I loaded all my fur and the little food I had left in the boat and let the current of the river carry me back to my trail leading to the Yukon. All I had to do was to keep the bow of the boat pointing in the right direction—so there was no effort spent in getting back. The walk over to the Yukon was also good, as most of the snow had gone due to the warm winds during the last two weeks and all the rivers were in full flood. Even at higher levels between the two rivers, most of the snow had gone so the dogs enjoyed chasing rabbits, squirrels and a few birds that had already come in from the south to find nesting areas. The birds in such areas can raise their young and spend a quiet summer away from civilization. It's remarkable how they seem to know the weather will be suitable when they arrive after flying several thousand miles. Some years the fly catcher species get caught with a late snow and cold. If this happens, many can die from lack of flies; however, normally, the mosquitos hatch in the shallow ponds by the millions in the marshlands which supply every fly-eating bird with more than they can possible eat.

On arriving back on the Yukon, everything I had stored during the winter was in good shape for the first run of fish, which normally come after the high water starts to recede. The current slows down as the run-off recedes, making it easier for the fish to swim upstream. I went to visit the natives in the village close to where I camp. It's only about three miles upriver. They were so pleased to see me and treated me like a long-lost brother and asked me to stay the summer. As soon as I came, the chief's wife put on a big 5-gallon kettle they had got from the Russians and started a big stew (which included moose meat, beaver, lynx and rabbits cooked whole with only the skin taken off and the insides left in, which the natives claimed made a good seasoning). This is fairly common practice and I must say it tasted good to me after a long walk. They added wild onions whenever possible, together with other vegetation growing in the area. It went well with the rice I had left over and which I had given to them. They were very interested about my going over to the Kuskakwim for the winter, as none of them had ever been there. However, as they had heard many stories about it they listened carefully to my description of the area and asked lots of questions about the Indians in that area.

Like most small villages, there is only one dominant family and relatives, with a few others who stay close by—mainly for protection against raids from stronger bands that think they are stealing their food supply. It seems that at least one band or another gets raided each year. The Upper Yukon bands got angry with a band near Nulato and nearly wiped them out, except for a few who were hunting at the time and one or two who escaped into the woods. This happened only a few years before I arrived so it was still fresh in their memory. We shouldn't be too hasty in our condemnation of their actions, as it's not many hundred years ago since different tribes and counties in England were at war with their neighbours—and, no doubt, the Romans wouldn't have succeeded in their invasion had England been united instead of fighting each other. This has also been true in most of Europe, Asia and the Middle East, where they have been fighting since the beginning of time. We saw a lot of tribal warfare in South Africa when I was there.

According to old-timers who have been in Alaska for many years, they maintain that the Native population from time to time seemed related mainly to their food supply and the number of predators, especially in the Interior where their main source of food was usually salmon, game animals and berries. Their numbers fluctuated a great deal according to the food cycle. Whole tribes would starve out if the salmon failed to come in along with severe winter conditions when they couldn't move to other areas where game numbers were still plentiful. A late frost that reduced the berry crop in the same year as the lack of salmon could mean a real disaster to many tribes. This would also bring tribal wars over the limited food supply.

The larger tribes thought the smaller tribes were getting food from what they thought was their territory, even though they hadn't had to use food from those areas for many years when food was plentiful elsewhere. Those on the coast were far more secure than those in the Interior and probably fewer tribal wars occurred in those areas.

Soon after I arrived back at my summer camp, a group of 25 prospectors arrived in four boats (one quite large boat holding 11 people, and the rest in three smaller boats). They decided to come to the mouth of the Kayukuk where it joins the Yukon and split up into small groups in their search for gold during the summer. They would then join up again at the same place in the fall and make their way to Nome for the winter. They made camp for the night and had their dinner of bannock and beans. They even brought two bottles of rum which they thought would give them a good send-off the next morning. Before going to bed, they all joined in a circle around the camp fire and placed one of the empty rum bottles on a grub box and gave it a spin. When the bottle stopped spinning the person at whom the top of the bottle pointed would have to make the farewell speech. That person slowly started by saying: "We are now in the land of cold, warm and mosquitos where no law has yet arrived. We don't know where we are going and the tears we shed when parting will be remembered long in the future if any of us return to our native land. I feel it will be the duty of the last one of us who remains alive to tell not only what we have done but also what we said to each other when we part tomorrow."

I could understand very well what he said, as I've thought of this many times when I've started off for a new venture. Would any of you know what happened if I didn't come back? This had also crossed my mind many times while in the war in South Africa.

Now that June is here, the river boats are back in operation and I hope to get this letter away. I've been writing bits and pieces of it during the 8-month winter I spent on the Kuskakwim River with no one to talk to except my prospector friend Slim, whom I hope to see again when he makes his fortune.

Hope all is well at home.

Jack

CHAPTER 6

SECOND TRIP TO ALASKA

The letters in Chapter 6 describe the second trip to Alaska. After a short stay in Vancouver, Dad sailed to Skagway, then walked from Skagway to Whitehorse. The final legs of the journey from Whitehorse to Dawson City, and hence to Fairbanks, were completed by riverboat.

May 6th, 1908

D ear Arthur,
      Hope this finds you all well and having a good year. It's really nice to get your letters to keep me up to date on the news from home. No doubt, letters from home will catch up to me when I get back to Fairbanks. I had a really good year trapping up until mid-April when a very warm spell hit the area. This wasn't good for trapping any more, as the warm weather soon makes the fur of the animals over prime (i.e. when the end of the hairs start to curl at the tips—making the fur lose its nice shine). When you hold a skin in the light, it looks ragged and the buyer (if he knows fur) will cut the price in half or even refuse to buy it at all.

      On April 28th I loaded all the fur and enough food to get out to Fairbanks on a sleigh and hooked up the dogs and left early in the morning. I followed the Salcha River, which drains into the Tanana. The ice on the river was still sound enough to travel at least down to the Tanana River, which was close to 130 miles downstream, then another 80 miles before reaching Fairbanks. The snow got soft late in the afternoon which slowed us down—the best time to travel with the dogs was in the early morning when the frost at night had hardened up the snow and the dogs could run right along on the crust as the sleigh pulled really easily—I didn't have to do anything to help them along.

When we reached Fairbanks and got our camp set up outside of town, my old Indian friend told me the fur buyers were offering very little as the market was down on most fur species, especially marten and mink (which I had most of). When I went into town the next day, this information was confirmed as correct when I talked with the buyers. I stayed in town for a while doing a few small jobs—building cupboards in a few new houses that had been built during the winter while I was away upriver trapping.

One evening after work I went to sort of a restaurant/night club with another worker to have a good meal for a change—as it was nice to get away from my cooking. As we approached the door, two drunks came out head first and landed face down in the snow. They were thrown out for getting too rowdy and making too much noise while others were enjoying watching the dancing girls (who had come down from Dawson for a week or so). We stopped and helped them get on their feet again and asked what had happened. One of them said, "We got tired of watching the girls dance, so we came out to see the Northern Lights dance in the sky—which can dance better than those girls in there."

While in the restaurant we got talking to a couple of prospectors who had made their way up the river from Nulato and reported the main Yukon ice looked pretty rotten and expected it would go out before the end of May. So, after a good meal and watching the girls dance, I decided to pack up the fur and make my way downriver as far as I could to Nulato and trade my dogs to the Indians in the village nearby for fur, then catch the first steamer of the season back to Nome and try the Russian fur buyers there to see if they would pay more than the buyers up at Fairbanks.

If not, I would hop on a ship going south to Vancouver to see what was going on there as to prices of fur, as many fur buyers move up and down the coast in the spring time when the ice on the rivers goes out and there is a little more competition. This is the time when most of the fur from the Interior moves out to market.

I stayed in Nome a few days and was able to book a passage on the next boat heading south to Vancouver. We had a very rough voyage most of the way, except when sheltered by islands. Many of the crew on the ship were seasick and the cooks had difficulty cooking, as utensils wouldn't stay put long enough. We made several stops on the way and because so many were sick, I got hired to help move supplies off the ship and other supplies back on. It was quite an interesting job, as I talked to so many different people along the way about what was happening in their area.

Better still, I arrived in Vancouver with more money than I had when I left Fairbanks and reasonably good meals all the way. It seems if you are willing to work, you can nearly always find a job travelling on both the ships that service up and down the coast—and even more so, on the riverboats that move supplies to many large and small settlements along the rivers. I'm quite surprised to see the volume of freight moved from June till the end of October. I get to know many of the people who work on the riverboats as they stop for wood at our supply camp and many buy fish from me.

Vancouver had changed quite a lot during the three years I'd been away and the value of the lots on Granville Street that I'd nearly bought in 1904 at $18 were already worth five times as much—so I'm kicking myself that I didn't buy before the price went up so much. I didn't try to buy anything as I still have visions of starting a farm somewhere in the Interior where there are not so many people around.

I rented a room during my stay from my landlady at 109 Hastings Street, where I had stayed before going to Alaska. She wanted me to stay, as there was a fair amount of work going on and she had an empty room she wanted to rent. While in Vancouver I contacted several fur buyers who were interested in my fur, and I finally sold them for a much better price than I was offered in Fairbanks; however, if you consider what I could have made working in Alaska rather than take the trip all the way back to Vancouver, I guess it was not more than a good holiday and to see what was going on elsewhere.

Even though there were many opportunities along the way, my heart told me to go back to Alaska and make a few more dollars trapping, fishing and hunting—money that could be used to locate farm land that could be developed into a nice homesite to bring up a family. While in Vancouver I read about all the land available for 50¢

to $1 an acre in the Chilcotin, Nechako and Bulkley Valley that could even be pre-empted where, with a lot of effort building a cabin and clearing a few acres, you could get title to the property—which sounded like a good deal to me. I wondered whether when I make a move to settle down someplace you might be interested in joining me in such a venture—which certainly would be different from your life in London working in the Post Office.

With my fur sold, I plan on staying only a few days as I want to be back in Alaska or the Yukon during the summer to catch the late runs of salmon, then get established for another season trapping. After this, I said goodbye to the landlady and two friends who had served in South Africa. I always find it interesting to talk to others who fought in the same war, as the stories are so different and especially those from people fighting on the other side. One thing it does is to remind us clearly how quickly oral history changes in such a short time. There is no question that without written accounts, the true story can be totally lost in less than one generation—which is not long when the average life is only a little over 60 years (and most of the Indians live under 50 years). After a good visit in Vancouver I gathered supplies needed for my next trip north.

I left Vancouver on June 14th, 1908 on board the *Amur* for Skagway. I'm looking forward to returning to Alaska, as there are lots of opportunities up there for anyone willing to work. The weather is nice, with not much wind so it's pleasant to sit out on the deck and enjoy the sun while talking to different people from many countries with a vast mixture of purpose. The majority are nice, hard-working people who want to find a good gold strike to enable them to set up a nice home, business—and then there are a lot like me who want to try their hand at farming in some remote area where the land hasn't already been claimed. All were confident that some day there will be a thriving community with schools, etc., in which to bring up a family in many of these areas.

Others on the ship are a mixed bag—high-rolling promoters and swindlers going north to make a quick buck with no conscience as to who they hurt and all the shattered dreams they leave behind. On board, there was a group of dancing girls that keep pretty much to themselves, who are heading for Whitehorse and on to Dawson City along with other towns that might want to hire them for Dominion Day and 4th of July celebrations, etc. These two days are big parties in all of the north. They usually start at daybreak with a flapjack breakfast, where they have big stoves that cook hot cakes till noon, then start on lunch and then to a big dinner and later a dance that lasts till the sun comes up next morning. Nearly everyone in the area turns out—even the prospectors in some far away creek will walk in 20 or 30 miles or paddle down the river 40 or 50 miles for the big days of fun. The Americans celebrate with English and Canadians on Dominion Day, then we celebrate the 4th of July with the Americans. No one seems to worry as long as they have a good time.

It's remarkable how peaceful these celebrations are, considering the amount of alcohol that is consumed. The big political issue at this time is where the Canadian and American border should be located—as it's not been settled yet. A lot of Americans like to work and stay in Canada simply because they like the Royal Canadian Mounted Police who they think administer law and order in a fairer fashion than the Police and Army on the American side. Law and order is really quite good on both sides where very few people hardly ever lock a door and most prospectors and miners leave the gold they find in a glass jar on a table in their tent--while they leave to go prospecting for a few days. It seems very few ever get robbed and, if such a thing happens, the thief most times is captured or shot—which certainly keeps crime down to a very minimum level.

It's not easy to get out of either Alaska or the Yukon without someone knowing why you left and which direction you took. Because there are no roads to the south, most have to go by ship after they get over the mountains or by river. The worst problem in both countries is the shyster—lawyers, gamblers and other crooks who make their fortune by employing claim jumpers who prey on those who work hard and discover a good claim and get led into a trap by such people. The latter often manage to find a technicality in the law in order to get their claim away from the legitimate owners.

On the way north we seem to pass dozens of islands while going through what must be the largest natural canal in the world (approximately 500 miles from Vancouver to Skagway), where, by the maps on board, we only touch the open sea twice—therefore, making the voyage very enjoyable as every hour there seems to be a different island or mountain to look at. Most of the coast seems to be covered by heavy timber, except where a fire went through a few years before, making feed very plentiful for game animals. We didn't see anything that looked interesting for farming. The few Indians on board tell me there are lots of nearly flat land over the mountains covered with grass as high as a man on horseback. When they told me this, I had a strong desire to get off the ship and walk inland following a river to explore the Interior and look at the possibility of starting a cattle ranch. The timber seems to get smaller as we get further north. In many places, it looks like mainly cordwood.

On Saturday the 19th, we came into Skagway, which had the reputation of being a rough town so I didn't intend to stay long. People tell me that Whitehorse is far better to find employment so I spent a day buying a bit of food to carry me to the next stop. A number of us went to the railway station to find out what it cost to buy a ticket to Whitehorse (120 miles away). When we were told $20.00, we thought it was far too much to go a little over a hundred miles, so we decided to walk via the railway line.

After a few hours walking, it seemed the railroad went a long way around in order to get a good grade, so we tried short cuts which we found to be the worst walking we had ever seen. There was so much skin-tangle (short brush of all kinds) about 2' or 3' high, which was terrible to walk through and took a lot of time. We went via White Pass and Bennett lake, which was very interesting to see—and to think of those early prospectors who struggled through here during the Gold Rush of 1898. There is still lots of equipment that was abandoned at that time to make their packs lighter so they could travel faster in the race to stake a good claim. We passed many very small (or altogether deserted) towns which once were quite flourishing as stopping places on the way north.

Carcross was a little more prosperous and we were able to buy a nice meal rather than cooking it ourselves when we were tired and hungry. Carcross got its name from the local Indians and means

Caribou Crossing—where hundreds of caribou passed while migrating from their summer feeding ground to their winter area. I was delighted with the various flora and animal species, which were far more numerous than I ever thought in this area. I was surprised to find both yellow and blue violets and humming birds after all the flowers. We saw rabbits, gophers (prairie dogs), which were very numerous—and it looked as if it wouldn't be so difficult to get a meal while travelling.

The first part of the trip was over White Pass, which is over 2,900 feet. We ran into snow and cold winds, but we were able to find an old deserted cabin to stay in, so we were able to dry out once we had got a fire started. The small streams were very interesting, as for a mile or so they were running quite fast, then there would be a dry creek bed for a mile or so where the stream went through what seemed like an alkaline-like deposit that soaked up the water as it passed through-- which acted as a huge filter as the water coming out was crystal clear. Most meals (where there is a restaurant) are 50¢, but there is only one choice—which is okay as it makes it easier for the cooks.

On leaving Carcross, we decided to build two log rafts to pile our packs onto and either pole them or sail--if the wind was right— down Lake Tagish and Mud Marsh Lake. We tied our blankets on poles as sails and they worked well as long as the wind came from the right direction. From there, we floated down the 50-mile river to Myles Canyon and the rapids above Whitehorse. We decided not to try and run the rapids with a raft, so we walked the rest of the way into Whitehorse. We arrived on June 28th and stayed two days. As there seemed little work that we were interested in, we decided to push on to Dawson City, where we were told there was more activity that might interest us.

On June 30th, I decided to join a party of six who had bought a boat. I paid my share ($6), jumped in and away we went with a limited supply of food as there wasn't much room with six of us in the open boat. We made good time and reached Lake Lebarge the same night. We stayed at the Mounted Police post, where we were called in to show passports and papers. The police check all travellers to try and find out if you are capable of surviving in the north—which is not a bad idea as they try and weed out tinhorn gamblers, undesirables, etc.

from going into the Yukon. They also have some information as to when you crossed the border, time of arrival at Lake Lebarge and Dawson City. This is very sandy country with small timber and fortunately numerous rabbits, groundhogs, ducks and geese. Everything went well next morning as we proceeded to paddle and sail down the lake until a strong crosswind got up and we had to make for shore as fast as we could, as the waves started to splash in the overladen boat. Three people had to bail water out as three of us paddle to shore in a sheltered bay where we made camp and dried out our clothes and bedding—which was wet by the time we got to shore.

Our captain was so scared on reaching shore that he decided to leave us with two others and walk back to Whitehorse. The two who stayed with me and the boat decided I should be captain as I'd had a lot of experience on the lower Yukon during my years in Alaska. We gave the three who walked back a good supply of food—which left us none too much to get down to Dawson so we relied on getting rabbits, ducks or grouse on the way down. We made good time as the boat was lighter and made it to Little Salmon by dark—which is supposed to be 30 miles from where we started so we were very pleased with our efforts and decided to take a short walk and see what the country looked like from the top of a small hill not far from the shore. On the way back, I shot three rabbits which turned out to be a good thing, because while we had been away, a bear came in to where we were camped and cleaned up on nearly all our food—except for some rice we managed to pick up with spoons that he had left behind.

Next morning, at daybreak, I went out and shot another nine rabbits, three ducks and a lynx which looked pretty good when I skinned it out. It looked pretty so we thought we would take it along for dinner and, hopefully, we could find enough game to get us through to Dawson City. We were able to find some wild onions which helped with the bit of rice to make a tasty stew with the lynx. However, rabbit stew for the next week—three meals a day—wasn't that exciting.

I was nervous about going through the Five Finger Rapids, but it wasn't as bad as we had expected. There was lots of water at this time of the year, covering some of the dangerous rocks—which, I think, made it better for us. We made good time with the fast flow of water in the river. It carried us in to Dawson City ahead of the time we expected to take.

The country in Dawson is covered now with patches of slightly larger spruce, lots of poplars, alder and rather small birch. The bluebells and dog roses are beautiful at this time of the year. Dawson City is now a town of several thousand people—with quite a number of frame buildings. However, most of the houses are log huts. There is a big handsome Government House and buildings, as well as the Police barracks. From the number of empty stores, Dawson City has seen its zenith and from now on will most likely gradually decline unless there is another big strike found somewhere close by to make it grow again. There is still plenty of prospecting going on up the various rivers and creeks in the area. There is a lovely view of the Yukon from the height of land above the town.

During the long summer days, the sun never sets—it merely dips the horizon at midnight, then starts up again. I stayed here for the Canadian and American celebrations—Dominion Day and the 4th of July—which everyone celebrates together. It doesn't matter where you come from! The best events of all are the pie-eating contest and the squaw race, where we placed our money on the one we hoped would win. It's surprising how many people come from far away for these events—and the dances last well into the next day.

I'm still unsatisfied and plan to keep moving—likely back to Fairbanks and the Tanana River again for the winter. There is quite a lot of cultivated land around here and a farm with 50 acres in vegetables would supply a lot of the area. I wish the town was booming and then I'd consider staying here and trying my hand at farming. I have thought of going overland—back to the Tanana, which is only 250 miles—and there is a trail most of the way. It would be nice to see the country in the summer. Yet I should also see all the Yukon River without ice, so I plan to take the 875 miles around by river and relax for a day or so and see for myself if there is an opportunity for wood-cutting. If I can find where a forest fire has gone through a year or so ago, there would be enough dry wood to keep our wood-cutting operation going for a year or two.

Tomorrow (July 16th) and I embarked on the *Florence S.* for the trip downriver. We put in at Forty Mile, then crossed the line into the U.S. When we got to Eagle City, we had to lay up for a week due to engine trouble. This gave me time to look around and do a bit of hunting. They have fine barracks for the Army or Police, as well as nice ranches in and around the area. On Sunday, we called at Circle, where the country is entirely different, with the river valley gradually broadening out to as much as 50 miles across the valleys. All the islands surrounded by sloughs are covered with poplars, cottonwood and spruce all the way down to Fort Yukon. There are numerous Indian encampments along the river—mainly family units and some a little larger which are all engaged in catching and drying fish for the winter. The Indians mainly travel in birch bark canoes. In total, it took us 11 days to get to Fairbanks and during this time we saw many fish traps, gill nets, fykes and other methods of catching fish. The weather was nice and warm, so we got a beautiful view of Mount McKinley, which is 20,000 feet high. Fairbanks seems to grow each year and now has over 3,000 people.

There are not too many good prospects for work, except in our wood-cutting business, which is doing very well. My partner has already sold two rafts of wood and another one is nearly ready. I will help him get it finished before I go fishing for the summer. All the wood is cut by either a crosscut saw or Swedish saw—with the undercut and limbing of the trees done with an axe. There are a lot of freight ships on the Yukon and they certainly take a lot of wood to keep them going. They amount to over 90% of our wood-cutting operation. Domestic wood for towns and villages wouldn't keep us going. All the trees close to the river and easy to get at are pretty well used up in the lower reaches of the river.

Last year I spent nearly 10 weeks cutting wood, which was taken to the buying stations in 14 rafts and averaging close to 40 cords to a raft. I tried fishing once I got settled with not much luck. A bad storm hit when I was up Clear Creek and Salt Jacket Slough—and I had my camp at the junction of the Slough and the Tanana. The storm hit the area so fast I had no time to get my nets out before several big trees came floating down and destroyed two of my nets—so I'll be busy every evening and other spare time making two new ones. I want to cash in on the late run before I go trapping for the winter. The salmon runs have been poor this year so the market is good if you manage to get the nets in at the right time. Some of these runs go by in a matter of days and it can be a week or two before the next run comes in. What makes it even more difficult is on the small rivers coming into the Yukon the runs seem to vary a great deal from year to year.

No doubt, the weather and temperature of the river seem to make a difference. Other people claim it all depends on the moon and won't go fishing till the right phase of the moon. I spent most evenings watching to see salmon jumping as they move upriver. One thing, I can do this while working on my nets till it gets too dark. My Indian friends mainly put one net out in front of their camp and sit to watch the floats on the net jump when a fish hits the net and if several hit at the same time they run to their boats and set the rest of their nets. Many other Indians take a good sized rock out in the river with a loop firmly tied to it then they run a light cord through the loop and back to shore, where they tie a net to the rope and pull it out to the rock. When they think there are enough fish in the net, they just pull the net back and the rope goes out to the rock—ready to use again. This is a very simple, yet effective, system where you don't even have to take a boat out to set a net once you get the rock and rope out as far as you want them.

There is no question that most of the fish migrating up to spawn travel close to the shoreline, as the river water is not running so fast as its speed is reduced by small points of land or trees that have fallen into the river. All of us who pole or paddle our boats try to see where the main current is running and try to avoid it if going upstream. If you are trying to make good time going down, you head for the fast water to carry you down. If you don't know a river and are going for the first time, it pays to stay close to shore in case there are falls downstream which you can usually hear before you get there—except on a very windy day.

I've had a good season and thought of going back to England for a visit. However, after much thought, I've decided to spend another season up here as wood is in great demand and we can sell all we can cut. I'm also confident I can do well salmon fishing now that I know most of the tricks of the trade. The most important of all is buyer contracts, as you have to sell them the day you catch them in order to get a good price. I keep my nets in until dark and leave the fykes in all night or until I'm leaving the area. I clean the fish by the light of the fire and catch the first riverboat at daylight in order to get the delivered the same day. If I'm fishing close to town, I take then in to town at daylight and deliver them to the buyers myself. The mine takes a lot of my fish, as they know they will be fresh—right out of the river. Restaurants also take a lot of fish in a month when the season is on.

I hear you left for Canada on April 24th, 1908, so no doubt you have seen a lot of Canada by now. I hope this letter will catch up with you. Also, you will let me know where you are working so that when I come out next spring I'll be able to find you before I leave for England. I know you will get to enjoy this new and exciting life over here in North America—and if you ever get stuck and hard up, be sure and come to Fairbanks. I plan to stay within a 200-mile radius of Fairbanks for the next year, as opportunity is good by the looks of it.

Jack

CHAPTER 7

TRAPPING UP THE KANTISHNA RIVER AND GOODBYE TO ALASKA

The letters in Chapter 7 describe Dad's feelings on reaching camp up the Chena (which had been well-supplied)—only to discover the camp had been robbed and nothing remained. Dad then had to make his way back to Fairbanks on one day's food and four days to get back. Once provisioned for the winter, he made his way up the Kantishna River (over 150 miles) and built a cabin on Minchumina Lake for the winter. Once the ice went out, Dad built a raft and floated back to the Tanana and caught a ride on a riverboat back to Fairbanks. After saying goodbye to all his friends, Dad left Alaska and travelled to England for Xmas with his family and Safie, who lived in Brackley, a neighbouring village. Dad and Safie discussed the future of possibly moving to Canada once he had found land that could be developed for a homestead.

Dear Mother,
My trapping season didn't start out very well after I decided to go back up the Chena for a week or two to get an early start and pick up a cache of traps and some supplies I had dropped off earlier after my trip to Vancouver. I ran into bad weather all the way, with snow mixed with rain—so my dogs didn't like it at all and it took us over four days to make the trip. We had to stop travelling early in order to find good shelter under trees that kept most of the rain out. When I reached camp late in the evening of the fourth day, I was in for a shock when I found nothing left in camp and all my traps gone. I was told by my old Indian friend when I got back to Fairbanks that a group of wandering Indians from outside the area had come in from up-river

and had stolen a lot of supplies as they travelled. Most of the local Indians were scared of these travellers and had hidden in the forest away from the river until word came in that they had moved back up-river.

I stayed the night in what was left of camp, then started back with the very limited supplies I'd brought for the dogs and that I thought would last until we reached camp. This only lasted for one day, so the dogs and I were pretty gaunt by the third day. We had had very little to eat, except for two rabbits and a ptarmigan that I had managed to shoot on our way out. It was surprising how fast the word of danger spreads that a gang of renegades was in the area and that Indian people should take care and disappear into the forests if possible. I'm told this sort of thing is not uncommon in some parts of Alaska, where outside tribes make trouble for local Indians. My friend is always on the look out for groups such as these. It is one of the main reasons why most local families don't try and build permanent shelter as the roving groups would soon know where they could be found and come in to burn down their shelter and steal supplies. The locals try to camp on the curve of a river so they can see both up and down stream for some distance in order that they and their families can scatter into the forest and never have all their supplies in one place.

Once I'd bought new supplies and traps I loaded up and started to move to a new area to trap for the winter. This is up the Kantishna River, which is a nice winding river to travel. By the time I got ready to go, the river in most areas was frozen over nicely for travelling, so I took my supplies up over 50 miles, set up a temporary camp in a sheltered area, then set out over 50 traps, and then went back and picked up a second load (and later a third load). For nearly a month, I kept moving further up-river and setting traps in areas that looked good for catching fur.

Fortunately, the weather stayed pretty good with not too much snow and not too cold to travel. As there was very little wind, I had little trouble keeping my supplies dry. After moving all my supplies nearly 100 miles up-river, I decided to try one of the branch streams in order to see what it looked like as a place to establish a base camp for the winter. After travelling all day and getting tired and hungry, I came around a bend and, to my surprise, I saw an Indian camp ahead in a patch of big trees on a point in the river. So I went in to talk to them and make sure I wasn't trapping on their line. I soon found there was a family of six; two of the children were boys (aged 14 and 16 years old), who were already good trappers and hunters. They were very happy to see me and I gave them some tea and sugar which they all seemed to like. Following a short discussion on where they trapped and my intention of going further up the Kantishna to the Minchumina Lake area, they were very happy and invited me to have dinner with them and to go back to my camp in the morning. I was so hungry after the long walk that I was more than willing to have anything to had to offer. They had a big stew pot on the camp fire. It looked good to me even after they told me it was a mixture of rabbit, grouse, muskrat and beaver, as well as dried nettles and other vegetation found along the river bank, most of which I couldn't recognize in its dried form. The Indian's wife scooped out a ladleful into a wooden bowl, which had obviously recently been carved by hand for that purpose. It thought it was great and polished it off in short order. One of the boys then motioned to me to have some more, so I dipped the ladle deep to get the thick stuff from the bottom. Suddenly, the Chief said, "Don't dig so deep. All the shit goes to the bottom!" So I took his advice and took a scoop from the top. I must say that I enjoyed that too. I finally got around to asking what he meant when he said, "Don't dig to the bottom." The Chief explained that in making the stew his wife only took the hides off the birds and small animals and cooked them up as they were because they had more flavour that way and were better for your health. I didn't ask any more because I was appreciative of their hospitality in asking me to dinner.

Later on when I returned to Fairbanks (after nearly seven months on the trap line) and was invited to a birthday party. At the party I related my story about the stew and how good it was, as well as how it was made—much to the amusement of the gathering. There happened to be a doctor at the party and he took a lot of interest in how the stew was made. Then he ventured to say that it made a lot of sense—something which made all of us sit up and listen. The doctor went on to explain that the most common cause of death in Alaska and the Yukon at that time was scurvy (incurred mainly as a result of a lack of vitamin C, which is found mainly in fruit and vegetables). Most people away from the towns rely far too much on meat for their daily meals while they are out for months at a time on their trap line or when they're prospecting. He went on to explain that rabbits, muskrats and beaver live on vegetation of some sort, while grouse eat mainly berries in the summer and fall and buds and needles the rest of the year. All of these things would be high in vitamins that are needed to keep us from getting scurvy—and probably my Indian friend and especially his wife were smarter than us in preparing a healthy diet, as all of the food eaten by these animals and birds would cook right into the stew. I'm not convinced that too many in the gathering would follow the doctor's advice (especially if watching the expression on the faces in the crowd is anything to go by!).

After the meal I was given a caribou hide with the hair inside and tied with leather lacing up the side, so that you had to slide down from the top. I found it so warm that I never took a blanket again during the winter. In the summer, it was far too hot. Later that winter, I shot a caribou and made one for myself.

Once I reached Minchumina Lake, I spent a comfortable winter in a small cabin overlooking a sheltered bay. It was very pleasant to sit and watch for wildlife. It was far better than a tent which I had used for several years. The worst thing about a tent is that if it snows a lot while you are out on the trail, the snow will flatten the tent and it takes time to shake the snow off it and put it up again. On most days that are so short, I seldom get back to camp before dark so it's a messy job to do it in such conditions.

Early in the winter, before the ice got too thick, I put a heavy string cord under the ice out on the bay. This was achieved by cutting holes in the ice, between 12 and 16 feet apart in a straight line for 70 to 100 feet. You tie the cord to one end of the pole and then shove it under the ice at the first hole and try and aim it towards the second hole. This is a cold job, as you have to shove your whole arm down the hole till you can reach under the ice with a 4' small stick with a notch on it to try and find the pole you aimed from the first hole. This is not as difficult as you might think, provided you line up the holes with care with a stick marker at each hole in order to help keep a straight line. I always choose a still warm day where I can light a fire on the ice and warm my hands and arms after each hole. Once you have the cord under the ice, it's easy to set the net by tying it to the cord and pulling it through from the other end. When you take up the net (hopefully, with fish in it), the cord is pulled back under the ice ready to set again once you run out of fish.

Quite often, I usually catch enough to keep the dogs and I going for a week. I get some greylin and a mixed lot of coarse fish like suckers, which is a bottom feeding vegetarian. I also catch squaw fish, which is a predator fish with a huge appetite—and some you catch, may even have three or four smaller fish inside! The squaw fish have a large mouth and can swallow a fish whole that's a foot long. Squaw fish taste good but have hundreds of little Y bones through the flesh. The name "squaw fish" comes from the Indians, where the men prefer the greylin or trout and let the women and children eat fish less desirable. Naturally, during the salmon runs, where they are very plentiful, all the Indians (male, female and children) all eat the same type of fish.

There is no question that the men are completely dominant in their family life—yet there is no doubt the women work harder than the men around the camp. The men's work is hunting and trapping. Both work at fishing, with the women doing most of the fish cleaning, as well as splitting and hanging the fish up to dry. Like any good managers, the Indians dry far more fish and meat than they can use in case something goes wrong, such as bears getting into a cache or some other disaster. It's completely survival of the fittest! Those who don't take these precautions soon perish.

I had a really good winter as the weather was kind and the fur animals were travelling. In early May, I loaded up and moved downriver. On the way through, I stopped to visit the Indian family who had given me the big dinner. I gave them all my traps and remaining supplies (which wasn't much). They were really pleased to get a sack full of about 80 pounds of fresh fish that I had caught the night before I left.

On the way down the river, I stopped to spend the night on a sheltered stream that came into the main river. When I came around the bend, I was surprised to see a little cabin and found a prospector at the bottom of a 20' hole digging for gold. He refused to stop what he was doing and talk to me until it got dark. When I told him to quit and come up for a chat, he answered by saying, "You may have lots of time, but I'm busy as I'll hit gold before dark—so go light a fire and wait, then we can celebrate!" Needless to say, darkness came before the gold. He proved to be an interesting fellow who came from the south of England, near Brighton. He had been digging all winter. After dinner he showed me his diary, which was completed until the end of June. When I told him he was a month ahead with his diary, he said, "What's the difference? I'll be doing the same thing for the next month—digging all day and thawing permafrost at night—and it saves a lot of time to bring it up to date once or twice a month."

Once I reached Fairbanks I had no trouble selling my fur, as I was out earlier than most trappers and the buyers seemed anxious to get fur ready for the spring market downriver once the riverboats could get going as the ice went out. I helped my partner Mike cut a lot of wood for a month. After this, I told him I would be leaving for England after the first big salmon run was over in late July, as I thought I might try my hand at farming some place in B.C. or Alberta. Mike thought I was joking till I told him that once I made up my mind I would want to sell my share in the wood-cutting business. However, I'd be sure and write and let him know for sure during the winter.

Love,

Jack

SAYING GOODBYE TO ALASKA

Dear Percy,
I gave Mike my five good dogs, who were excellent to work with, and told him to take good care of them as they were like old friends. They would leave a hole in my life as they had pulled heavy loads of my supplies for many hundreds of miles while I'd been trapping during the winter. I gave my small riverboat to my old Indian friend who had camped close by during the spring and summer for several years. He and his wife gave me a lot of good advise, especially the first year I spent in Alaska when they showed me how to dry fish, moose and caribou meat (making it light to carry on the trap line). They were happy to get the boat as it was far better to carry supplies in than their canoe. They moved to different areas to hunt, fish and pick wild berries. They also told me which Indian tribes I should stay away from, as they were scared of some of the nearby tribes. Most of the Indian families don't seem to travel far during their life and generally stay within a radius of less than 60 miles. A few travel farther, looking for better prices for their fur. On thing for sure—they certainly knew every inch of that area and what they could expect to find to keep them over the long winters, whether it was fish, moose, caribou, bears, beaver, rabbits and other small animals, birds of all kinds (especially grouse, ptarmigan, ducks, geese, cranes and swans). They also knew where every berry patch and other plants they would need could be found and which month they would be available. None of the Indians have a calendar but they know as well as any of us when the seasons of the year will change. When the leaves start to colour, they know winter will follow and the signs for every other season change.

The night before I left, quite a number of the friends I'd met in town and out at the mine put on a farewell dinner for me. It was really nice to see them one last time before moving on, as they felt sure I wouldn't be back. Mike gave me a lot of advice on what not to do when I got to England. The last, and most important of all, was "Don't get married and not come back to us. We need you here to build the new cupboards in the new houses we will build when we strike it rich!" He then proceeded to read the Ten Commandments that circulated around the bars in Alaska and the Yukon:

1. Thou shalt have no other claim but one on any one creek.
2. Thou shalt not make unto the Recorder any false statements concerning thy discovery for thy Uncle Sam is a jealous uncle, visiting thine inequities upon thy head in case of contest, and showing mercy unto all such as keeps His laws.
3. Thou shalt not take the name of the Lord God in vain when thou breakest thy windlass rope, for it doesn't do a damn bit of good.
4. Thou shalt not go prospecting again before thy claim givest out; neither shalt thou take thy gold dust to the gaming table for Monte, Faro, Roulette and Poker will prove to thee that the more thou puttest down, the less thy takest up.
5. Thou shalt not remember what thy friends do at home on the Sabbath Day. Six days shalt thou dig or pick all that thy body can stand, but on the seventh thou shalt wash all thy dirty shirts, darn all thy socks, tape thy boots, make thy bannock and boil thy pork and beans.
6. Thou shalt not grow discouraged, nor think of going home to thy Father and thy Mother until though hast made thy stake.
7. Thou shalt not salt thy claim to sell it to a Cheechako.
8. Thou shalt not commit assault and battery, unless thy neighbour jumps thy claim.
9. Thou shalt not bear false witness about "good paydirt in the creek" to benefit a friend who has boats and provisions to sell.
10. Thou shalt not covet thy neighbour's cash, nor his tools, nor pick nuggets from company's pan and put them into thy mouth.

After the party was over, which was just before daylight, I loaded all my worldly belongings in my boat and decided I wouldn't rush. I decided I would take an easy trip downriver by letting the river currents carry me downstream without too much work. I went downriver to Nulato, which was close to 400 miles with all the bends in the river. There were many moments as I floated downstream with little to do but think, when sadness came over me. I wondered whether I was doing the right thing leaving Alaska when things were going so well with me—hunting, trapping and fishing.

The slow, easy trip floating downriver was one of the most enjoyable trips in my life so far. I just watched all the birds and animals along the shore. There were hundreds of families of ducks and geese in the eddies and small streams entering the main river. Most of the young hadn't been hatched long and they looked so cute, dodging in and out looking for something to peck at and eat while, at the same time, keeping close to their mother. I saw several moose cows and calves on the islands along the river. The cow moose are really smart when having their calves. They go to islands where they are fairly safe from wolves that prowl along the rivers hunting anything they can get. At this time of the year, some of the main prey of the wolf are beaver, muskrats and young calves. During the fall and winter months because of the heavy snow, while travelling in large packs the wolves can kill any animal or groups of animals with little difficulty.

The wild flowers along the banks of the river are lovely, especially in burned over areas where nearly every flower imaginable comes up—especially the fireweed which thrives after a fire along with berries which come later during late August and early September, depending on their location from Interior to Coastal climates. The ripening of berries is opposite to what I expected, with many of the Interior berries ripening first, due to the long days during such a short season after the snow goes till it returns. Nature has to do everything in a hurry, while down on the coast it can take its time. It's remarkable how plants can adjust to the exact amount of days free of snow. Upon the mountains close to the glaciers where the snow goes late in July, the plants come up, grow and seed all before the end of August when the snow returns for the winter!

On arriving at Nulato, I spent an interesting day telling my friendly Indian family all about my travels down to Vancouver, back up to Alaska by way of Skagway, and trapping up the Kantishna River and back down the Yukon. They were quite impressed, as they hadn't been to or heard of these places. However, when it came to their local area they knew every foot of it and which animal or fish could be found at any given time of the year. I spent two weeks fishing for the big Spring salmon and did very well with the fish wheel, fykes and gill nets which kept me cleaning fish till well after midnight by the light of the fire. It was fortunate that I was able to sell most of them to the riverboats and others moving up and down the river. Once the first run was nearly over, I decided to move on so I gave my fish wheels and fykes to my Indian friends, who were very happy as it would help them to catch a supply of fish for the winter as well as helping them to sell some to the travellers on the river. They were so happy to get the fish wheel as they could now impress their friends that they were the people with the big wheel.

From Nulato, I got a free ride downriver with one of the riverboats after giving them 500 pounds of salmon and also helping them to load or unload supplies at several locations along the river. From old Hamilton, I travelled on a larger ship over to Nome—which had changed a lot since I first saw it five years ago. It is quite a modern little town with hotels, restaurants, and several general stores. There are still a lot of ships coming and going from Nome to Siberia— mainly traders bringing supplies. They are an interesting lot and many speak English because they are anxious to get contacts in Alaska who can help to collect furs from distant points upriver as well as isolated areas of Alaska. I was offered a job which would mean spending the next year or so buying fur for the Russian-America Fur Company. However, I'm anxious to go back to England and visit for the winter— which will be a break from the long winters up here.

I had a long letter from Safie asking me to be sure and come to visit them while I was in England. The trip from Nome to Vancouver was very enjoyable, as I managed for the first time to get a small cabin. This was really nice as it rained most of the way. It wouldn't have been pleasant sleeping out on deck with a blanket and canvas over me (which I've done before on other trips). While on board, I spent most of the time reading about world affairs in the newspapers, which were only two weeks old—so I was able to catch up on what was going on in the world.

In one paper that came out of Vancouver, it described the lovely Bulkley and Nechako Valleys and the opportunity for future farmers with the railroad being built from Prince Rupert on one end and Prince George on the other end. It all sounds so exciting that I will bring the report with me and show it to all of you when I arrived. I will stop in Vancouver for a few days and go up to Powell River and see Arthur, as I gather he is doing well in the logging industry. It will give me a chance to see another area of B.C.—but I doubt whether it will be interesting as far as farming is concerned.

After fishing, hunting and trapping for the last five years, I would like to try my hand at farming because I'd like to settle down and get married rather than travelling so much in riverboats, dog sleighs and snowshoes—which has been very interesting and I've done very well. However, I'm ready for a change.

Vancouver certainly has changed a great deal since I came here in 1904 and built several houses on Hastings Street. (I stay at 109 and I helped to build others.) I went to look at them the other day and they look great—with lawns and flowers in front and vegetable gardens at the back. Vancouver is sprouting up into a nice little town and likely has quite a future in the years ahead. I should stay and build houses but I don't want to get stuck in a town for the rest of my life. Therefore, I will keep moving till I find the right spot.

I had no trouble finding a supply boat that was going to Powell River. When I arrived I found Arthur washing his clothes beside a donkey engine, which had lots of hot water and is the best place in camp to wash clothes. He was very surprised when I appeared on the scene, as he hadn't got my letter letting him know I would stop over and stay for a few days and see first hand what life was like in a logging camp.

I was simply amazed to see the meals they served up in camp. There were three types of meat. so we had a choice of having beef steaks, pork and roast chicken. It sure beat my dinners that I cooked up for myself! There was also a comfortable bunk house that would hold about a dozen men in each. They seemed to have lots of room for me and didn't charge me a cent for either meals or lodging.

The first night Arthur and I spent telling each other all about our experiences in North America. The second evening I spent hours exchanging stories with a fellow called Raffles, who was a Boer and who had fought against us at Rustenburg and Lindley during the war in South Africa. Raffles had also been in the Yeomanry. He was quite a character and said, "It's so nice to see you here but glad we didn't meet in Africa." I also found several people in camp who had spent several years in the Yukon and Alaska looking for gold—but they'd never made any money at it and found far better money in the logging camp. The latter was not too far from town where they could spend their money and have some fun. It seemed that most of the men weren't interested in saving money for some other venture. They only wanted to go to town and have fun.

The trip back to Vancouver was good, with the weather so nice that most of us tried to find a place where we could lie down in the sun and have a nap. However, these small supply ships that run up and down the coast don't have much room for that kind of thing. On arriving in Vancouver, I went back to see if the landlady at 109 Hastings Street had room for me till I was able to arrange passage on a ship back to England. I also plan to leave most of my things in a shed she had at the back of the house.

I'd only been there overnight when a builder came begging me to come to work as he needed cupboards built so he could sell the house. The pay was good, so I went to work at noon. As soon as I finished one job, there were three or four others waiting for me. I could have stayed all winter working on construction projects.

In fact, it's six weeks since I came here and winter is on its way. Snow is falling on the tops of the high mountains and will stay all winter. We have had two flurries of snow down here, but it soon goes. Hastings Street still has lots of mud around in many areas; however, it is far better for walking as much of it in this area has plank sidewalks.

I'm booked on a ship to leave Montreal on November 28th, so plan to leave here by train ten days before that so I have a day or so to look around Montreal before boarding the ship. I'm looking forward to seeing you all for Xmas, which will be the first at home since 1902—when I came out of Africa. I hope there are lots of mince tarts, Xmas cake and all the other goodies that go with Xmas—all of which I've missed out on the trap line with no one to talk to except my squirrel, camp robbers and dogs (which were always good company).

I'd better get this letter away as I've been working on it every time I got a moment all summer.

Love to all,

Jack

Evenley
April 1910

Arthur Shelford
Powell River, B.C.

Dear Arthur,
It was so nice to have a good visit with you in Powell River. You are lucky to have such a good camp to live in. I never saw such good food with so many choices in my life—I didn't realize there was such a place on earth.

The trip back from Vancouver to Montreal took six days, which I thought was good—and the meals were excellent, even though there wasn't as many choices as you have in camp. I've already put on nine pounds since leaving Alaska. We got delayed for a while with fog after leaving Montreal in the Gulf of St. Lawrence. The fog horns seemed to blow all night and we could hear others in the distance. Other than that, the trip to Liverpool was enjoyable as I met many knowledgeable people on board which made the time go quickly. Some of them had been in Alaska or the Yukon, so we soon found we had a lot in common to talk about.

The trip by train down to Evenley took only a little over three hours and all the family, plus many friends, came to the station to meet me on arrival—and best of all, Safie cycled from Brackley with one of her sisters, Dorothy, which made my home-coming just perfect. It seemed nearly everyone in Evenley crowded into the old home to hear about life in Alaska, especially about living in a tent during the cold winters. I told them that thousands of people tented out, especially during the first year of a gold strike. They went prospecting and trapping during the long winters when the sun only comes up for a few hours during each day. In some locations, you don't see the sun at all if a high hill or mountain is to the south which blocks out the sun—the latter is so close to the horizon even at noon.

I hope all is well with you; however, I doubt you had the lovely Xmas dinner that Mother and Flora cooked so well—and Dad even splurged on a bottle of champagne to propose a toast to all. Old Pots wanted to know how far my trap line was from the nearest pub, the most important thing in his life. When I said it was over 300 miles, he said, "I'm not leaving England!"

Dad and Mum said Xmas was good but would have been perfect had you been there, as they missed you a great deal. To make it worse, sister Flora said, "I just might go to Canada once you settle down and stay a while in one place—which I've pretty well decided to do."

Two days after Xmas I had a second Xmas dinner at Brackley Fields with Safie and her family. Fortunately, they have a big house to hold Safie, her Mother and Dad, four sisters, three brothers—as well as uncles and aunts, together with the Morton family who seemed to be getting over the loss of their son John who was engaged to marry Safie and who died not long before the wedding was to have taken place. The dinner was excellent, with a 25 lb turkey, six different vegetables, cranberry sauce, Xmas pudding, hard sauce, mince tarts and Xmas cake with eight candles on top (one for each year I'd been away).

We had one really bad spell of weather in January with quite a bit of snow and strong winds which piled snow 6-8 feet high in some of the roads which blocked them for horses and sleighs. As a result, very little mail could be delivered, except close in to the railway lines and stations. The wind came in from the north east and with the damp salt air, I found it colder than a winter in Alaska.

Safie and I made a trip to London by train and stayed with Aunt Elizabeth, who lived just outside of London and easy to reach by train. We enjoyed the shows in London and the various historical buildings and sites around Piccadilly Square.

Later on in March I went by train to Kendal, Westmorland, in the Lake District, which is a very nice place in northern England. It's full of lakes and streams which is a lovely area to walk. The main attraction was Safie, who is the same age as me and who was working for Aunt Ann and one of her aunts who ran a tiny store in Kendal, where she worked many years for board and 6s (six shillings) a week. Because there was such a large family, Safie was sent to work at 15 years old, which seems to be quite common. There are not many jobs available for girls and many had to find work with relatives.

We spent many happy hours looking out over the lakes and streams, which are much smaller than those in Alaska and the Yukon; however, they are just as lovely. We spent a lot of time when she was not working talking about farming, as Safie knows far more about farming than I do as she was brought up on the farm which is called Brackley Field. (This is a good name as there are many lovely meadows covering the countryside over a large area of that area.) No doubt, you know much of the area while cycling before you came over and you were visiting Dorothy when you two were pretty sweet on one another. During that time, I was giving you lots of advice in my letters and now I find myself needing advice as to what I should do.

There is no doubt Safie is not keen on the thought of going to Alaska and certainly won't move out of England till there is a fairly secure place to go—so I'll have to do an awful lot of thinking during the next few months about whether I should go back to Alaska where I can make good money or take the plunge and buy a farm in either Alberta or B.C. and settle down in a nice location where I could raise a family. I'll be asking a lot of questions when I see you next as to whether you want to join me and embark on a new way of life.

I'll see you early this summer.

Jack

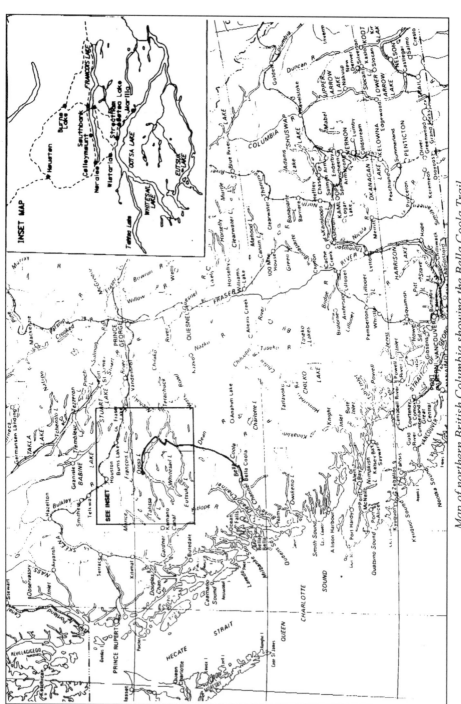

Map of northern British Columbia showing the Bella Coola Trail

CHAPTER 8

IN SEARCH OF A NEW LIFE IN THE WILDERNESS OF BRITISH COLUMBIA

The letters in Chapter 8 describe Dad's trip back from England and joining up with his brother Arthur in Powell River. Dad then said to Arthur, "How would you like to join me and look for land in northern B.C.?" Dad and Arthur then went to Vancouver and caught the steamer Henriette *for Prince Rupert. On reaching Prince Rupert, the two changed to the riverboat* Port Simpson *for the trip up the Skeena River to Kitselas Canyon. At the Canyon, they had to walk around and board the riverboat* Hazelton. *The latter then made its way through the fast waters to Hazelton, where the two brothers bought a horse to carry their supplies. They walked with an 80-pound pack on their backs up to Houston, then south to Ootsa Lake. Here they found land near the west end of the Lake, after searching the whole 42-mile-long lake. This is the place where they staked their claim—and thus began a new adventure in Central British Columbia.*

Houston, B.C.
September 1910

Dear Mother and Dad,
I certainly enjoyed my stay in England and spending Xmas with the family and friends. It made me realize it would be nice to settle down in a comfortable home and quit moving from one place to another every season of the year—from the trap line in winter, wood

cutting in the spring, fishing on various rivers during the salmon runs
in the summer, then hunting moose and caribou during the fall while
getting supplies ready for another long winter on the trap line alone,
except for an occasional meeting with a prospector or Indian along the
river. Every time I go on one of these new ventures it crosses my mind
that if I failed to return, no one would ever know what happened and it
might relieve your worry somewhat if I stayed in one place.

The journey from Liverpool in the spring of 1910 back to
Montreal was very enjoyable and lovely weather all the way—and
plenty of new people to talk with. They were mostly immigrants going
to western Canada to stake out some land before it was all taken. They
were very interested learning about how to locate land and being able
to describe it to the land agents so that they could record it in the right
place. Many people staked land and found much later when surveys
were made years later that they had given the wrong description and
had built a house and cleared land miles away from where they
intended. I have to give credit to the Survey groups who tried to
accommodate the new settlers as much as they could.

I took the train back across Canada and stopped off in Calgary
and spent some time looking in different areas for land that had not
been claimed. It seemed that most of the best land was already taken,
as well as the opportunity to do some trapping in the winter to make a
few dollars to carry you through the rest of the season which many new
settlers in all parts of Canada have to do in order to feed their family. I
stayed with some of my schoolfriends who had settled near Red Deer.
They were having a struggle surviving, as they had two dry years with
poor crops. I could see the dust cloud a mile away where they were
tilling the land. On good years, when enough rain came in late May or
early June they could sprout the seed and get it started. They seemed to
get enough rain later on to grow a good crop. Prices for wheat seem to
fluctuate from year to year and if the crop is good, the price is low—
which makes it very difficult to plan ahead. Many go broke after
spending their savings trying to get the farm going. When this happens,
they are forced to sell out for next to nothing to land speculators, who
turn around and sell to some unwary new settler for three or four times
what they paid for it. I soon realized it wouldn't be easy to establish a

farm unless you had lots of money to get started or could find other employment to supplement your income for the first eight or 10 years. A freakish early snow storm had flattened their grain crops on the 24th of August the year before.

After a good visit with my friends, I moved on to Vancouver and then back to Powell River on the first steamer. I wanted to meet with Arthur to see whether he was ready for a move to start a new life in the Interior of B.C. As soon as I found him getting the steam engine ready for a day's work, I gave him a jolt when I said, "How'd you like to come with me and look for land in northern B.C.?" However, I was surprised when he quickly said, "Sure" (especially when I knew he was making $85 a month and board). Fortunately, there was another engineer who came in on the same boat who was looking for a job, so Arthur was able to quit that morning. We had to wait two days for the next boat to Vancouver, so I had several good meals in camp free of cost and a nice bunk bed to sleep in. I was lucky to find such a generous company as the Powell river Pulp and Paper Company, which was just starting to build a new mill right on the coast at the mouth of the river (an outlet of Powell Lake). Powell Lake was a ready-made-to-order reservoir for a really good hydro-power plant to run the mill.

We stayed in Vancouver for two days to gather up a few supplies that I'd stored before leaving for England, including two blankets, a frying pan, two pots to cook in, a small tent that two people could sleep under if it rained, a saw, an axe, two wood planes that I had brought out from England and had used in Alaska, as well as my .30-30 and .22 rifles with shells, which we would need more than anything else to keep us in meat of one kind or another.

We left Vancouver on the steamer *Henriette*, which stopped at two logging camps on South Moresby and at Queen Charlotte City and Skidegate on Graham Island before taking us over to Prince Rupert.

Before we left on our trip up the Skeena River in search for land somewhere in the Bulkley Valley region, Arthur and I were well aware that that would be no easy task—as various Government Bulletins warned that settlement in the area involved moving on long trails as people were moving in long before the railroad was projected to serve the area. Also, the closest stores with supplies were still in Hazelton and Fort Fraser to the east.

In *Bulkley Valley Settlement, Bulletin No. 3*, they describe travel on the Skeena as follows:

> *Navigation on the Skeena opens about May 1st and lasts for six months. It is one of the most difficult rivers in the Province to navigate as the current is swift and the route of the river tortuous and consequently progress is slow up the river and rapid on the way down. (p. 10)*

In their "Introductory Remarks" they make it very clear about what we will face when settling in the area and state that a word of warning is necessary:

> *It is not desirable either in the interests of the Province or the Colony itself that the development of the enterprise should be hampered by men and women who are unused by experience to the trials of pioneer life, unfitted by training to take up the work of actual farm development and unable by physical endurance to withstand the hard labour involved. It **must** be understood that settlers who go in there will for some time be wholly isolated and that for three years at least their property will be unproductive. The prospects for success are long and hard without pluck, intelligent effort, self-reliance, physical endurance and some capital, disappointment and failure are sure to result.*

Once in Prince Rupert, it was easy to get a ride on a riverboat up to Hazelton, as there was a lot of railroad construction going on up the Skeena River. We hardly had time to look around when we got on board the *Port Simpson*, which was a well-made flat-bottomed sternwheeler owned by the Hudson Bay Company. It was not too different from some of the riverboats I rode on in Alaska and the Yukon.

Most of the people on board were like us—land-seekers—travelling to Hazelton, then walking to different areas before deciding where to settle. The Skeena is a very fast-flowing river running between high mountains. It would be a difficult river to pole a small boat laden with supplies, so I was glad we decided to pay our fare rather than try to paddle and pole a small boat the 190 miles up to Hazelton. Arthur and I were well aware that we might have a long walk before we found the location where we could farm for the rest of our lives.

The first 100 miles up to Kitselas Canyon was a pleasant journey with nothing unusual happening. However, the Canyon is about a mile long and looked from the bottom that it was absolutely impassable; however, the Captain told us that during medium high water some riverboats did get through—but not in June when the main run-off of snow water was at its height. Everyone had to get off in the rain and carry supplies up to a rough wagon road where teams of horses and oxen pulled the wagons and supplies above the Canyon— and all the passengers had to walk. Some who were not equipped for walking in the rain, got soaking wet before they reached the top of the Canyon and got on board the steamer *Hazelton*, which was waiting for us. Everyone cheered when they saw the steamer tied to the shore and ready to leave once all the supplies had been stacked on board.

The river above the Canyon was fast-moving—unlike the first 100 miles—so travel was much slower. In some places, the riverboat couldn't move upstream against the current. The crew, therefore, had to take a small boat with a cable attached and paddle and even pull the boat from shore upstream above the riffle and attach the cable to either a big tree or a dead-man fixed firmly to the shore above high water. Then, with the paddle wheel churning at full speed and its winch winding in the cable, the steamer literally hauled itself up the riffles. We all admired the skill of the Captain who, with great care, was able to navigate some very tough areas. Several times we thought we were in for trouble—yet he seemed to manage until we seemed to be heading straight ahead one minute and a cross-current caught the bow and swung us right around (just missing a big rock bluff on the shore as the bow went by). Fortunately, we ended up in a quiet eddy downstream, where the Captain managed to get us through and on up the river.

When all this was happening, I was talking to a pretty nurse who was en route to the Hazelton Hospital. She screamed all the time as the boat swung around. I was scared to death myself but assured her that all would be well and that I'd experienced this sort of thing in Alaska and the Yukon. However, I never did see a boat missing a 30' high rock bluff by inches as the fast current took it around—and hope I won't see it again because with the speed of the current had we hit the bluff it would have shattered the front end of the boat and all on board would have been in the water.

We were told by the crew that there had been similar incidents where riverboats had been smashed up on the Skeena River— especially when the river was at full flood, like it was now. From there to Hazelton, we only stopped twice to pick up wood. We had to tie up every night, as it was impossible to travel at night under such conditions.

Hazelton was much as I expected—being composed of three hotels, two fairly good stores, a post office, a bank, a few houses, two churches, and lots of tents. This was to be expected as it was more of a trading centre than anything else. There were lots of Indians who came in from outside areas at this time of the year to sell their winter catch of fur and to camp on the junction of three rivers (the Babine, Bulkley and Kispiox) to catch salmon and dry them for food for the coming winter. Quite a number of them had horses, so it was easy to buy one to help pack our supplies. Arthur and I didn't have many supplies, as we wanted to find a suitable location before we moved our supply for the winter. We wanted to make some sort of shelter before we bought too much—especially a safe meat-house built eight feet off the ground with the four posts wrapped with stove pipe so the bears, wolverines, and other climbing animals couldn't get in.

By the time we got to Hazelton, I was starting to get worried about the supply of meat, as every morning, at daylight and just before dark at night, I watched to see what game animals we could expect to keep us supplied while on the trip. I never saw one animal or track along the shore when we tied up for the night. The new railroad being built was on the side of the Bulkley River, so Hazelton didn't get as much business from the men in the camps as it would have done had the line been on the same side of the river.

We bought the horse for $8.00 up at 2 Mile (east of Hazelton), where most of the Indians from out of town camped. We named our horse Tom—as that was the Indian's name we bought him from. The next requirement was a pack saddle, which I thought would be easy with all the pack trains coming in with supplies for the railroad camps up and down the line, and all the prospectors and Indians who came in from distant points—some over 150 miles away. Some of the pack trains had as many as 35-40 horses. When we came into the Hudson's Bay Company store I told Johnny Boyd, the manager, what I wanted and he said, "Sorry, there isn't one in town. I had 35 last week and they all sold the same day they came in." However, he did have one Mexican-type Aparejo pack saddle, which I knew nothing about—and it wasn't many days till I wished I'd never seen one!

Nearly everyone who came along gave us advice about how to pack it—but every try failed to hold the pack more than a mile. Also, on every steep hill (either up or down), the contraption gave way and the supplies rolled down the hill. Finally, we tried our own hitch, which was little more than a toggle, and were surprised when it held the load on. It seemed that every Indian who met us on the trail had a good laugh and would walk away shaking his head saying, "White Man, him stupid."

Our next place of interest was Hagwilget Canyon, where the trail crossed a bridge over the Bulkley River—thanks to the ingenious work of the Native people. It was a fine specimen of a primitive type of cantilever bridge constructed over the canyon using poles cut from the woods and telegraph wire salvaged from the telegraph line that was to be built to Alaska and over to Siberia. (This was never completed, due to the underwater cable that was successfully laid across the Atlantic and took away the need for the line to Siberia.) This bridge gave definite proof that the Indians possess good brains and common sense once they got hold of some of the White Man's inventions.

The story was told many times as we travelled up the valley that once the bridge was completed the Indian women were allowed to cross to ensure it was safe for the others to pass. The bridge swayed as you crossed and our horse Tom didn't want to set foot on it. It took a lot of pushing and pulling to persuade him to go. Our supplies consisted of two blankets each, a small tent, beans, rice, rolled oats, flour, baking powder, sugar, some bacon, salt, pepper, tea, and my two guns that I had had in Alaska (as well as over 100 rounds of ammunition). We travelled through good land as we proceeded east along the Bulkley River. However, most of the good land was already staked by professional landstakers from the United States and Britain, who had come in ahead of the railway to take advantage of the very low prices set by Government to bring in settlement.

Hudson Bay Mountain taken from the pack trail
from Hazelton to Telkwa in the Bulkley Valley

The land was far better than what we ended up staking on Ootsa Lake. We travelled less than 15 miles a day, as the trail was very muddy in low ground and we had wet feet nearly every night and had to dry them over the camp fire for the next day. You sure have to take care of your feet when carrying a heavy pack of close to 80 pounds. Some of the Norwegians, Finns and Swedes carried much more and would stop to ask why we travelled so light. The one who suffered most was poor old Tom—as the stuffed pads of the Aparejo didn't fit his back and we didn't know enough to try and work the padding each day to try and get it to fit the shape of his back. Fortunately, he didn't get saddle sores, which was more good luck than good management as he groaned every time we came to a hill. I think he soon learned we didn't know much and if he groaned loud enough we would stop and give him a rest. If we weren't looking, he would lie down and quickly roll to get rid of the pack.

Fortunately, there was good feed for him, but we didn't do so well getting meat along the trail. There was only the occasional grouse and several days we had to rely on squirrels or rabbits, which weren't plentiful in many areas. The farther we travelled the more concerned I was about the lack of game animals over a very wide area—which would make our meat supply far more difficult than in Alaska and the Yukon. Some days we even stopped early to try and get some fish out of the river or little lake along the way. The fish sure were good! All we had to fish with was a hook tied to a 12' piece of light string or strong thread tied to a willow stick and a piece of bacon or large horsefly (of which there were lots—with all of them trying to bite poor old Tom). The horseflies didn't bother Arthur and me much, but if they did bite, it sure hurt. There were thousands of mosquitoes, deer flies, black flies and "no-see-um" (Indian name). If you sat down for a minute in the shade, they would cover you in seconds. While walking it wasn't so bad, but at night it was near impossible to sleep unless you either had a mosquito net or pulled the blanket over your face—which I didn't like as I liked the fresh air too much.

We met Charlie Barrett, when we stopped to camp. He had had a long day and was ready to camp, so he stayed the night with us and gave us some good advice on how to get started. He had come to the area several years before and was early enough to get some of the best land in the Bulkley Valley. Just before dark, another old-timer, Hank Raymond, who had settled near the east end of Ootsa Lake, came along and had a big 25 lb. salmon he bought from the Indians near Morice town. He had never seen us before but he walked right up to our big fire and proceeded to kick the fire logs around and said, "Yep, the fire is right to cook the salmon if you fellows will cook the beans and bannock." After doing this, he stopped to introduce himself and said,

"Why don't you stake some land near me at the foot of Ootsa Lake. It's not far to Bella Coola. I go down there twice a year for supplies. It isn't very far from where I live. It's less than 200 miles!"

We had a lovely feast of salmon before moving on with him next morning. After a long day and a lot of mud on the trail, we finally reached Telkwa, which was one of the early stopping places for pack trains moving supplies to the numerous camps building sections of the new northern rail line (which would end in Prince Rupert which would become the second port to move supplies between central Canada and the Pacific Coast). Much of the fish caught on the north coast will move to the eastern United States and European markets.

Our next stop for two days was at Houston, which was a thriving little village with a post office and store owned by Harold Silverthorne, who also had a nice farm a mile west of town. He told us how to find the trail going over to Francois Lake and Ootsa Lake. Wild animals were not plentiful. A high population of wolves, we were told by both the Indians and settlers, that had been around a few years had cleaned out most of the deer and caribou, which, at one time, had ranged over large areas of the Central Interior. There are no moose in this area. For this reason, I thought I should buy a shotgun which would be better for shooting duck, geese and cranes which migrate through the area in large numbers in the spring and fall. Some ducks and geese also nested in the area.

I knew I couldn't afford to buy a lot of shotgun shells and carry them along, so I also bought a self-loading kit with shot caps and powder that I could soon learn to load myself with the right amount of powder and shot for different species. For rabbits and grouse, a light load was all you needed, while for ducks and geese you required a fairly heavy load. Arthur stood well back when I took the empty brass cartridge and used the hammer to drive the cap in before adding the powder. I covered it with a felt or paper wad, then added the shot with another wad to keep everything in place. The brass cartridge could be used hundreds of times as long as you were careful to keep the empty shell after firing. If in a hurry to shoot again, it is easy to forget to pick up the empty shell case.

On leaving Houston, we took the Buck Flats trail, which went over a hill leaving Houston then joined the Buck River again above a canyon, which was more than difficult to travel. The trail followed the Buck River for 8-10 miles. The river is full of salmon when they come up to spawn (mainly in late July and August); however, they are starting to get red after their long travel from the ocean at the mouth of the Skeena River. Some are fairly good to eat but nowhere near as good as at Hazelton, where thousands are caught—mainly by the Indians and some by the settlers and travellers who pass through on their way north by going up the Kispoix then north to Atlin on their way to the Yukon and Alaska (which is a long hike).

On leaving the Buck River, we travelled through heavy pine country over to Trout Lake. We arrived at the lake on a lovely day, so we went for a swim after the long day from Houston. While in the water, I saw a nice buck deer standing looking at old Tom, who was grazing on a small clearing. I crept up the shore for my gun and was able to shoot the first deer we had seen on our long journey. It was nice and fat, so we skinned the deer out and hung it up to cool out. We were very pleased with ourselves until we started to think about how we could carry it over to Ootsa Lake. After much thought, I told Arthur to gather a lot of alder wood that grew along the lakeshore and the creek leaving the lake. While Arthur was busy doing that, I started to slice the meat off the bones in long strips that could be laid over the tree branches and poles to dry them. This worked well but took a lot of time so we had to stay over three more days to get everything dry—so that it wouldn't weigh too much for us and Tom to carry along with our other supplies.

While waiting for all this to happen, we enjoyed catching rainbow trout out of the lake—the latter holding large amounts of small fish that weighed less than a pound. I had a glorious time fishing, as you could catch a fish nearly every time you tossed the bait out. Deer meat seemed to work fine. We dried and ate a lot of these while staying on the lake.

The next day we travelled from Trout Lake to the head of Francois Lake, which is 72 miles long. This is where the Nadina River comes in to the lake and there are huge meadows that are too soft for the horse—except right along the lake where there is mainly sand which is good for him to travel on. First of all, however, we had to get the horse and supplies across the river without getting everything wet so we had to find dry trees and get Tom to drag them down to the shore. Then we nailed them together and loaded all the supplies. After this, we had to persuade Tom to swim the river. It was less than 100 yards wide and he could touch bottom most of the way. While we were doing this, Mathew Sam and his son of about 14 came to see what we were doing. (His trap line was up the Nadina River.) Once we told him we were going to Ootsa Lake, he was happy and if we needed help, he would come and work for us.

The next day we got our first sight of Ootsa Lake and the mountains to the south and west, which looked like good trapping country—so we were impressed at first sight. After setting up for the night, Hank Raymond caught up to us again and insisted we go with him to his place near the foot of Ootsa Lake (which is about 45 miles long). This took us nearly three days and we saw some nice land. Unfortunately, most of it had already been staked. Hank insisted we go on as it was closer to Bella Coola and he wanted us as neighbours, so he wouldn't be so lonely. There were few houses in the district and most of those that staked had to work on the rail line coming from the east and west and still many miles apart. The people, therefore, only came in when work was slow.

After getting to his place, we stayed for two days and staked two possible areas (if we couldn't find better). When leaving his place, we retraced our trail back up Ootsa Lake to Wistaria and put Tom in a pasture which was surrounded by windfall trees where he couldn't get out. This was also not far from the cabin belonging to Bob and Jim Nelson at Wistaria. (They happened to be away from home at that time.)

We saw other cabins belonging to the Bennetts, Ellisons, Morgans, Mitchells, Olaf Anderson and Mark Brennan. The only people we actually saw on our 30-mile trip down Ootsa Lake were Mrs. Eakin and young son Sammy who were living in the Ellison cabin. As we had done a lot of walking and carrying a heavy load on our back, we thought we should take it easy for a day or so. We, therefore, decided to build a log raft that would carry the two of us and supplies and let the east wind, which was blowing nicely, carry us up to the west end of Ootsa Lake, if we put up a blanket or two for sails. All went well for the first hour, then the wind went down in the early evening. We, therefore, poled the raft along till dark, then camped for the night. We thought the wind would get up in the morning and carry us to the head of the lake. To our surprise, the wind did get up but, as it was blowing from the west, the sails would be of no use.

We worked for several hours and gained about a mile. This was more work than walking and packing our supplies, so we tried tying a thin rope we carried to the raft and one of us pulled from the shore while the other kept it from shore as the waves tried to push the raft in. This worked a little better till noon when the west wind got so strong we couldn't keep the raft off the shore. At this point, we gave up and waited till evening when the wind went down and we poled the raft along the still lake by the light of the moon.

The mountains to the south of Ootsa Lake looked nice in the moonlight and we thought this had to be a good place to trap in the winter when the lake froze over. We travelled most of the night till the moon went down. After we had camped and had a few hours sleep, we tried again the next morning and thought we would soon be there. But—the wind once again came from the west and blew up a blinding rain storm, which lasted all that day and night before the sky cleared and the wind went down enough for us to be able to travel once again.

When we got to within a mile of the head of the lake, we saw a tiny 1-room cabin which belonged to an Indian family by the name of Jim Andrew. He had a son, Jimmy, a 14-year-old boy, who could speak a little English and who was happy to see us and try out his English. Jimmy had learned English from a fur buyer who came up from Bella Coola once a year in the spring, once travel was possible over the mountains. Jimmy was proud as could be to take us around in a small dug-out canoe to see the head of Ootsa Lake over to where the Tatsa River came into the lake (which was a mile and a half from their cabin. Jimmy also showed us the big meadows in the delta land, where they hunted for ducks and geese in the spring and fall and where thousands of them came in for a stay before migrating south or north in the spring or fall. Most of these meadows were over 100 acres with old river channels winding between them. They flooded with over two feet of water in early summer when the water was high and dried up in mid-August when the high run-off of melting snow went down.

I thought what a beautiful place to cut wild grasses for cattle and horses. We were surprised that very few Indians had any kind of a garden, except a few at Hazelton who grew some vegetables. They seem to rely mainly on wild berries and edible plants, like wild onions that grew on the gravel or loose rock slides in the hills. I find it amazing how they are able to live. However, there are very few families in this area and we have only seen two so far: Jim Andrew and his family at the head of Ootsa Lake and Mathew Sam and his family at the head of Francois Lake. We are told there are other families on the other end of the lake which we haven't seen yet.

If these two families are any example, they are very friendly and glad to see us. Young Jimmy liked our raft and wanted it so he could anchor it out in the bay—which is nearly half a mile across in a perfect moon shape with small meadows and willow all the way around. He wants to sit out there in the evenings when the deer come down to water. From the middle of the lake there's a nice view of the shoreline and lake but very few deer, so he may have to sit a long time to see one.

We didn't see anything along the shore when we came up from Wistaria. Coming up along the lake, we could see high tree-covered hills to the north and one peaked hill to the northeast, which looked like a good place to go and be able to see the surrounding country to the east. It was obvious there was nothing to the west or south, except high bald mountains and dense timber apart from areas burned by a recent forest fire.

We took all our supplies that we had left (which was little except for some flour, beans, rolled oats and rice and my .22 rifle). As the hills looked as if they were not more than six miles away, we thought we could get there early in the day and thus be able to look around for a good spot to see the surrounding countryside. The walking was reasonably good, with open pine and spruce most of the way and thick balsam all the way to the top (which was over 1,000 feet above the surrounding country). Once we got there, we set up camp under a big tree that would keep us dry if it rained. Fortunately, the weather had turned hot so everything went fine.

Looking east, we could see heavy timber and beaver meadows and swamps for the next six or seven miles. However, there looked like two big meadows, a number of lakes, and large poplar areas which looked good from a distance—so we stayed the night and got an early start next morning. After walking about two hours, we came to the peaked hill we could see to the northeast from the lake. We climbed it to get a better look at the area that looked good and a better idea of how to find it while going through the thick forest where you could only see a few yards ahead. From an open area on top of this hill, we got a better look and found we were at least going in the right direction. However, there was a large lake at the other side of the hill that blocked our path, so we had to walk miles either way to get around and decided to cross a creek at the north end. However, when we got there, a large area (a half-mile across) had been flooded by the beaver, so we had to go another mile up the creek—to a place where we found a high beaver dam we could get across.

There were only a few old deer trails that hadn't been used for several years. They took us over to another two lakes, and then on to the open poplar to the east. I was anxious to get settled and liked the area before we even set foot on it—simply because it looked good for trapping and I didn't see a blaze on a tree or any sign of trapping trails or stick trap houses. This indicated that it looked as if the area was unoccupied by anyone and I know I'll have to trap in order to buy food and supplies for several years—before the farm will support me.

Arthur and I spent a day looking around and I was satisfied there were two potential areas that, once cleared, would feed a small number of cattle. Both areas had big beaver meadows that could be drained to grow crops, as the soil was good in this bottom land. One meadow is over 80 acres and the other over 50. There is a nice creek that drains out of the two lakes we passed on the way in which runs through both meadows. This will ensure a year-round supply of water.

The following day, Arthur went back about eight miles to where we had left old Tom, our horse, and also back to our claim the same day. I spent the day staking out and finding a suitable place to build a cabin—which wasn't difficult, as there was an acre of clear space in the poplar where a fire had burned three or four years previously. This overlooked the meadow where there were numerous ducks ready for the stew pot.

The next day, we blazed a trail and cut down trees to make a trail to join the trail over to the head of Francois Lake that we had come in on. This trail would cut off over two miles on our next trip. We blazed the trees along the new trail so we could find our way back.

I'm going to mail this letter from Houston and send any letter to me at General Delivery in Houston and I'll pick them up when I go out in the spring for supplies. I hope you don't mind me rambling along about our travels. However, I have nothing to read so spend any idle time writing to the family. I only wish it was possible for all of you to come and see the lovely postcard view from the farm where I want to stay till I die as I've travelled enough.

Love to all,

Jack

CHAPTER 9

MOVING SUPPLIES TO HOMESTEAD FROM HAZELTON

The letters in Chapter 9 describe the freighting of needed supplies to the ranch, especially heavy, bulky items that were difficult to carry long distances over narrow pack trails. It took a very quiet and steady horse to carry such loads up the mountain out of Bella Coola and to cross five rivers. This chapter also describes the building of the big log house, which was the family home for many years. Also mentioned is the sale of the first cattle raised on the ranch to a railway contractor near Houston. The cattle were driven nearly 50 miles to Houston over the Buck Flats trail before being butchered on the Silverthorn Ranch and hung overnight on a stout pole held between two trees. The following morning they were delivered to the contractor's camp.

January 1911

Dear Percy,

After a full month of travelling and searching for land, we finally got back to Hazelton to pick up supplies for the winter and record the land we had staked. In total, we staked over 10 pieces of land that looked good. With our lack of experience, we were totally unaware of the type of soil under the land we had staked and we didn't even dig down to see how many rocks there were under the soil. The vegetation looked good, so we thought the soil had to be good. We sat around the camp fire all night trying to decide how to pick the best of the 10 pieces staked. I finally chose the big meadow, as I was sure it could be drained and would make lovely hayfields. There was also a secure supply of water running the year round, which made it so attractive. In addition, there were miles and miles of dense forests to the west and mountains to the south, where the Andrew family told us there were caribou less than seven miles away. This looked like the ideal location where I could stay on the farm to feed the stock in the winter and run a trap line, starting at the door and going west 35-40 miles, if needed. My line would be located between the Andrew family trap line and the Mathew Sam trap line to the north, which wouldn't come in conflict from anyone (just what I want to keep friendly neighbours all around). Arthur decided to record 20 miles away down Ootsa Lake, just east of the Bennetts' place, which is closer to 8-10 people.

Recording land was not simple, as there were no survey lines and all we could explain to the agent was that it was about a mile and a half on the north side of Ootsa Lake and about eight miles down from the head of the lake. It was surprising there wasn't more conflict, as there seems to be stakes all over the area. Once the land was recorded, the next step was to buy supplies to carry us through the winter—but even more difficult than buying the supplies was getting them packed to the homestead. I had made out okay buying for myself in Alaska, but with the two of us it made a difference as Arthur wanted a few things that I hadn't bothered with.

The basic needs have to come first to see if there is any room left for luxury items. We, therefore, started out with 600 lbs. of flour, 200 lbs. of beans, 200 lbs. of rice, 200 lbs. of sugar and 100 lbs of bacon. There were also 100 lbs. of rolled oats and two boxes of dried applies, as well as cans of baking powder, baking soda, salt, pepper, some candles and a stable lantern which could be fitted up to burn fat (especially bear fat which is so soft). We took extra tea and sugar to give to our Indian friends, who thought such items were the height of luxury. I bought six dozen traps. (They are heavy, so we couldn't take more.) My boxes of carpentry tools had managed to reach Hazelton after being shipped from Vancouver. I decided to store half of them to be picked up later but had to take a cross-cut saw for cutting wood, two folding sheet iron stoves, nails, three pans for cooking and two 5-

pound cans of lard. We needed the cans after the lard was finished as they make good pails in which to cook your tea. Because these containers have handles, you can hang them on a stick over the campfire. They are also good for making stew in on the trap line if you're away from the base camp. (If I'm in camp, I try to use a saucepan, because it'll last longer.)

Old Tom, our horse, who was tied to a tree outside the store, looked worried and started to groan when he saw all the supplies being piled up—probably thinking he would be expected to carry it all! We bought two more horses, Billy and Romeo, from Round Lake Tommy. These two came with proper pack saddles that were getting old—but we hoped they would last one more trip. After that, I could make some new ones once I got all my carpentry tools brought in. I also bought another one from an Indian who was returning to the coast, as he had had enough of the winters in the Interior and wanted the money to get home on the steamboat.

Our four horses couldn't pack all the supplies, as even the canvas used to cover the packs and keep out the rain added a lot of weight to the load—so we hired an Indian, Tom Campbell, who had several pack horses to travel with us to take all the supplies. It cost 5¢ a pound to take them to Houston (90 miles) away. There, Campbell was due to pick up another load for railway camps on the way back— so he did quite well packing all kinds of supplies to various camps out of Hazelton.

Tom tells the story of going to the first bank that located there to get a loan to upgrade his pack train which needed new equipment. The new manager refused the request as he didn't think there was enough security to grant the loan. However, he did ask Tom how many horses he had. When Tom told him he had 65 horses, the banker became interested in a partnership. The Indian thought for a few minutes and then asked the banker, "How many horses and saddles do you have?"

On reaching Houston, we had to relay three times with our four horses, which took a long time, and so we took ages to get back to the homestead. We took it in turns taking the horses back for another load while the other guarded the supplies from bears or other wildlife that might like a taste of something new.

When we reached the Nadina River, Arthur went back for the last load while I built a big raft that would hold all the supplies. After that, we swam the horses across the river and let them graze on the wild grass until they got dry so we could go on. We then packed them up and moved on.

It was nice to get all our winter supplies over to the homestead and packed away under big trees to keep most of the rain off—and with canvas on the top, we had little problem keeping things dry. However, I knew from experience in Alaska, that we had to build a shelter of some kind before the wet snow came in the fall. Such snow would find its way under the canvas before many days were up. Before we could spend time building a cabin for ourselves to live in, we must first build the shed to get the supplies off the ground, as moisture comes up from the ground when the wet weather starts. It requires a log floor to keep everything at least a foot from the ground. We, therefore, worked 16 hours a day cutting logs for the floor and walls, before splitting shingles to put on the roof. We only got it finished just in time, as an early snow covered the area in the middle of October. Fortunately, it soon disappeared and we had two more weeks of nice sunny weather, where we worked from sun-up to sun-down with two scythes. We needed to get enough hay for our three horses before the deep snow came. We had to rake and pile into hay stacks, as we had nothing to haul it with. Fortunately, there were areas on the meadow that weren't flooded by the beaver, so there was no shortage of hay—it was only a matter of getting it cut and piled up.

Once this was nearly completed, Arthur decided he would stake an area a mile north of mine and walk back to Hazelton to record the new claim and drop the one he had staked 20 miles away. (It seemed like a good idea to be closer together, as we hadn't seen anyone else since we came here.) I had plenty to do, getting a small cabin built so that we could live in it for the winter. It would be easier to keep warm than the shed we had built to keep our supplies dry. There was always wood to be cut and piled in the shed to keep dry for the long winter. Fortunately, there was a good supply of dry trees that had been burned by a small forest fire. They were dry and light, so that either Tom or Billy could pull them in without any trouble. Once in close to the shed, I cut them into the right length to fit in our stove. I also built a small boat and cut a trail down to Ootsa Lake, which was only a mile and a half away. I was able, therefore, to take one of the horses to pack the fish back, as I set my net every three days to help the meat supply. As there was no deer, we had to rely on beaver, ducks (where there were lots of them) and grouse (of which there were plenty). There were also porcupines and muskrats, so we never really went short except when we were very busy and didn't take the time to go out and hunt something.

Ootsa Lake is not a good fish lake and most of what I catch are suckers (bottom feeding fish), an occasional nice lake trout, squaw fish (predator fish that eat anything that comes along). or ling (which also feeds on little fish). Both the squaw fish and the ling have a large mouth and can swallow whole a fish not much smaller than they are. If you happen to catch one shortly after they have swallowed another fish, both are edible. It must take well over an hour before they start to digest, as the skin seems to slow down the digestive process.

Arthur was gone nearly three weeks on his walk to Hazelton and back. There was over a foot of snow by this time, so it was difficult walking. Even though he bought a pair of snowshoes for me from an Indian in Houston, he didn't know how to use them, so I had to give him a quick course on how to use snowshoes. Soon after Arthur got back he went trapping west of the homestead about 20 miles away on the north slope of Mosquito Hills (which was named by old Andrew after going up there in the late summer with his family to pick huckleberries). The mosquitoes were so bad, the family gave it up and came home to look for a better place. I didn't blame them, as the flies were bad when we were on a hill just north of there when we were looking for a location to settle.

You can tell Mother she needn't worry about her youngest son, as he is quite able to take care of himself. He comes home once a week to pick up a few more supplies and often stays two or three days, depending on the weather conditions. If it's really cold we all soon learn to stay put till the weather moderates again. I keep myself busy fixing up the cabin with two bunk beds made of poles, with a large gunny sack filled with dry hay, which is known as a "palliasse" or "dryass" (which is used to keep your bottom dry when driving a sleigh loaded with firewood or supplies). I also made a small table and two chairs, which is real luxury after trying to balance a plate on your lap while sitting on a block of wood with only your hat on it to make it softer.

The horses are doing really well and seem to be quite at home. I find they do well pawing through the snow for slew grass that lies on the ground nearly 6" deep. They do very well till a thaw comes, which is followed by cold weather. This makes a hard crust and it is difficult for the horses to paw, so you have to feed them from that time until spring. If horses are working, then they need feed all the time (except when the grass is young and luscious in the early summer).

We are having a fairly good winter and the food supply looks as if it will carry us through till we can get out for more supplies in May when the trails will be fit for horses to travel. The snow stays in the deep timber on the north slopes till late May. Most of the creeks and small rivers are in full flood sometimes well into June.

I'll mail this letter when I get to Houston and hope there is news from home. Hope all is well in Evenley and that you all had an enjoyable Xmas.

Love

Jack

Houston
1911

Dear Mother,
It was nice to get your letter and hear all is well when I made my first trip out to the Silverthornes' store for supplies and to pick up any mail that had come in during the winter. I rented two horses from Old Sam, as we lost poor old Tom this spring when he walked out on the melting ice and drowned—a great loss to us. He was not only a good pack horse but also a trusted friend who would always walk up to you when needed for a job of pulling in fence rails or wood for the stoves.

As soon as the weather got good, I dug out a plot of land for a garden, which would save freighting a lot of food if it can be grown at home. There is no doubt a vegetable garden is the number 1 secret of survival in an isolated place like this, as you can't afford to walk or ride a hundred miles or so any time you run short of vegetables.

We were told by Harold Silverthornes that the best products to grow in this climate are potatoes (on higher ground where there is less summer frost), as well as carrots, turnips, parsnips, cabbage, cauliflower, onions, beets, Brussel sprouts, lettuce, radish, peas, etc. These grow abundantly nearly anywhere. They told us to be **sure** to build a warm roothouse dug into a hillside with a log roof and two feet of meadow peat on top and a double door spaced two feet apart with a small air hole that can be closed during cold weather. In this way, vegetables will last all winter and many will last till the new crop grows the next year. This certainly was good advice and served us well.

While planting the garden, young Jimmy Andrew, who is around 18 years old, came along. No one knows his age for sure, as there are no records of birthdates because there is no church nearby. (Churches are the only ones that keep any records.) Young Jimmy was curious about what we were doing scattering seeds in the ground. His comment was, "Him plenty good for birds!" Jimmy only spoke a little English but loved sitting around a campfire drinking tea and eating a piece of bannock we'd made. He was always anxious to help with whatever we were doing, so we hired him to clear land. All we had to clear land with was an axe and a grubhoe, which was used to cut the roots of a tree underground and pull the stumps out with the horses. It is very slow clearing land and can take several weeks to clear an acre. Jimmy got quite good at it, so we liked to have him around to look after things if both of us were away on a trip. Once the garden came up, we showed him how to weed and cultivate it.

During the summer we spent a lot of time clearing land and building fences to protect our crop and garden, as we planned to go to Bella Coola in the fall to buy some cattle once we had a good supply of hay put up to feed them during the winter. In order to make haying a little easier, I made a 2-wheel cart with a rack on it to carry the hay. The wheels were made of poplar and the axles were made of birch, which worked very well and saved a lot of time carrying hay to the barn for winter use.

Near the end of August, we left for Bella Coola with our four horses. It took three days to get to the east end of Ootsa Lake, where the trail crossed the Ootsa River (which is about 160 yards wide where it leaves the lake). Fortunately, the river is low at that time of the year, so we had little trouble getting the horses to walk across. We camped the night there and while Arthur was making supper, I found a better place to cross lower down.

In the morning, we proceeded on our journey to One Eye Lake, where a small Indian village is situated with not more than 10 Indians. They kept a few horses on a meadow which grew excellent wild hay. From there, we followed a jack pine escarpment along the Chislaslie River till we crossed with little trouble as the river was low and hardly came up to the horses' knees. From the crossing, it's only about 10 miles to the Tetachuck River, which connects Tetachuck Lake to Euchu Lake. The river falls 150 feet in four miles, with a succession of four falls (the largest being 25 feet high). We had to build a raft for supplies and swam the horses across. On the way back, we found there was a shallow ford just above the high falls, where the horses could walk over with not more than two feet of water. We passed the little Indian village of Algatcho, half-way to Bella Coola, which was deserted. On reaching the coast, we found all the Indians from the area had moved to the coast for salmon to keep them in food for the winter. From here, the trail crosses the headwaters of the Algatcho River, which is easily fordable except in June and July during run-off when the snow is melting.

The trip over the mountains was lovely, with the late flowers that cover the open high country. Here we saw our first herd of caribou. There were numerous ptarmigan that we flushed out. They were very colourful, as they were changing their summer plumage to their winter plumage which is snow white. We had a lovely feed of them for dinner. The view from the top of the mountain was spectacular, looking down into the Bella Coola River winding through the valley from nearly 3,000 feet above the river. It looked so close that we thought we could be there in less than an hour. We, therefore, proceeded down the winding trail. It turned out that it took hours—and it started to rain. The hill was so steep there was no place to camp. We, therefore, got drenched before we reached the little ferry, which is closed after dark. Fortunately for us, the old ferryman heard us coming down the mountain and was kind enough to come across and pick us up. The ferry was an interesting contrivance, which worked by the front end being winched until it pointed upstream. The ferry worked by the current forcing the boat across the river.

Once across, we had to pitch tents for the night, which is not very pleasant in the blinding rain. Next morning, Bill Eakin turned up and he had it worse than us. He had had to travel in a blinding snow storm across the high country before coming down to the river. We were starting to wonder whether we could get back before winter came, but Bill Eakin assured us that the snow would go and travel would be good at least until the middle of October—and, furthermore, the cattle would drive better. They wouldn't want to leave the trail so often when they saw some nice grass or wild mushrooms, which the cattle seem to like.

We looked around Bella Colla for the cattle we wanted—12 cows that would have calves in the spring, and one bull. This proved to be a difficult task, as none of the farmers had more than one or two they wanted to sell because all the farms in the valley were small and the cattle, except a few dairy cows, were a mixed breed lot.

There was another problem (as we soon found out). Because the cows came from different farms, they didn't know each other and, at first, all they wanted to do was fight. Fortunately, one of the farms had a good fence and the farmer was kind enough to let us use one of his fields until we got all the cattle collected together.

Another problem I hadn't counted on was that most of the settlers were Norwegian and had a number of pretty daughters—so I spent nearly as much time rounding up Brother Arthur, as he enjoyed having tea at the various farms and visiting the girls. For several days, I thought I'd be going back to Ootsa Lake by myself!

I bought two more horses and pack saddles, so that we had five to pack more supplies. While in Bella Coola, I managed to find a plough share and coulter in a little hardware store. I figured I could take it back to the homestead and find a strong birch tree from which I could make the plough frame and handles. This would mean I would save a lot of work digging the garden plot and the area I wanted to plant with a few oats for the horses and some rye—which we hope will ripen before the frost sets in. The reason we want to get a little rye is so that we can roast it and grind it (in a hand coffee grinder I found in Hagensborg, while rounding up the cows. I'm not sure Dad would approve of the rye coffee for his breakfast, but you could try it some time without telling him and see what happens!

After keeping the cattle from several farms together for two days, we thought they might all follow if we led Briggey, a very tame cow, on a rope behind the pack horses. We had no sooner let them out of the corral, when they took off on the run following different trails back home. All we had left were the horses and the one cow we had on the rope. We took them up to the ferry landing, where an American family asked us to stay the night. We put the horses in a small pasture with the one cow. The following day we put ropes on two more and managed to get two others to follow. On the following day, with the help of a farmer and his two sons, we managed to get the other seven up to the ferry landing and left them overnight with the others. After we got them across in the ferry and away from their home range, they decided to follow.

In many ways we were sorry to leave the Bella Coola valley, as we enjoyed the local apples, the salmon we bought from the Indians camped on the river, and all the friendly people who were so helpful which made our stay enjoyable. We looked forward to coming back in the spring on our next trip for supplies to visit all the friends we had made while staying in the valley. We moved out at daylight in the morning, as we were anxious that snow might fall on the high country and feed would be very scarce for the horses and cattle. In some areas, there wasn't much feed, as the pack trains using the trail had grazed off most of the grass during the late summer. We were concerned whether the cows would want to climb the steep mountain trail leaving the Bella Coola valley, so we followed Harry Morgan's advice and took the Burnt Bridge trail, which wasn't as steep as the one we had come down. The trail climbs nearly 2,000 feet before we reached the open high country, which is very pleasant to travel—and, by this time, the cows had learned to follow old Briggey, who was still tied to the last pack horse.

On the second day, a herd of 18 caribou came close to take a look at us, then turned and ran at top speed till they were over half a mile away. Then they stood on a hill and watched us go. We had just got out of sight when they came running towards us to take a second look. Some came as close as 25 yards. We wished we could have shot one and taken it back for the winter supply of meat—but as there wasn't room on the five pack horses, we left them alone.

After passing Majuba Hill, Algatcho and Coal Meadows (which all had a good supply of water and meadow grass for the horses and cattle), we had no trouble getting a good supply of ptarmigan on the high country over the mountains, and grouse the rest of the way. They would fly up in front of the horses and land in a tree, and sit and watch. It seems they come to the pack horse trails in the early morning and evening and peck for grit on the horse trails.

When we reached Tetachuck Lake, already there was ice on some of the sheltered bays. We had no trouble getting the pack horses to swim the river and we took the supplies on the raft. But the cows didn't want to come, even after we led one from the raft and she swam behind. It took the best part of a day to get them all across. For the old bull, we had to have one person pulling on the rope and two pushing from behind before he agreed to swim across. We should have taken them downstream to just above the Tetachuck Falls, where the water is only knee deep. However, it looked a long way down the falls. Also, we didn't want to lose all our cattle if they slipped on the rocks under water or bunched up and pushed some over, so we didn't try it. Most of the pack horses came this way, so we decided to use it ourselves on future trips for supplies.

Pack horses on the Bella Coola Trail

In the spring the river is a fast-flowing river over 100 yards across—which is quite a swim for the horses. It also takes some skill to get across on a raft, as the fast current washes you downstream close to 100 yards before you reach the far shore. Therefore, you have to start upstream and push with long poles as fast as you can. If you got washed down over the falls, you wouldn't stand a chance. Several people (including a local Indian) lost their lives by starting across too close the falls and getting washed over.

After crossing the Tetachuck River, we had no trouble crossing the Chislaslie River or the Ootsa River as the cows seemed to know what they were supposed to do. These rivers have a lot of water in them in the spring and flow very swiftly, as most of the melting snow runs out of this area in June and July. By August, they are easy to cross with less than three feet of water on many riffles which makes it easy to walk across. Therefore, one can lead the first horse and the rest follow—so that most of the packs you have don't need to be taken off. Exceptions are things like flour, sugar, rice, rolled oats, etc, which you have to take care of and it's safer to put them on a raft with a foot high platform to make sure the water doesn't get to them.

Crossing the Ootsa River on the Bella Coola Trail

The last 30 miles up Ootsa Lake to the homestead were no trouble and it took us less than three days to get there. As soon as we came in sight of the big meadow down on the flat, the cows ran down and made themselves at home, feeding on the thick grass which is over two feet tall. This was something they seldom saw in the Bella Coola valley, where they browse much of the time on willow and other brush.

Soon after we got back, Arthur and Herbert got ready to go trapping for the winter on the south side of Mosquito Hills. They took my boat and a hand sleigh I had made to take their supplies in. Their journey was close to 35 miles up Ootsa Lake and the Tahtsa River. They only got a little more than half way by boat when they ran into ice in sheltered areas and where the river current is slow. They had to pull the boat up on the bank of the river and leave it till spring when they came out.

From there they had to load what they could on the hand sleigh and pack the rest in two trips, going only three or four miles a day in very difficult going as the river was still open without ice on the swift riffles. Where there were swift riffles, they had to pack all their supplies on their backs around the open water before they could use the sleigh again.

After they got past the Mosquito Hills and up to Red Top Meadows (which was a large area of open meadows that was an excellent area for mink trapping and the higher levels for marten), they gave up going any further and built a small cabin—where they stayed all winter. They did very well trapping, as there was no one else in the area. They stayed till the ice on the river went out near the middle of May. They expected an easy trip home after building a raft to load everything on and floating down to the boat and paddling their way home. Unfortunately, after they got past the swift currents, past Mosquito Hills, they found the river still frozen solid. Once again, they left the raft and loaded on the sleigh their catch of fur and a small amount of supplies left after the long winter (November-May) and got down to the boat after several days and stayed for nearly 10 days. After this, the ice on the river finally went out and they could float down to the lake, which was still frozen over but unsafe to travel on. They managed to find their way out by following the north shore of the lake, where the sun in the daytime managed to melt the ice for 8-10 feet out.

The Andrew Family, who lived at the head of Ootsa Lake, had caught enough large trout to give them sufficient to get home. They swear they will never go up there again—but likely will next fall. However, they will go a little earlier before the ice starts to form on the river.

I'll mail this from Houston when one of us goes out to pick up a few needy supplies in the spring before we venture out to Bella Coola. We will do this after the garden is all planted and the fences are all up to keep the cows out.

Love to you all,

Jack

D ear Flora,
     We are starting to get the homestead organized, especially bringing in supplies to last us a year. This requires two trips: one in June when the spring flush in the rivers is high and we have to raft all the supplies across four rivers. When we reach the the fifth, the Bella Coola River, there is the small ferry—which makes it nice, as we don't even have to unpack the horses, the journey only taking a few minutes to cross.

The second trip is in the fall. We try to do this one in late September after finishing haying and before the snow comes to stay on the high country over the mountains. It's a lovely area to travel when the weather is nice—but can be miserable if you hit an early snow storm, where you can't see 20 yards ahead. The best thing to do, therefore, is to find a sheltered spot with available firewood so you can sit out the storm (which usually doesn't last more than 3-4 days).

We can now grow a good garden which saves freighting in a lot of food. The garden gets better all the time as we now have lots of manure from the horses and cattle, which more than doubles the crop on just over an acre. This pretty well keeps us going, except for flour, sugar, rolled oats, rice and a few other items (e.g., baking powder, salt, pepper, tea, and other small items). We seem to manage to keep ourselves supplied with wild meat and fish.

It's still a struggle during the winter when the ducks and geese are away, and the beaver are under the ice. Deer are still very scarce and we seldom get more than two a year. They are the only large game animal with a 5-10 mile radius. There are mountain goats in the mountains and a small herd of caribou up on the "Dome," Mt. Wells (which is close to six miles away)—and we have to go nearly to the top, above the timber line, to find them.

I took my hand sleigh (once the lake had frozen over) and went over the top where there is a lovely view of the country on a nice day. I managed to get a fat caribou on the second day—just before a heavy storm came in. Therefore, I had to sit it out for two days in a small valley where the wind couldn't get in. During this time more than 18" of snow fell, so I had to break trail on my snowshoes and then come back to bring my sleigh and the caribou. It took me a full three days to get back to the homestead—and it looked pretty good to settle down with a roof over my head. We were very pleased to have the caribou, a welcome change from grouse, rabbits, and muskrats (which we caught in their houses on the meadow and small lakes nearby).

During all our spare time in the summer, we clear land (which is still a very slow process, even since we got a hand-winch stump puller and used two horses to pull the small stumps). We still have to cut the big roots with an axe or grubhoe before the horses could move them If we have time during the winter, we ring the bark on the big trees with an axe, which kills the tree and once the roots rot in about two years, the wind will blow them over. After this, they can be piled by hand and burned in the fall when they are dry.

Another method of clearing land is to try and get a small forest fire burning in the spring when the ground dries up in the area you want cleared. The fire will kill the trees, which make good firewood for the following year. Occasionally, these fires get away and burn an area larger than you expected. However, it isn't all bad—as it makes a good feeding area for the deer, bears, rabbits, etc. The wild berries soon come in , which can be picked for jam during the winter. The first to come in is the raspberry, which starts to come in the second year after the fire. This is followed by blueberries, huckleberries, wild high-bush cranberries, which make lovely jelly. In some areas, the wild gooseberries, blackcurrants and strawberries come in. Most years, we can always find enough wild berries of some kind to keep us supplied with jam, jelly and preserves for the winter.

I hope some day you will come out to Canada, as there are plenty of things you could do to keep you more than busy. It's even possible you might want to stay as the area gets developed. The railway construction is coming along well and we hear from travellers that there are less than 80 miles of track to finish—it will then join up between Fort Fraser and Houston. This will make travel a lot better than it is at the present time. Most have to trek from Bella Coola, Hazelton or come in from the East by riverboat to Prince George or by land across from the Cariboo Trail at Quesnel through the Blackwater River Trail to Fort Fraser. The railroad will reduce the time of travel to a matter of days. I'm sure when this happens I'll be able to persuade

Safie to come to Canada. It would be nice if you could come with her and be here for the wedding—once I get a house built.

Travel will not be difficult when you can come by rail to Houston—which is only 50 miles away and the pack trail from Houston is getting better all the time. When I was last out to Houston, there were several new settlers in the Buck River valley southeast of Houston and they already have a rough wagon road into the valley—which is only a little over 30 miles from here. We plan on helping to cut the trees to widen the pack trail from here to the head of Francois Lake to make it passable for a sleigh or wagon. There is a small, covered boat powered with a small outboard motor which brings fur buyers and some supplies up to Nadina. Hopefully, this will develop into a regular service—could be helpful if someone starts a small store where we could get a few things that we need from time to time.

I finished building a two bobsleigh last winter. This has two sets of runners and is handy to bring in firewood, as it will carry 10 or 15 good-sized trees—saving a lot of time gathering firewood. The next thing I will have to work on will be a wagon. I can make most of it, except the axle and the steel rim. I'll try and find something like this the next time I'm in Bella Coola or Houston. Some heavy wagons are being used on the railway construction, which I may be able to buy. It would be nice if I could find an old one that was wrecked. Then I could get the parts I need to make one.

I don't think it should be difficult now that I've had all my tools shipped in from where I left them in Vancouver. I didn't have much trouble making the plough after bringing the plough share and coulter from Bella Coola last fall. It was a good winter project and we were able to plough nearly two acres of land in the spring, as well as the garden. This should grow quite a bit of hay next year for the cows. We now have 11 little calves, which seem to be doing well. We lost one when it was born. We don't know what happened, as it seemed good for a few hours. We suspect the cow may have lain on it.

With love to all and hope all are well.

Jack

1913

D ear Mother,
       Time seems to go by so fast, with so many things to do on the
farm—planting the garden crops, etc. and with the cattle herd
growing—we decided to buy a horse-drawn mower which will save a
lot of work cutting the hay with a scythe. This was not easy to pack in
from Hazelton. The two wheels were easy to pack with one wheel on
each side of a horse and various parts on top. However, the centre
section was very difficult—even after everything possible was taken
off to make it lighter. It was still heavy and awkward to load on a horse
and keep the pack balanced with equal weight on each side.

I'm sure we loaded and unloaded it six times a day. We had to
change loads to different horses, so it wasn't too hard on one horse.
I'm sure it proved the most difficult thing we've ever tried to pack over
the years. We were sure relieved when we unloaded it for the last time
on the farm. After this, all we had to do was put it together, which was
not a big job. Therefore, it was all ready for hay time in July.

During the summer, other than haying, we spent nearly all our
time cutting down some big logs (over 12") to build a house. It was to
be 26' x 24'. To find such trees, we had to go nearly a mile from the
ranch. Cutting them down was the easy part—hauling them home
proved to be a difficult task, as all two horses could pull was one log at
a time. Had we done this in the winter time and slid them on the snow,
there is no doubt the horses could have pulled two or three at a time.
Finally, after lots of hard work and little progress, we built a ramp,
where the trees were cut and the logs pulled out to a place where they
could load them. We then put the heavy end on the wooden cart I had
built and bound them on with a chain and let the small end drag. This
all worked quite well as the horses could pull the logs without too
much trouble. Once we got them to the building site, we tried our hand
with the broad axe and, with a lot of practice, we managed to square
the logs on three sides. This made the logs much lighter and easy to
handle.

During haying, if we got wet weather and couldn't hay, we cut
lumber with a whip saw for the roof, floors, partitions and stairs. All

the floor and ceiling joists had to be squared with the broad axe, which took a lot of time. We had to make sure the logs were all the same size. There is no question we could have saved a lot of time and work had we cut the logs during the winter, when we could have hauled them home with the sleigh. However, we thought we should be trapping to make enough money to buy supplies for another season. One thing was that once we had got all the material cut, it was easy to pile in layers with a strip of wood between each layer, so that the logs and lumber would dry till next spring (when we planned to put the house up).

We were lucky in another way we didn't expect—due to our lack of experience. However, logs piled in this fashion with the weight and layers of logs piled on top—it took a lot of bends out of the logs while drying and they sat flat on one another while building.

We had a good spell of weather in late August and so we were able to get the hay up sooner than we had expected. It helped a great deal to have Jimmy Andrew work with us most of the summer. He didn't have anything else to do, so he was pleased to make a few dollars to buy himself a brand new .30-30 rifle, which he could use when hunting deer and caribou. Once he got it, he had to walk the eight miles back to his family at the head of Ootsa Lake to show them what he had bought.

More and more people are coming in, so a meeting was arranged by the two ladies in the area—Mrs. George Lawson and Mrs Harold Bennett. They wanted to try and get a doctor to come to the area so that anyone needing medical attention wouldn't have to go all the way to Hazelton. The discussion was going well until Jacob Lund, a Norwegian, who had moved in three miles from us, got up and asked why anyone would want a doctor in a place like this as no one ever has time to get sick in a new settlement like this. I tried to explain that a doctor would be a great asset to the area, as only last month Arthur had cut the side of his instep while using the broad axe and I had had to put four stitches with a glover's needle to close up the wound. (Fortunately, Arthur survived my patch job.) Jacob wasn't about to give up on his argument and said, "Well, that's no big deal. I stitch up my horse's foot quite often when it steps on a sharp snag and you don't need a doctor to do that sort of thing!"

In early September, we left the farm for Bella Coola. We set out early in the morning and stopped to visit two neighbours, Bob and Jim Nelson. We hadn't met them as they were out on the railroad working any time we went by. We had a pleasant visit and found they came in from Northern Ireland with their partner Kelly, who was an Irish Canadian. We had a cup of tea with them and told them where we were going. They, therefore, offered to loan us two horses and pack saddles if we would pick up a few supplies they needed for the winter. We gladly accepted, as we had a heavy load to bring back from Bella Coola. The weather was good and everything went well until we bought a hay rake, which could save us a lot of time while haying next year—as it takes lots of time with pitch forks to pile the hay up after it's dry following mowing.

We had to take the rake all apart and tried to load the two large rake wheels on one horse—but it seemed next to impossible until we put one wheel on one side and a 100-lb. sack of flour on the other to balance the load. It worked quite well, except it gave a lot of trouble along the trail as the wheel was up so high we had to take care every time the horse went under a leaning tree or a big branch. The whole frame of the hay rake (10 feet long)) couldn't be taken apart and proved to be even worse than the big wheels to carry. We picked Pinto to do the job—as, even with only one eye, he was the most reliable of all our horses to tolerate an awkward pack and this was the very worst we had ever tried to pack. The rake, at 10 feet long, had to be balanced on top of a regular pack, composed of light items that wouldn't be damaged easily. This meant that the rake frame would be brought higher, as it had to stick over the horse's tail and head—which meant the horse had to walk over 180 miles with his head slightly down. He adapted to it so well and we felt sorry for him. Therefore, we didn't try to go far in a day—and it took us over three days longer to make the trip back home.

Another bit of excitement on the way back was when we came over a ridge at the same time that a grizzly bear was coming up the other side. The bear let out a loud snort, which frightened the horses and they all ran away, except Pinto, who froze in his tracks and didn't move an inch. The horses with the two high rake wheels ran under an overhanging snag and broke the cinches on both saddles and one sack of flour was scattered all over the ground. After catching the horses when the bear was just as scared and had run away, we spent the rest of the day repacking the loads to try and get the right balance after losing the sack of flour. We were grateful that none of the supplies we had bought for Bob and Jim Nelson were damaged. This was the first time we had had a problem with a bear along the trail.

Also in the pack were two big bear traps, as we wanted to supplement out meat supply when we got home. A bear is very good eating, especially after living on blueberries and huckleberries for 4-6 weeks. They are also good in the spring when they come out of their den. At this time of the year, bears live on vegetation growing along the south slopes of hills or mountains, where the sun faces and melts the snow and the plants grow quickly. The feed comes on these slopes while there is still two feet of snow left on the north slopes, so it makes bear hunting really easy at that time of the year.

Due to a late fall, we were able to collect 12 big flat rocks, which were over two feet square, for a solid foundation for the house to sit on. Once we got all of these level, we were able top put the first round on without any trouble. This being the case, we decided to keep going till the snow came. (Snow makes it very slippery to work on a building.) The weather stayed really nice for over a week, so we were able to get the walls up to six feet before weather stopped us from doing any more. One thing, though—it will give us a good start in the spring.

I hope I can find someone who can take this letter out to Houston before winter sets in or you won't get it till spring.

If things turn out well during the winter, I may decide to take a quick trip to England in March or April to make arrangements for Safie to come out to Canada once the railway is linked up to Fort Fraser. It will make it easy for her to come to Houston or Burns Lake with all the things she wants to bring with her to Canada. I hear there is a rough wagon road that can be used in the summer from Burns Lake to Francois Lake when the ground is dry. It also makes a good sleigh road during most of the winter if the snow doesn't get too deep for the horses to travel. This may prove the best way for Safie to come in, providing there is a boat travelling from Francois Lake landing up to the head of the lake (35 miles away).

With love to all,

Jack

Eutsuk Lake from the portage to Whitesail Lake

Kendal, Westmoreland
England
March 1914

Dear Arthur,
        I thought I'd better drop you a line and let you know I got to
England safely with no problems on the way. The snow condition was
quite good most of the way when I left the homestead on snowshoes,
February 10th. In going to Fort Fraser (which is over 120 miles), I
decided not to go over to Nadina at the head of Francois Lake, because
the snow condition for snowshoes seemed good. I thought if I travelled
northeast through the bush I could cut 10 or 15 miles off the journey.
        Fortunately, I didn't find any deep ravines or high hills that
would slow me down, so made pretty good time travelling through
mainly well spaced pine and spruce country—with no windfalls caused
either by bug kill areas or recent fire. It seems this area over to
Francois Lake was all burned over 50 or 60 years ago, so the forest is
still quite young and not much old growth falling down to hinder
travel.
        I reached Francois Lake about half way down, roughly 30 miles
from the east end, so all I had to do was follow the lake till I reached
the Stellako River which drains out of Francois Lake and goes down to
Fraser Lake, which is a very short river of less than 10 miles. I
followed this river down to the new railroad grade, which seems to be
nearly completed in this area. I walked, therefore, on that till I reached
Fort Fraser. The latter has developed into quite a nice village, which
has a nice store, Government Office and small hotel (which I stayed
at). There are several Indian settlements nearby, where they took me
across the Nautley River which must be one of the shortest rivers in
the world, as it's less than half a mile long and joins the Nechako
River (which drains the Ootsa Lake system).
        Again, I paid for a ride across the Nechako and walked into
Fort Fraser. Had I known the area, I could have continued following
the rail line and could have walked across the new rail bridge, which
was nearly complete and saved myself two miles and the cost of
getting a ride across two rivers. The Hudson's Bay have a trading post

here, which was established in 1806—before the turn of the century. Quite a few of the Indians and white settlers work mainly for the Hudson's Bay and on the railway, with others developing farms all along the Nechako River. Some of the farms look good and are far easier to develop than where we established, due to nearly level country and very few rocks. Most of the area is covered with poplar and some willow, none of which is very large (seldom more than 7" or 8"). It looks as if a huge forest fire swept through this whole area 30 or 40 years ago. I didn't see much large pine or spruce after I left Francois Lake—and most of this along the south side of the lake.

It took me a full four days to walk through with lots of sheltered areas and plentiful wood supply all along the way (as well as plenty of rabbits and grouse to eat). I didn't see many other animals, except a few deer along the north shore of the lake and a few coyotes crossing the lake. I also saw where they had killed three deer out on the ice and left a bit of hair and bones.

I had to wait in Fort Fraser for two days before I could get a ride on a supply train with one passenger coach. I enjoyed my stay, as there were plenty of interesting people who had recently come to the area from many parts of Europe. Most of them came in from Quesnel through the Blackwater country and could tell some good stories about their travels. Quite a few had been working in the gold mines around Barkerville and Wells before coming in to work on the railway line. It seems they expect it to link up with the line coming from the west this year, which will make it easier for me when I come back from England. I hope to be able to get my ticket right through to Houston and only have to walk 45 miles to get home.

The trip across Canada seemed long as usual; however, the food and service were excellent—especially after batching for so many years in remote areas where only the bare essentials are packed in. I had a three-day wait in Montreal before we set sail for England. I must say I enjoyed it, as I had time to take in two shows, which I thought were very good. I also spent a lot of time walking around to explore the different areas of the city. I sure wouldn't want to live here but do enjoy a few days in a city. I can look at all the things I'd like to buy but can't afford.

The trip across to Southampton was good, with no rough weather so I could eat all I wanted without feeling sick even once. I talked to a lot of people like me who were going back to England to visit girlfriends and arrange plans to move them to Canada or Alaska. I find it surprising how many people travel back and forth. It seems the ships are full to capacity.

Once in England, I took the train north to Kendal where Safie was working and stayed with her Aunt, who was always good to me and who tried to talk me into staying in England—as there seemed such a demand for finishing carpenters. During the week I stayed, Safie and I spent hours trying to decide what items she should take with her when she came over. We finally decided to take one large clothes cabinet and one large trunk, where a lot of things could be packed and shipped ahead of time, together with two large suitcases which she would take when she came. I thought it was going to be so easy to get everything in until I saw the list growing every day—and I began to wonder whether the new house we were building would hold everything!

We went down to Manchester by rail one day and up to Carlisle another to take a look for things we thought we should ship to Canada. Thank goodness, Safie knew more about what might be needed than I did, as the only things I thought were necessary were blankets, a stew pot and a frying pan! In less than a week I realized how little I knew about what a woman might like to take.

After a week I went down to visit the family in Evenley, where I got advice from both Mother and sister Flora, as she was trying to make up a list of things she intended to take when she came out to Canada. I had to beg that they wouldn't give the lists to Safie, as I could envisage four big crates (4' x 3') on top of our little pack horses setting out from Houston—and what would all the packers say when they saw us coming!

Before returning to Canada, Safie and I decided we should go to London and take in a show or two and look around the shops in London to see if there was anything we'd missed in Manchester or Carlisle. I couldn't possibly go back without spending a week with her family, the Mattisons, at Brackley Fields, so we had to look over the big farm and especially the 48 milk cows which were the very best. The four brothers wanted to know how far it would be to deliver all the milk if I got a dairy herd as large as theirs—even though there was a pamphlet circulating around England with lovely pictures of milk cows on one side and a dairy plant on the other. The dairy plant was planned by a big promotional firm that was going to lay out a town site at the head of Francois Lake. The firm was going to process the milk from hundreds of milk cows providing enough people bought one of their lots where there was lots of work, putting in running water, street lights, etc. It looked good on paper and they were quite disappointed when I stated my doubts that it would ever happen. They weren't so sure that they would want their sister to go to such a place that couldn't support a 50-cow dairy herd. Other than that, we had a great visit and they were disappointed that you didn't come over with me—and hoped you would pay a visit before too long.

I'm booked to leave in another three days and should arrive back in a little over two weeks, if all goes well—hopefully, before the middle of May, which should give us time to put the house up before haying starts and I can make the windows and doors on rainy days when we can't do much else.

Hope all is well on the farm.

Jack

June 1914

Dear Mother,
Just a short letter to let you know I got back home on the 2nd of June after another enjoyable trip. I met with many nice people who were emigrating to Canada. Many of the people on board had no idea whatsoever about what to expect when they got there. Quite a few from Eastern Europe couldn't speak English at all. Members of the crew set up meetings to help them pick up some English before they landed—which certainly helped them quite a bit. During those few days, many picked up enough English so at least they could ask which train went to Edmonton, Saskatoon or Winnipeg—which seemed to be the places where most of them were going. There were several families with children. Most of the young ones sure picked up English words really quickly and would soon be a great help for their parents. They had to learn enough English to get by on before they would be taken into many schools, which made them work hard. The parents all wanted the children to learn English as quickly as possible so they could get work after school whenever possible to help the family get by during the first few years. Most of these people were moving to the Prairie Provinces to join relatives or friends who had come out earlier and had established themselves on the Prairies.

Once people found I had been out in Alaska, the Yukon and had a homestead in northern B.C., they asked me to sit in on question-and-answer sessions so that people could ask questions and others could listen to the answers. I found these sessions a lot of fun, as so many didn't know what to expect. Many expected there would be electric lights and running water. I told them that the only running water would be if they ran down to the lake or river and got a bucket of water. One fellow, who became very friendly, had no idea about the size of Canada. When I told him our farm was in northern B.C., he said, "That's great! We are moving north of Winnipeg. We should get together for lunch as soon as possible!" I carried an old map, which soon made him realize that it was three times as far from Winnipeg to Houston as it was to travel from Brighton to the very north of

Scotland. Many others had done a lot of research on Canada and knew more about it than I did.

All of this made for an enjoyable journey to Montreal. It continued during the rail trip across Canada, even though our numbers got less and less. By the time we reached Jasper, there were very few left. I had to wait there for three days before I could get on a train but was happy to learn when I went to the ticket office that the last spike on the Grand Trunk Pacific had been driven near Fort Fraser on April 7th, 1914 while I was away in England. This joined the railway coming from Prince Rupert with the other being constructed from Prince George. They told me I could likely get through to Houston but they were having early trouble with soft spots under the track where they crossed swampy ground and were having to put a lot of rock for fill in a number of places. They were all very nice and said I could go as far as I could go—but that they wouldn't charge me a fare past Fort Fraser. They were sure we would get there as many work and freight trains had been going there for some time and the track was standing up well that far.

Even though they travelled very slowly, we managed to get to Burns Lake. Beyond that point, they had problems in some spots where the track was sinking down as the frost came out of the ground. The lines were expected to be working most of the summer.

Once in Burns Lake, I enquired about travel south and found a ride on a wagon that was hauling freight out to north Francois Lake, where some of the freight went across the lake and the rest was picked up by a boat that had a small engine and took freight or passengers, if any, up to Nadina at the west end of the lake. Things were changing rapidly with the coming of the rail line.

We partly chose Ootsa Lake as a place to settle as it was closer to Bella Coola, which had replaced Hazelton as the main place of supply for the new settlers in that area. Now all has changed and it looks as if Houston will be our main supply base and shipping point when we sell cattle in the fall. We now have 10 nice steers we want to sell and keep more heifers to increase the herd.

I took the boat going to Nadina the next day as I wanted to see whether it might be the best way for Safie to come next year when she plans to move out to join me. The 38-mile trip up the lake was very enjoyable, even though we had to pull into a sheltered bay as the storm coming from the west was more than the little motor could handle. We had, therefore, to stay the night and early next morning we could get going again and arrived at Nadina, where I stacked my supplies under a good spruce tree. This would keep the rain out till I came back the next day with the pack horses to pick them up. It's just over two months since I left and all was well at the farm—with 15 little calves to add to our herd.

I hope this finds you all well in England and will try and get another away before winter.

Love

Jack

November 1914

D ear Percy,
Since I got back from England, many things have happened—
especially the outbreak of World War I in August which, no doubt,
will change the lives of most of us. Hoping it won't have too much
effect on Safie coming out to Canada in the spring of 1915 as now
planned. We have been so busy building the house, haying, and
bringing in supplies that we didn't get out of here during the summer.
We didn't hear the war had started for over six weeks. We heard about
it when a prospector came by on his way up the mountains and told us
all about it. He had come in by rail from Edmonton and had brought
with him several news reports from the newspaper there. We had a
long discussion after he left and decided to carry on developing the
farm till spring, as it seemed by the paper report that the war wasn't
expected to last long.

Soon after coming back from England we got busy putting the
rest of the logs up, which proceeded quickly. Once up to eight feet, we
put the ceiling up so we could stand on it while putting another five
feet of logs up to make the bedrooms upstairs. From there, the roof
went on with not too much trouble. Once the roof is on , you think it's
nearly finished—yet you are only starting. You still have to deal with
all the partitions to put in, the stairs to build, all the cupboards to be
built and put in, the table, chairs and bed frames to make, all of which
take a lot of time. Fortunately, once the roof is on, it's pleasant to work
inside in any kind of weather.

I set up a work bench in the big living room facing south, with
a view of the meadows and the mountains in the distance. It was,
therefore, a pleasant place to work as all the whip-sawed lumber had to
be planed a lot as it's not all even in width for the full length of the
boards. It took me more time planing the boards to get the correct
width for making the windows, doors, bed frames, cupboards, shelves,
etc. than it did to make them. Most of this was achieved during rainy
days during haying.

Even though it is shorter to get supplies from the railway at
Houston or Telkwa, we had to make one last trip to Bella Coola to pick

up supplies I'd ordered the last time I was there. One of the most important items was glass for all the windows, which has to be crated very carefully with a sheet of paper between each pane of glass or they would break while being packed back to the farm. I ordered some extra, as I expected some breakage. We were, therefore, surprised when we got them all home safe and sound. I was glad we did have extra as I needed something to bring light into the chicken house, as we now had 16 hens and one big red and black rooster who thought he was boss of the farm—and even chased the cows to keep them away!

We arrived back from Bella Coola in late September. We took up all the produce in the garden and stored it safely in the root house. Soon after, I rode out to Houston to try and find a market for 12 nice fat steers. When I got to the Silverthornes I was asked to stay the night—and luck was with me. The cook from one of the railway camps came in to visit and when he heard I had cattle he said, "I want them all, providing you bring them out to Houston and butcher them for us. It will be far better than trying to get beef from Edmonton, as the rail line was still unreliable." He didn't want them delivered until the end of October or November when the colder weather set in as they had a big meat house where meat would keep a long time. This suited us just right, as the steers would be relying on hay by this time and would want to follow the horses and sleigh loaded with hay. That way, the steers could grab a bite of hay as they walked along.

To get started we tied one to the sleigh and the others followed. There was already six inches of snow, so once away from their home range the steers followed without any being tied. In driving cattle any distance, you have to go slowly or else they start to break away to get a rest when they see a comfortable tree with no snow under it where they could lie down for a spell. It took us nearly five days to drive them out, then two days to butcher them, and another two to deliver them in our sleigh to the camp. The railway contractor paid us 12¢/pound, as that is what it would cost them to buy in Edmonton and pay to freight it to Houston. This was our first real sale of beef from the farm—which made us feel very good.

The winter months were spent finishing the house so it would be nice when Safie arrives next spring. When all the windows were in,

Peter Kerr, his wife and Mrs. Lawson came eight miles to look at it. They couldn't believe that the lovely big window facing to the south was handmade and that we had brought the glass in by pack horse. When they took a look at the big bed and the soft down mattress, they wanted to know where I had bought them from. They found it hard to believe when I said that we had kept the down from every duck we had shot. Then we stuffed them in a strong cotton bag. there were long periods, especially in the spring and fall, when we had to rely on ducks as there was little else for our meat supply. If I was really busy, I didn't take the time to get to the lake to catch fish—so we shot lots of ducks instead.

Hope all are well.

Jack

*Cattle from Bella Coola on the ranch, with the new house
—waiting for Safie to come from England 1915*

CHAPTER 10

A BRIDE BEHOLDS HER NEW HOME

Chapter 10 describes in a letter to his Mother how difficult it was for many of the women who came from a nearly modern culture to join their husbands from places such as London, Glasglow, Paris, Oslo, etc. Such cities had many modern conveniences, including bus and rail transportation, lights, running water, shops, etc. The only available running water available was when people ran down to the lake or stream to get a bucketful. It must have been quite a shock to adjust to a harsh way of life and to shoulder alone far more responsibility of minding the children and feeding all the livestock, etc. in the wintertime.

Chapter 10 also describes how the women kept things going while their husbands were away trapping to get money to buy food and other supplies during the coming year. It certainly was a heavy responsibility to stay home with the children— and their closest neighbours several miles away in many instances. The dread of fire was the greatest concern, with no trails open even for a saddle horse during heavy-snow winters.

1915

Dear Mother,
      Certainly 1915 has started out with a rush—trying to get the new house in order for my coming bride, and Arthur and Herbert are trying to get everything together so they can join the Army. Therefore,

it looks as if I will be left alone to run the ranch until the war ends—which we all hope will be soon. However, we get very little news unless one of us goes out to Houston, where some people manage to get a letter or an old newspaper. The newspaper is usually a week or 10 days behind the times—but it's better than nothing (when you don't get anything else).

War news and letters from home are what we all live for. I got a shock recently when I was in Houston and got word of the sinking of the passenger ship, the *Lusitania* by a German submarine. It certainly changes the outlook of future wars where women and children are at danger as much as the fighting men. Soon after this happened and the news of the sinking were headlines in papers around the world, Safie was getting nervous about crossing the Atlantic because there was so much talk about it. She, therefore, sent a cable to me, which came to the nearest telegraph office 60 miles away at Burns Lake. It was given to a traveller who was coming out to Ootsa Lake—so I got it three days after it arrived.

Safie was asking advice on what to do and should she cancel the trip until the war was over—or come, as planned, and take the chance. I thought about it day and night until I decided I would walk out to Burns Lake and send a cable back. I said I was really looking forward to her coming as I'd be alone on the farm after Arthur and Herbert left. However, if other passenger ships were sunk, she had better stay where she was till the danger was over. I stayed in Burns Lake all week. After the exchange of several cables, it was agreed I would come to Montreal in May and meet her when she arrived. We would then get married in Montreal and cross Canada by train for our honeymoon (which wouldn't be quite as exciting as we had planned). Fortunately, Safie made friends with several other women on the ship who were also coming to Canada to meet their future husbands. One of these was a lady who would become Mrs. Braithwaite—after she married John Braithwaite, who settled in Fraser Lake.

I arrived in Montreal two days early (on July 24th) and found a young Anglican minister, who agreed to perform the wedding as soon as the ship came in—providing that I gave him half a day's notice. It was quite an emotional day when the ship did come in, as all on board were so relieved to land safely. They were all laughing and crying at the same time.

Jack and Safie Shelford 1915

On July 26th, we had a quiet little wedding ceremony with a total of 14 people in attendance. All were passengers from the ship which Safie had only met days before during her voyage. It would have been perfect had all the families been there to celebrate with us. After the ceremony we had two hours before the train left, which gave us sufficient time to go to a French restaurant. The manager gave us a small banquet room, which held all of us. And, to our surprise, he had even arranged for a violin and an accordion player to play soft music and sing two wedding songs—which we all enjoyed so much. This was all done with the compliments of the restaurant manager. He just refused to accept anything and invited us back if we ever came to Montreal.

The trip across Canada was very interesting, even though I'd done it several times before. But Safie was thrilled with the trip and couldn't believe how big Canada was. It was a beautiful day and the Rocky Mountains stood out with a clear light blue sky as a backdrop. I tipped the black porter $10 and he managed to arrange for a small

Certificate of Marriage

John Leo Shelford (bachelor)   *Residence* Ootsa Lake, B.C. Canada.

Occupation Rancher   *Son of* Charles Shelford

Residence Evenley, Brackley, N.Hants, Eng.   *Occupation* Schoolmaster

and of Elizabeth Plumb   *his wife.*

and

Sarah Frances MATTINSON (spinster)   *Residence* Windermere, Westmorland, Eng.

Occupation +++++++++   *Daughter of* Joseph Mattinson (deceased)

Residence Brackley Fields, North'shire, Eng.   *Occupation* Farmer.

and of Mary Anne Morton   *his wife, were married at Trinity Church*
in the City of Montreal and Province of Quebec under authority of License
~~after due publication of banns~~ *according to the Rites and Ceremonies of the*
Church of England on the twenty-sixth *day of* July
A.D. Nineteen-Hundred-and --fifteen.

Contracting parties: *Witnesses:*
   J.L.SHelford   Arthur H.D.Hair.
   S.F.Mattinson.   Esther Davis.

By me, G.Quintin Warner.
                 Priest in Charge.

The above is a true copy taken from the Register of Trinity Church in the
City of Montreal and Province of Quebec this twenty-seventh *day of* July
A.D. Nineteen-Hundred-and --fifteen.

By me, G. Quintin Warner
            Priest in Charge.

room—much better than the bunks in the sleeping car. He certainly did his best to make our journey a time to remember. We were very sorry to see him go on to Vancouver, as we had to get off the train in Jasper and wait two days for a train leaving for Prince Rupert.

Once we got to Burns Lake, we were fortunate to find a wagon that was empty and was going out to the Keefe and Henkel ranch at Francois Lake to pick up a load of grain (which was grown on the north shore of the lake). This was Safie's first rough ride (15 miles)—and showed her what the pioneer women had to put up with! The road still had the stumps cut off at ground level, which the wagon wheels bumped over as we moved along. We stayed the night in an empty cabin which had only been used by the bush rats for the last six months and they didn't want to move out for the Bridal Couple! I tried my best to hit one with a rock—but with no success. I then tried a 6' stick but he just played games by running outside through the cracks in the corners of the poorly notched logs. I would chase him out and he would stay till all was quiet, then he'd sneak in and sit on the small table and thump his tail and foot to see if all was safe. Much to my disgust, he survived till morning when we boarded the little boat going 40 miles up Francois Lake to Nadina. At Nadina, we were met by Mathew Sam, the son of our friend, who was around 14 years old. I asked him to get on his horse and ride the 14 miles over to the farm and get Arthur to bring three pack horses and two saddle horses the next morning. We also wanted some food, as we hadn't brought much with us because of all our luggage. Mathew Sam was always more than willing to help and his eyes lit up when I gave him $5.

Once we had finished unloading from the boat, we set up camp under a large tree and made a soft bed of spruce boughs—on which we could put our blankets. Fortunately, the weather stayed nice, so it was pleasant to sit on a log close to the campfire and look up at the thousands of stars glittering in the sky above. The loons were flying around making their call, which usually indicates a storm is coming. We hoped that storm would hold out till we reached home and had got settled in the dry, warm house—which would look pretty good after the long trip from Montreal.

I picked our tame horse Pansy for Safie to ride as he was so gentle. I'm sure she didn't mind which horse she rode, as she was better on horses than I was. Safie rode a lot back home at Brackley Fields, where there was lots of room. I'm sure the highlight of her trip was watching the pack horses navigate through the timber on such a narrow trail—especially the last two miles. She couldn't believe how Grey (one of the larger horses) managed to carry the two big trunks through such a narrow trail without smashing them to bits. He would carefully ease his way between two trees and if he touched, he would back up and try to get around where there was more room. He was by far the best of our pack horses. Some of the others would just walk and didn't care if they hit a tree and smashed everything up. The third big trunk was carried on Romeo. It was difficult to find supplies that would equal the weight of the trunk for balance. Balance is extremely important in order to avoid saddle sores on the horse and prevent the load from slowly moving to one side and finally tipping over. If the load tipped over, some horses would kick it to pieces or else it would break the cinch belts on the saddle.

Before reaching the farm, we rested the horses for a short time. This was a good opportunity to look over the countryside from the height of land between Francois Lake and Ootsa Lake—one of the best views in the country. From this vantage point, you could see our new home looking over an 80-acre meadow. At this time of the year, everything looks so green with the new leaves on the willow and poplar trees and the wild grasses in the early growth. The Dome Mountain (Mt. Wells), to the south, where I go to hunt caribou, stretch from the west to the eastern horizon, while the Coast Range to the west with its snow-capped mountains (where snow stays all year) stretched out for 40 miles overlooking the Tatsa, Whitesail and Eutsuk Lakes— the most beautiful picture. Safie stood there, without saying a word, for at least five minutes. Then she said, "This is the most beautiful sight I've ever seen—and when facing difficulties in life ahead, I can always walk up to this spot and remind myself how fortunate we are to live in the most beautiful place on earth. This will give me the strength to face all difficult problems that, no doubt, both of us will face in such an isolated area."

View of Mount Wells and the Shelford homestead that greeted Jack's new bride Safie

From there it didn't take long to reach our new home. I always felt indebted to Jimmy Andrew, who knew I was going a long way to bring back a wife, because he came by and lit the fire in the house to make sure it was warm. He also put the tea kettle on the stove, so that we could relax and have a quiet cup of tea. I'm sure he had visions about the future, as Safie was so impressed with him. There is no doubt he will get tea cakes or cookies whenever he comes by.

The very first thing she did after tea was to go out and hoe the garden, as she loved gardening and knew that the garden was the most important thing that stood between us and starvation during the coming winter. No doubt, it will take time for her to adapt to such a new lifestyle—a different one to what she was used to in England with shops nearby and a bus or train close by if you wanted to get to a larger centre. Even the clothing and footwear are quite different, as rubber boots or moccasins have to be worn for almost six months of the year.

During this period, heavy sweaters or coats are also worn to keep out the cold winter winds. So far, with the lack of good maps of the area, it must be difficult for you to grasp the vastness of the area in which we have to travel for supplies. The area in question would reach from the south of England to Scotland—and most supplies come in only twice a year. However, this will change soon, as little shops will develop in all these small farm communities and along the railway line, where a few people have settled.

Lots of love to you all.

Jack

Eutsuk Lake

October 1916

Dear Flora,
    Since writing home after Safie's arrival, quite a number of things have happened to improve our communications with the outside world. No. 1 is mail delivery once a week to Wistaria Post Office (which is only eight miles away). Therefore, it only takes a day on horseback to pick up the mail. Bob Nelson was chosen to act as Post Master. We may still not get mail during the winter if the snow gets too deep, because the horses and sleigh may not be able to get through from Southbank, on the south side of Francois Lake. High drifts pile up over grassy plains, where there is so much open country with farmers' fields and recent fires, all of which allow the wind to sweep through.

Camp at Morrison Lake on the trail to Wistaria

    Safie is doing just fine coping with a new way of life on the farm. We had a very long cold spell that lasted nearly five weeks— with temperatures seldom getting above 20 below zero, even in the day time. We have been busy trying to keep the house warm because the upstairs, where we have the bedroom, is still not finished. Therefore, we had to close the top floor off with canvas boards and anything else we could find and bring the bed down into the living room close to the fire. I would stoke up the fire at 11 o'clock before going to bed and get up at 2 o'clock to keep it going—and again at 5:30. This method kept things from freezing too much.

To make things worse, the cold weather froze the creek solid to the bottom, half a mile from the house, so we had to melt snow on the stove for three weeks until the cold spell ended. Then the water found its way down again under a recent blanket of snow. We had to use water with care for cooking and bathing, as it takes a lot of snow to make much water. When the snow is powder dry in cold weather, all the water we get out of a bucket full of snow is about one inch in the bottom of the bucket. Having the snow on the stove all the time certainly cools the house down—which takes more wood. I was out with the cross-cut saw cutting wood nearly every day to keep a supply ahead in case of sickness. Safie kept busy packing enough wood in to last the night; then she would do the same thing the next day.

When spring came and we were able to move around again, we found everyone else was doing the same thing. Very few of us got out trapping for most of the winter, so there was very little money around by spring. In early April, I snowshoed the eight miles down to the Post Office and found some of the people down there were having a get-together at Billy Kerr's place on the next Saturday. I came home and told Safie, who hadn't seen another woman since she came in. Safie quickly agreed we should ride the eight miles to get acquainted with our neighbours.

Fortunately, it was a very warm week and a lot of the snow had melted, so the horses had little trouble in walking. Unfortunately, there were only three women there: Safie, Mrs. Lawson and Mrs. Harrison— and 11 men. One thing, everyone had a good time exchanging information about how they had come in and where they came from. We stayed the night with Billy Kerr, who gave us a black bear hide and two blankets for a bed (which was just fine). Before we left in the morning, five men came back for coffee. It seems Billy Kerr's place is the hospitality centre in the community and most of the community projects got their start over his kitchen table. The Nelsons, Kerrs, Blackwells, Harrisons, Herbert Plum and my brother Arthur agreed to get together the following weekend and set up a camp by a small stream on the trail from Wistaria to Nadina at the head of Francois Lake. We would widen the trail so that wagons and sleighs could be used to bring in supplies—either from the boat that comes up Francois Lake or from Houston, where most of the supplies still come from.

This was completed before Arthur left to join the Army. Everyone worked hard and I brought the team and wagon to carry needed supplies (e.g., food, nails, axes, cross-cut saws, logging chains, a broad axe, etc.). This would leave the slashing crew free to move ahead in groups of three for safety reasons. (If there are more than three, it's easy to fall a tree on someone.) The 3-man crew was spaced out every 100 yards. In some shaded areas on northern slopes where the sun is shaded, we had to leave most of the trees. This was because there was still too much snow and we couldn't get the saw close to the ground. In those areas, we only cut just enough for the wagon to wind between the trees. By the time we came back and the snow was gone, we could finish cutting those areas. The trees were cut at ground level either by axe or cross-cut saw. It is difficult to saw that low to the ground. A road like this in the winter is great with a team and sleigh, as the stumps are all covered and the sleigh trail becomes smooth. However, with a wagon in the summer, it is rough. This is why, in pictures of wagons, you notice the driver is usually standing. It's too rough sitting down. While he's standing, the driver's legs cushion the bumps if the knees are relaxed.

There are six creeks that have to be crossed, so I was skidding with the horses the big logs that hold the deck of the bridge up above high water. Jacob was a powerful Norwegian fellow who was as strong as a mule—though I was too slow using horses. He just picked up one end of a log and slid it across the creek himself. He also carried two of the deck logs at one time. The reason he was in such good shape was that he had spent the last three months carrying 200 pounds on his back half a mile uphill to a mine that would save making two trips. The crew were paid by the number of pounds they carried in a day.

Jacob loved to argue as long as it stayed peaceful and no fight started. He would take either side of any discussion, which was his favourite pastime around a campfire at night after work.

Safie and Jacob had fun discussing the need for a doctor in the district. They both held very strong views. Jacob saw no need and said, "No one gets sick in this country, we are all too busy." Safie, on the other hand, was firm in her belief that accidents could happen and we needed a doctor since the only one was Dr. Wrinch in Hazelton (200 miles away), who tried to do his very best in such a vast area.

With nine men, it's surprising how far you can go in a day with axes and saws. The bridges over the creeks, which were 10-15 feet long, took a lot more time. The willow and other brush were cut and the ground levelled down to firm soil. The stringers were firmly in place and the logs for the deck were blazed flat, either with a broad axe or an adze. Once flat, they were laid on the four stringers. The top was flattened and then spiked solid. We got seven kegs of 6" spikes very cheaply from the railway crews once they had finished the rail line around Houston.

On the way back after three weeks hard work with no pay, the sections that had been left because of the snow were finished. This completed the 45-mile wagon or sleigh road from Southbank to the Nadina River. The 10-mile section left to complete from the Nadina River to Buck Flats, south of Houston, was finished by community work gangs after haying. This was completed by people from both ends.

Safie kept herself busy cooking cakes and cookies along with the few other women in the area. They would often ride out on horseback from the various locations to see how far we had completed and how long we would be out there. I find it quite exciting to see how well people coming from different countries can get together and work as a team, without any problems when it comes to making life easier for all. The completion of this road now makes it possible for women having babies to go out to the rail line at Houston by wagon or sleigh, then by rail to Hazelton, which has the only hospital in the area. Up until now, the only way to go the 45 miles was by saddle horse.

It was also nearly the end of the pack trains, except to remote areas and mining camps, as it's now possible to bring as many supplies in one wagon load as it took six or seven pack horses previously. I took two of my pack horses and sold them to my Indian friend, Sam, who was freighting supplies up to a mineral deposit near Sweeney Lake. This lake is not far from Tahtsa Lake, so he was glad to get them. I was pleased, as I walked out to Houston and bought two larger horses from a railroad contractor who was moving on to other areas now that the railroad is complete through this area.

I'm very pleased with the development of the farm and things are going really well. However, we still miss Arthur and Herbert. We have a pretty big field cleared, which must be close to 25 acres. This clearing was all done by axe, pick and stump puller—and it takes a long time to clear an acre this way. I hired Mathew Sam and Jimmy Andrew to clear another field up on the highest bench overlooking the meadow and close to our north line. This was to try and find a better place for growing potatoes. The summer frost is hurting them in the garden by the house which is not very high above the meadow and is, therefore, more likely to get frost than up higher, where there is better air drainage. The new field of 12 acres soon became Sam's bench, because he worked on it all summer after Andrew quit to help me with the haying.

Safie soon developed the love of going out into the newly cleared area and picking up all the small sticks and logs to build a fire. She often made lunch and we would sit by the fires and look at the lovely view of the mountains now that the field has been cleared. Safie is also busy making butter and cheese from the three cows we milk. She learned how to do this in England before she came to Canada. The cheese she makes is excellent. As I haven't had much for quite a number of years, I'm getting spoiled. Safie is also picking wild berries for making jam—strawberries, gooseberries, blackcurrants, high-bush cranberries, raspberries and blueberries. They are very plentiful in two small burned-over areas close by. Huckleberries are really good but not as easy to get as they mainly grow closer to the mountains. We have, therefore, either to walk or ride for some distance to get a good supply for the winter. Every time I go for supplies I have to bring back a dozen or so jars and more sugar, as Safie makes a lot of jam and bottles a lot as preserves for dessert or making pies.

Yesterday we were out picking in our favourite spot and watching all the birds coming in to get a feed. Suddenly, we saw a mother black bear with three cubs come out of the forest into the burn for food just before sun-down. We watched them for some time. Then the the wind changed direction and the mother bear was able to get our scent. She let out a deep growl and two of her cubs took heed and climbed up a burnt tree. The third cub, however, took no notice and continued to play on an ant hill. The mother quickly moved to her offspring, swung her paw with a powerful blow and knocked the cub rolling till it hit a stump. We both thought she had killed her baby, but the cub slowly got up with its head down in shame and quickly climbed the tree to join the other two. We had good reason not to trust the mother when protecting her young, so we slowly backed up over the knoll and moved away.

I've seen this happen with other animals, especially a mother skunk who also disciplines her young very severely till they do as she wants. Then, minutes later, she will forgive them and show her babies her love by licking their faces and necks. I've also seen a mother moose trying to get her calf to follow her across a stream. When the baby didn't want to follow her, she came back out of the water and up the bank of the creek and gave it a butt with her head and knocked the baby right into the water. After this, the mother had no trouble getting the baby to follow. No doubt this is nature's way of teaching both discipline and survival!

In the early summer I went by rail to Edmonton to buy eight more cows—Shorthorns. These are a better beef cow than the mixed cows we brought in from Bella Coola. The mixed cows from there were part Holstein, Jersey and Hereford. Some of them were very good, while others had long legs and not much meat on their bones. Safie rode out to Houston with me and stayed with the Silverthornes while I went to Edmonton. I was only away a few days and was lucky to buy the cows and a small Shorthorn yearling bull. Charlie Barrett from west of Houston also bought 15-head. so we loaded them together and marked mine with blue paint on the left hip so we would get the right cows. Once we got back to Houston, we separated the cows and left mine at the Silverthornes while I helped Charlie drive his cattle the 10 miles west to his ranch. Charlie's is a lovely ranch, which was made possible with the money he made selling hay and grain to the railway contractors. The latter had lots of work horses to feed that made the grade for the rail line. All the money Charlie made went back into the ranch to clear more land. He was situated in the right place close the rail line, where, during slack periods, he could hire good men who were hardened to hard work for little more than board in return for clearing the land. Had the railway gone between Francois Lake and Ootsa Lake, as expected by early surveys, we would have been those who benefitted the most. This was thought to be the best grade from Fort Fraser to Chislatta Lake and west to the Nadina River. It would then follow Owen Creek down to the Morice River and cross half a mile upstream, where there was a rock formation that crossed just under the river. This would make an ideal foundation for the bridge. On the south side of the Morice River, there is a rock formation over 20' high which was considered essential for the bridge approach. It would also be high enough to avoid flood problems when the Morice was in full flood during late May and June. From there, it was to go north to the Telkwa River, then up the pass to the height of land. After this it would follow the Copper River down to Terrace. This was, no doubt, the shorter route. However, Hazelton was pretty well established and had some political clout—which may have had some bearing on the final decision.

Another good reason for taking the rail line to Hazelton was an expected line that would go up the Kispiox Valley on to Dease Lake and then on to the Yukon and Alaska. There is no doubt that many of us early settlers in the Ootsa/Francois Lake area believed the roll of the dice would bring the rail line their way. Others like Harry Morgan, the Bennetts, Ellisons, and Mitchells firmly believed there would be a road from the foot of Ootsa lake to Bella Coola which would become one of the major seaports on the Pacific coast. All of these possible development routes made for lively discussion at all community meetings.

After leaving his cattle on his ranch, Charlie Barrett came with us to help Safie and me get ours started on the 45-mile drive back to our place. This went very well, as people seemed to come from everywhere to give us a hand. The first night we stayed with Tony Reapel on the southeast end of Buck Flats. He had a small pasture which he let us put our cows in for the night. The next day we got to Trout Lake early in the afternoon and thought we should go further so we could reach home the next day. However, Safie saw all the trout jumping and wanted to learn all about catching them. I had some small fish hooks I got while I was in Edmonton and she had some strong thread which I tied to a 10' willow stick. With the hook on the end were some white ant eggs. They worked really well—in fact, too well! I couldn't get Safie moving from the lake till the next day. We couldn't eat all the fish she'd caught, so I had to split them and hang them up in the sun till it went down. After this, I put the fish on branches over the campfire to smoke and dry so we could take them home.

Getting the cows to follow the horses across the Nadina River was not easy, but old Sam and his son Mathew came to help and with a lot of persuasion, we got the cows to the other side. I'm sure the best part of the trip which Safie will remember forever was when we caught up to Mike Gallagher with his wheelbarrow. He was bringing it in from Houston with all his supplies. He had a little rack built up so that he could get more supplies piled up. He then put a rope over the top to stop things bouncing out when he went over the tree roots and other bumps. Mike told us a small store is starting up at Nadina. It handles some needed items and opens two days a week when not bringing in supplies up the lake. Mike is, therefore, very happy that he will only have to wheel his wheelbarrow a little over two miles. He proudly refers to the little store as "right next door"!

I'm very happy to see the area building up so nicely with the railway in and supplies coming closer all the time. It appears the district has a very bright future providing the cattle prices stay up. I'm confident the next step forward will be a doctor somewhere in the area as there is already a dentist who comes through the area once a year on saddle horse and one pack horse to carry equipment. It seems from reports of the area in the city papers that the men get all the credit for their hard work and hardships going out trapping in the winter to make money to help build up their farm in a short period. However, in my opinion, the Pioneer Women in the district deserve most of the credit for adapting to the hardships of building up a new area like this. The women are often left alone for weeks on end, while their husbands are away—trapping or freighting in supplies. In most cases, the closest neighbour is three or four miles away—with not even a snowshoe trail during much of the winter. With two or three small children, they must have lain awake at night many times with a fear when stoking up the wood stoves to keep the house warm in cold weather. The chimney going through the ceiling and roof was kept away from the wood by only one piece of tin. This could get too hot and set the roof on fire—which can happen with a chimney fire. They must have all wondered what they would do if such a thing should happen and the house burned down and neighbours so far away.

Firewood for the winter was usually piled in a shed close to the house, but water is mainly brought in from the well, creek or lake with buckets, one in each hand to keep balanced, along the narrow snow trail. This is a chore every day—not only for cooking but also for washing clothes on a scrub board. On top of this, there are the cows, horses, pigs and chickens to feed and water. Nearly all of these duties the Pioneer Women do day in and day out—and they largely go unnoticed by the reports in the city newspapers. I hope in the years to come that future historians will dwell on the hardships willingly accepted by the hundreds of pioneer women—especially in the northern regions of North America. Their efforts more than anything else made the development of these areas possible.

It's almost impossible to imagine the changes in lifestyle that all the immigrants had to learn to accept. First of all, governments played absolutely **no** part in the lives of people in all rural areas and settlements—whether they were white or Native. Very few earned more than a few hundred dollars a year—mainly from trapping or packing supplies by pack horse to distant points hundreds of miles from railway lines or rivers. A few would pack supplies on their backs into mine development sites, if such developments were in areas too steep to be reached by horses. This is the same situation faced by early settlers in all northern regions of North America across both the United States and Canada. Only the very hardy survived this way of life for more than a month or two. Others had no way they could turn back.

Very few people (certainly less than 2%) had wells in the early day where they could pump water with all kinds of hand pumps. The others had either to pack water in in buckets from the lakes, rivers and creeks, or build what was known as a "Go-Devil" and pulled by horses. A "Go-Devil" is made of two logs (7' or 8' long) with the front of the log blazed off at a slope so that it wouldn't catch under the roots of trees or rocks. A rough board platform is then nailed to hold two 45-gallon water barrels (made mainly out of old gas barrels). A 4" pole was nailed around the platform to stop the barrels sliding off when it was going up or down a hill.

There was no such thing as cold storage to store food, so cooked food couldn't be kept long and was mainly kept in a cool room on the shady side of the house or under the floor. Generally you could lift up a trap door and reach under to lift out what you wanted. Another important storage place was the meat house, which was usually a small building (6' x 6'), with a roof on to keep out the rain. All four sides were covered with fine screen wire to keep the flies, birds and small aniamls out. A bear could easily tear the screen out and gobble up everything inside! If this happened, the bear usually ended up in pieces for use during the next few days as bear stew, roasts. The hind legs were cured as ham, which was equally as good as pork.

Another much used place of storage was a 45-gallon wooden barrel dug in the ground in a shady spot behind the house. This would have a lid on top and was used to keep things cool such as butter, cheese, milk and cream. Nearly every family has a cow or two and makes their own butter, cheese, cottage cheese, etc. When it was brought in from the barn, the milk would be strained with cheese cloth into containers and then placed on a shelf in the cool room for 24 hours to allow the cream to rise to the top. After this, the cream could be skimmed off and stored in 2-quart bottles and kept in the barrel outside until there was enough to churn into butter. If wanted for cheese, the milk was strained into large containers and warmed on the stove till the temperature was right and the rennet was added to the milk and stirred in to be left to cool until the curds were set firmly. It was then placed in containers of various sizes depending on your needs. The most used container was usually 5 lb. or 2 lb. coffee cans with nail holes a half-inch apart in the sides and bottom of the cans. Once the curds were in the cans there had to be heavy pressure put on the them to force the whey out through the holes. This was done by cutting a block of wood slightly smaller than the cans which was set on top where the weight of rocks on the blocks would force the block down on the curds. It was left like this for five or six days until the curds in the coffee cans were firm and could be pushed out and wrapped in cheese cloth. They would then be dipped in warm wax to seal the cheese and left to age. This time period would depend on the taste of the user—whether they wanted medium or well-aged cheese. If properly made, the cheese could be stored in a dry, cool place for up to a year.

Scrub boards were the only method for washing clothes—requiring a big tub filled with warm water, soap and strong arms to get the clothes clean. The clothes were then hung out on the clothes line to dry in the wind.

Safie and I are very happy on the farm, which is being developed a little each year. This is such a beautiful place to live and we must be the most fortunate people in the world to be able to live the rest of our lives in such a lovely valley with snow-covered mountains the year round to the south and west.

Love,

Jack

EPILOGUE

The coming of the railroad and the completion of rough wagon and sleigh trails to Houston and Burns Lake brought to an end the first chapter of early settlement in the Lakes District of British Columbia.

The next chapter of life in the area brought many changes with mail delivery once a week. Several 1-room schools were established and the teacher boarded with one of the families close by and, in most cases, had to walk 2-3 miles to the school in the morning. The pupils had to take turns as janitors. Their duty was to light the wood stove in the classroom. In the winter, this required them to get to school one hour before class time in order to be able to get the room warm before the others came to class. After school they had to sweep the floor and tidy up before going home. During the short days in the winter the children had to walk or if further away, ride saddle horses before light in the morning and after dark in the evening.

The teacher was paid $25 or $30 a month—$10 of which she had to use to pay board in one of the farms in the area. One thing, the teacher was one of the most highly respected people in the area. There were not many eligible girls in these areas, so the lady teachers had no trouble getting a date to go to the local dances or other community functions being held. Many of them received several proposals to marry young bachelors in the area. Most of the men trying to date the teacher would "fancy up" their sleigh, buggy or wagon. In the winter they would heat up a good-sized rock and wrap it up in a piece of blanket to keep their feet warm and provide a heated blanket to put over their knees to keep them warm during the drive to and from the dance. Some would travel seven or eight miles to one of these functions, so they would have to leave an hour and a half early in order to arrive at the dance on time.

The very hardy type would ride saddle horse 10 or 20 miles to special functions in wool slacks, a man's warm winter shirt and heavy coat with a parka to keep the face warm. They would take their fancy dress and change somewhere before going into the hall. In some locations, the only private place in which to change was a nearby barn—and even the outhouse back in the trees!

The Christmas concerts were organized by the teacher with help from some of the local women—and they were the big event of the year. All the students had their part to memorize and many of the plays were excellent. Everyone in the surrounding area came—even bachelors in faraway locations. They would come even if there was a snow storm! After the concert was over the dances lasted till daylight so it would be light to ride or drive home. The younger children would sleep in a corner with a blanket around them; others would sleep around the walls.

We lived too far from the closest school, so we took correspondence school and sent all our work each week to Victoria for corrections or to do the work over again. We lived over eight miles from school but would be asked to take part in the concert.

My brother John was born in 1916 in Hazelton Hospital, where my mother went by wagon the 45 miles to Houston and then by train.

Hugh was born on December 13th, 1917, also in Hazelton. This time, Mother went by sleigh to Houston during a heavy snow storm, then by train to Hazelton which she thought was the very ultimate in comfort. On the return journey the sleigh trail from Houston was closed due to deep snow and she had to come by train to Burns Lake and back to Wistaria Post Office with the mail sleigh. This journey took another three days as there was so much snow that the driver had to change horses often to break trail. There had been no one travelling since he had used the sleigh trail the week before. My Dad was to meet Mother at the Post office eight miles away and knew travel with the sleigh and horses would be slow, so he broke trail for five miles and returned home for the night. Dad knew he could make fairly good time the next day on the first five miles and the next three he could break through before the mail stage arrived. Unfortunately, Dad had a long wait at the Post Office and it was nearly dark when the mail stage arrived. Bob Nelson, the Post Master, therefore, insisted that Mother and Dad stay the night and get an early start the next morning. From this experience coming home, Mother would often tell newly married couples, "Remember this advice: Never have a baby in this country during the winter!"

Myles was born in Hazelton on June 26th, 1919 when travel was good across to Houston.

I was born in a tiny, 3-bed hospital at Southbank, on the south shore of Francois Lake, on April 8th, 1921. My mother travelled the 45 miles by sleigh without any trouble, as there was still sufficient snow for easy travel.

The full story of life in the Lakes District after this time in 1916 is available, including my book *From Snowshoes to Politics* and *We Pioneered*, which was written by my uncle, Arthur Shelford. He gave a copy to many friends and schools in the area and after he passed on at the age of 96, I had the story printed so that many other readers would have the pleasure of reading it. Several other people have written books about the Lakes District which are well worth reading.

My parents lived a happy life on the farm and never thought times were tough, as they grew everything they needed. They often spoke of how lucky they were to have so many friends who were just the same as family because they would all help each other to make life worthwhile. There was hardly any money in the area, yet people enjoyed a very happy lifestyle.

My mother died in 1945 before the war ended and Dad passed away in 1951. They are both buried on the farm they were so proud of—on a little knoll overlooking the 80-acre meadow and Mount Wells, Tweedsmuir Peak, Mitchell Mountain to the south and Shelford Hills to the west. This is one of the most lovely areas in the world in which to live and die.

Cyril, John, Dad, Mum, Myles, Hugh. 1939

OTHER BOOKS BY CYRIL SHELFORD

From Snowshoes to Politics

Think Wood!

BY ARTHUR SHELFORD

We Pioneered